❧ The Testing of Hearts

The Testing of Hearts

A Pilgrim's Journal

A new, revised edition, including the
journal of Donald Nicholl's final
months

Donald Nicholl

Edited by Adrian Hastings

DARTON · LONGMAN + TODD

First published in 1989 by Marshall Morgan and Scott
Publications Ltd

This new edition first published in 1998 by
Darton, Longman and Todd Ltd
1 Spencer Court
140–142 Wandsworth High Street
London SW18 4JJ

ISBN 0–232–52285–5

A catalogue record for this book is available from the British
Library.

Designed by Sandie Boccacci
Phototypeset in 10/12.25pt Times by Intype London Ltd
Printed and bound in Great Britain by Page Bros, Norwich

For silver, the crucible
for gold, the furnace
for the testing of hearts,
Jerusalem.

(adapted from Proverbs 17:3)

Donald

How describe the debt?

When one tear alone
warm on my cheek
seeps from the silence
of an interior grief,
and I know I am comforted
by an embrace
calm, unthreatening,
never requiring explanation;

and when, in the darkness
following small sounds and scents,
I stumble into the place
I can only, sparsely, recognise
as the next,
and know, retrospectively,
I was accompanied;

and when, utter without merit,
I feel mercy's breeze
flicking dry the damp tendrils
of neglected hair
and the resolution that has carried
softened into acceptance of grace

and thus joy;

then, oh then I see you
with discipline beyond my understanding
kneeling,
bowing your tall frame
supplicating for my waybread.

(Hilary Elfick, 1988. First published in
The Horse Might Sing, *Envoi Poets*)

ɛ̀ Contents

This book has been written
in gratitude for all those
who shared testing of hearts with me
in Jerusalem,
both those whom I tested
and those who tested me,
especially
the staff and scholars of
Tantur,
and the Maryknollers,
who
made all the difference.

❧ Foreword

The rectorship from 1981 to 1985 of the Ecumenical Institute for Theological Research at Tantur, between Jerusalem and Bethlehem, represented the climax of Donald's life in several different ways. It was his final full-time employment. A unique position of potential Christian influence at one of the world's central points, it was easily the most significant post he ever held. But, still more important, it provided the possibility of a consummation of his entire intellectual and internal development. Here, the pastoral, the spiritual and the theological were able to come together to furnish a ministry at once religiously profound and humanly reconciliatory.

In 1964, as a medieval historian at the University of Keele, Donald, aged 41, published his life of Thurstan, a twelfth-century archbishop of York. It was a thoroughly professional piece of well-researched scholarship. But once it was completed, he came to the conclusion, perhaps not fully formulated at the time, that this was not the sort of thing he wanted to go on doing for the rest of his life. He switched fairly dramatically from medieval to twentieth-century history, but also, if less overtly, from a classically academic to a much more applied and user-friendly model. It is not that he had failed to find a contemporary resonance in the writings of Aelred of Rievaulx, or in the Welsh and Irish religious texts which had increasingly enthralled him – far from it; still less is it true that his study of modern Russian religion or the attitude of the German Catholic bishops to Nazism was not very carefully researched. But it was certainly more practicable to make modern history a starting-point for the pastorally informed intellectual care of students – whether school-leavers or middle-aged frequenters of the Penny University in the Café Pergolesi – and of fellow academics as well, for all of whom he felt a responsibility which was never purely scholastic.

It remains a pity that Donald never published anything considerable derived directly from the Celtic studies which were so important to him in the later period of his medieval teaching, and that for 15 years after *Thurstan* he published very little at all. *Holiness*, his next book, only appeared in 1981, the year he went to Tantur. Written, initially 'with great reluctance', at the instigation of John Todd, it was the first large fruit of the period in which he extended his field of study from Christian history to the wider interpretation of religion, especially after moving to Santa Cruz, a campus of the University of California. In Santa Cruz he filled, through most of the 1970s, a chair at once of history and religious studies – and, from then on, the two would constantly rub against one another in his mind. This steady enlargement of academic area – an enlargement entirely reflective of a concern for the totality of things which had always characterised his work (*Recent Thought in Focus*, published in the early 1950s, had been 'a book about everything') – was a further reason for the lack of publications throughout Donald's middle years, given too his inability to put pen to paper on any subject he had not worked over very intensively in mind. He himself felt this lack. As he remarked in his journal when packing up his books to go to Tantur in August 1981:

> Oh! The fragility of human life and aspirations! Seeing and handling those series of Celtic books and Russian books and books about church history and many others also made me feel miserably how little I have to show for all those years of learning and reading – *Holiness*, for instance, seems very small fruit for all that endeavour.

Tantur arrived in Donald's life at the ideal moment to reap what, over many years, he had so diligently sown. At the appointment committee one German professor apparently queried his suitability – 'Was he *wissenschaftlich* enough?' He need not have worried. Donald was ever so *wissenschaftlich*, but, still more important, he was also extraordinarily *geistlich* with a near preternatural power to read the heart. At Tantur, he could bring his vast knowledge and subtle insight to bear on a ministry at once of interpretation and inspiration, presiding over a group of learned but often awkward scholars of a contrariety of views, but at the same time standing tall and free between Jews and Arabs, Judaism, Islam and Christianity in its many forms, the rector of an institution absolutely *sui generis*. To an Israeli colonel who recognised that he tried to be 'neutral', Donald explained that he disliked the word 'neutral' because it suggested a lack of concern. What he tried to do was to be 'on both sides', a position flowing out of a sense of compassion for Jews and Arabs alike, 'caught in a situation largely not of their own making'. It is fascinating to see him at work in this ministry through the pages of his journal. After leaving Tantur he sorted out his journal notes, until in 1989 they were ready for publication under the title *The Testing of Hearts*. Only someone with Donald's remarkable combination of academic and spiritual experience could possibly have written this book – certainly his most original and memorable.

Over the next seven years, in between frequent visits to America and the numerous retreats and lectures he was invited to give in Britain in universities, convents and study days of every sort, Donald put together – somewhat slowly, as was his wont – a work on religion in modern Russia which focused on the four highly contrasting figures of St Seraphim, Nikolai Fyodorov, Fyodor Dostoevsky and Pavel Florensky. He wanted to reveal the face of a very different Russia from that of the 'evil empire' of Stalinist tyranny and popular Western abhorrence. He wanted to do so because he loved this 'other' Russia so very much.

Just at the moment when *Triumphs of the Spirit in Russia* was at last completed, at the end of July 1996, Donald was diagnosed as suffering from an inoperable cancer, having a life expectancy of only a very few months. That autumn he and I were able to put together a collection of his best papers, something he had long been wanting to see. It was published shortly after his death under his chosen title, *The Beatitude of Truth*. The Russian book was already well on the way – in fact, the first copies arrived just a few days before he died. Looking at it was one of his last joys. Donald regarded *Holiness, Triumphs of the Spirit in Russia, The Beatitude of Truth* and *The Testing of Hearts* as a quartet, containing all of his writing that he wished to remain accessible. These four books constitute the harvest of his reflections from Keele, Santa Cruz, Tantur and all the retreats and lectures he had given in later years while theoretically retired. Together they surely do not suggest any poverty of publication. Rather, they witness to the value of allowing the mind to mature before setting its mark too solidly in print. Yet one should not neglect his early work – *Recent Thought in Focus*, the two symposia, *Selection I* and *Selection II*, the translation of books on Thérèse of Lisieux and Edith Stein, *Thurstan*, an edition of Dante's *Monarchy*, together with numerous articles scattered around a range of periodicals – all evidence of the progress of his own spirit from the moment he left Oxford at the end of 1947.

The Testing of Hearts is about many things – community, conflict, reconciliation, friendship, prayer; how to be a Church both divided and united; how to encourage hope within a particularly hopeless situation; how, above all, to be a Christian, a scholar and a human being – and all three at the same time! It is especially, I would judge, a book about pastoral direction. Donald, the layman with no formal training in *pastoralia*, provides, across a multitude of incidents gently described, an almost inspired casuistry for modern life – not a formulation of principles sucked out of events, nor imposed on events, but just a sense of the way in which a good pastor ought to handle the multiplicity of meetings, disagreements, rituals, chance encounters and human tragedies which constitute life today, so as best to encourage a body of humanity which can also be a sacrament of divinity: this, all of it, is my body. In Tantur he was surely a teacher, even a professor, but he was a learner too, and he tells us at the end of the book what he had learnt that mattered most to him – a fresh understanding of the gospel story, relived in numerous ways. Thus, for instance:

> Since I have met the peasant women of Galilee ... the image [of Mary] that comes spontaneously to my mind is of a woman with strong hands, sinewy through much work; and of a face whose skin is rough from exposure to the sun and the wind; of feet that are broad-spread through climbing the hills around Nazareth barefoot; but, above all, of eyes that are steady and a mouth that is firm through enduring the sorrows of the refugee, the poor and the oppressed.

That image of the mother of Jesus is what 'as much as anything', Donald tells us, he gained by living in the Holy Land.

One thing that mattered enormously to Donald throughout his life was friendship. He both experienced it and reflected upon it as the greatest of human gifts. Perhaps it was even Aelred of Rievaulx's treatise on spiritual friendship which originally drew him to the study of twelfth-century Yorkshire, about which he wrote in his one deeply researched academic work. We see it again and again in many different forms – in *The Testing of Hearts*, for instance, in the account of the burial of Ruth, a Jewish friend, assisted by Abu Jihad, a Muslim friend, Yakoub, a Christian friend, and Günther, her German husband, graduate of a concentration camp. Ruth and Günther were unbelievers. Donald had been asked to preside over the burial, and his words, while the words of a believer, could not presuppose belief. 'Every word you spoke, Donald', said Günther, 'seemed to come out of my own heart.' For Donald, the task of friendship was the building of bridges between hearts, even such as to make it possible for the believer to speak for the unbeliever across the bridge of death.

In friendship heart speaks to heart, and the testing of true hearts becomes possible – proving that they are what they are meant to be. The poem of Hilary Elfick, one of Donald's old and dear friends from Keele days, has been placed at the beginning of this book because it was written by her and sent to Donald just at the time when he was compiling *The Testing of Hearts*. He replied, 'Your poem touched me . . . I thank you with all my heart.' Eight years later, Hilary was praying in the chapel of the Princess Alice Hospice with two of its other trustees at the very time when Donald, unknown to her, was in hospital undergoing his final diagnosis. A poem came into her head and she sent it off to him, as was her custom, the following day. Its final lines were these:

> my cry is the sound of one hand clapping
> the single sound of the hole in the rood
> the purest heart only wills one thing
> and to will one thing is to will the good.

It was waiting for him when he and Dorothy arrived home 'feeling very emotional'. When he called to tell her the diagnosis, he referred to the poem, saying softly 'Beautiful. Beautiful.' Later she gave it its title, *Litany – for Donald Nicholl.*

In March 1997 I visited Donald when he was still able to walk quietly around and have lunch with Dorothy and me. After lunch he produced a very large cup and asked smiling if I remembered it and who had given it to him. It was my mother, because back in 1947 he had so often visited our home at Oxford in the Banbury Road and liked to have his teacup refilled again and again, that my mother had bought him this special cup to solve the problem at one blow! He still used it 50 years later, a symbol of remembrance of one of his very special friends. Friendship feeds on memories. It is striking how Donald ended *Thurstan* on the note of the archbishop's 'genius for friendship':

[It] had won for him the confidence of every sort of person from the unworldly Christina of Markyate to the very worldly Bishop of Durham who had tried to seduce her, from the Popes at one end of Europe to the semi-barbaric king of the little Isle of Man at the other. Thurstan's biographers are fond of comparing him to a strong tower; perhaps he is better thought of as a bridge over dividing gulfs, as one who could truly say with Bran the Blessed: 'He who is chief, let him be a bridge'.

The Testing of Hearts witnesses to Donald's own qualities as 'a strong tower', but still more to his 'genius for friendship' which enabled him to act 'as a bridge over dividing gulfs', so it was supremely appropriate that, when I visited him for the last time as he lay dying, he asked me to fetch him from the shelf on the stairs his copy of *Recent Thought in Focus* and pointed to a quotation from Aelred of Rievaulx on friendship in heaven. How could I not remember that, 50 years before, in the early summer of 1947, we had walked together across Yorkshire to visit Rievaulx? Donald was most anxious in his last months that *The Testing of Hearts* should be reprinted, as its original publication by Lamp Press had been unfortunately over-shadowed by the closure of the publisher almost immediately after the book's appearance. It has in consequence been too little known. He did not, I think, envisage much change in what had first appeared. However, while David Moloney of Darton, Longman and Todd was keen to do a new edition, he, Dorothy and I agreed that it would be far better to include within it Donald's final journal, his reflections while terminally ill, a small amount of which appeared in the *Tablet* (5 July 1997) soon after his death. These reflections represent the ultimate earthly testing of his own heart and will, I am sure, be widely welcomed. Their inclusion did, however (given the publishing requirements about the length of the book as a whole), mean cutting back to some extent on the original text. Some 46 pages have been omitted in consequence. Dorothy and I have thought very carefully about these cuts and we do not believe that they impair the character of the book or the lines of Donald's reflections in any significant way. Rather the contrary.

The omissions relate almost entirely to three things: the first, problems about the celebration of the Eucharist and shared communion inside the Tantur community. Inevitably, given the range of Church and national background represented by the scholars in residence, this issue produced regular tensions. No one involved in the modern ecumenical movement will be surprised at that. While this matter inevitably loomed large in Donald's work and worries at Tantur, we feel that, in retrospect, too much space was given to it, even tediously for some readers. While quite enough remains to make the problem clear, still more has been removed. The second area where some material has been cut concerns public issues and political figures of the day, much of which, 15 years later, could seem ephemeral or obscure – at least without extended notes of explanation. Finally, Donald's thoughts about two inter-religious peace conferences, one in the Sinai Desert in March 1984 and one in Nairobi the following August, have been left out as reflecting rather less on the central themes of the book while taking up quite a lot of space.

Donald's final journal is not something on which I feel able to comment at any length. It is too personal for that – flashes of insight, memory, the resurrection of things held dear by a dying man for whom that phrase of Pavel Florensky was very true: '*proshloe ne proshlo*', the past has not passed, only the dross passes. But it is something to be shared. It came in two parts: the first, composed in the early days of his illness, was recorded on tape, while the greater part, from October up to the last entry of 31 March, was written in his increasingly feeble hand. His voice had become, perhaps, too low to be recorded. Both parts were typed up by Dorothy. These broken 'jottings' provide something of a final earthly validation for all he had earlier written and done, a validation produced while he was climbing spiritually what felt to him like an ever steeper mountain path, an ascent across pain, the sense at times of being 'utterly abandoned', the ultimate loneliness intrinsic to dying. Such climbing must bring with it a final purification of heart, the ultimate surrender of acceptance to being no more and no less than 'God's business'. The purest heart wills only one thing. Blessed are the pure in heart, for they will see God.

As Donald lay in his dug-out, as he liked to describe his study (borrowing the term from David Jones), with his books on the walls around him – the Russian books opposite, the Celtic books to the right, a great mix of church history and religious studies on the shelves behind him – his eyes turned particularly to the pictures of the friends and heroes who had meant most to him in life – Edith Stein, Conrad Pepler, Anthony Ross, St Seraphim of Sarov, among many others. It had pleased him greatly that Julia de Beausobre's life of Seraphim, *Flame in the Snow*, had just been republished with his own introduction to both Seraphim and its author, herself a remarkable woman in many ways. Biographer of the most miraculous of modern saints, she married Sir Lewis Namier, the most secular of modern historians. I recall how, on that March day when I last saw Donald up and about, Dorothy told me that the night before she had had a dream of huge happiness – she and Donald were walking together in the woods of Sarov. What more congenial image of eternity? But though, as he approached death, Donald had to go almost alone up and up that mountain, he never lost interest in those about him. On the contrary, he repeatedly affirmed what he had learnt in those months of his vocation for eternity: to help others through their deaths. The duty of friendship remained paramount.

It was good that Donald could die at home in his dugout (3 May 1997) at 'Rostherne' in Betley, with Dorothy and his children around him, exactly as he had hoped to do. It is good too that he is buried among friends in the churchyard at Keele nearby. This little corner of Staffordshire had become, more than anywhere else, the home of a Yorkshireman who, at a deeper level of experience, had often felt the strains appropriate to the homeless, the 'wandering scholar'. Dorothy had ensured, however, that, despite the wanderings, there was always very much of a home as well – in their flat at Tantur as much as anywhere.

It has been one of the great privileges of my life to have shared Donald's friendship for over 50 years, ever since our first meeting in Oxford in November 1946 and the subsequent visits to his parents' home at Claremount in Halifax. Remembering the kindly hospitality invariably offered to me by his parents and Bertha, his sister, I felt it inescapably right, at his funeral Mass in Keele University chapel, to read the story of his father's sharing an apple with him in a childhood outing and its fulfilment in the Anglican Eucharist celebrated in his father's bedroom in Claremount as he lay dying. These first pages of *The Testing of Hearts* provide one of the supreme ecumenical parables, and Donald may well be remembered above everything else for giving us this wonderful story.

That story begins this book, and recalling it can best conclude this foreword, except to add two things. The book itself now ends with two further poems written by friends as Donald lay dying, one by Hilary Elfick, the other by Charles Evans, both former students of his at Keele – final tokens of what Donald's friendship has meant to many. The second is that, a couple of nights after Donald died, Dorothy had a most powerful dream in which he was talking to me. Awaking, she at once took a piece of paper and wrote down what he had said: 'Nothing can separate us from the love of God which is in Jesus Christ'.

ADRIAN HASTINGS

৶ Introduction

Anyone who starts to read the Introduction to a book naturally
expects that it will enable a reader to grasp more easily what the
book is all about. Let it be said immediately, therefore, that
the present book, as the title indicates, is about the testing of
hearts in three concentric spheres. The outermost of these spheres
embraces all the peoples who live in the Holy Land that is centred
on Jerusalem; the next sphere is defined by the Ecumenical Institute for Theological Research at Tantur, situated on the road
between Jerusalem and Bethlehem; the innermost sphere is the
heart of the author of this book, who was rector of the Tantur
Institute from 1981 until 1985.

A word about each of these spheres seems desirable.
Much of what appears in this book concerning the peoples who
live in the Holy Land was originally composed for a series of
'Letters from Jerusalem' which I regularly wrote for the *Tablet*.
My intention in those letters, an intention maintained here also,
was not to deal with the political issues which tend to obsess
commentators on the Holy Land, but rather to touch upon the
struggle going on in the hearts of ordinary people for a decent,
human, dignified and peaceful life. Already in 1976–7, when I was
a scholar at Tantur, I was amazed to discover that almost nobody
in authority seemed to pay heed to the aspirations and sufferings
of the ordinary people, whether Jew or Arab, Muslim or Christian.
Knesset politicians, Arab rulers, US diplomats, the PLO leaders
and Christian hierarchs all appeared to move in a stratospheric
realm far removed from the day-to-day grind of life in, say, Beit
Shemesh, the Musrara or Hebron. It took the *intifada* of 1987 to
bring such people down to earth.

As regards the Institute at Tantur, it is helpful to know
that the inspiration to found it came out of the second Vatican
council. On 17 October 1963, the observers appointed to the
council met with Pope Paul VI in the pope's library and there
agreed to establish an institute where Christian scholars of every

1

tradition might live together and work towards establishing Christian unity. The site finally chosen for the institute, Tantur, was at that time under Jordanian control. Nowadays, according to international law, it is just inside the Occupied Territories; according to the Israelis, however, it is just inside Israel proper. Although it was originally hoped that all Churches would contribute to the Institute's finances, in the event the financial burden has been borne almost entirely by the Catholic University of Notre Dame, Indiana. Not surprisingly, therefore, the splendid building of the Institute reflects an American conception of architecture. And when I first set eyes upon it in 1976 I spontaneously characterised it in my mind as a Crusader castle. I then asked myself whether the Institute might not therefore have inherited the mentality of a Crusader – that is, an inclination to look down from the heights of Tantur upon the concerns of the local people. Be that as it may, since the inhabitants of Tantur enjoy a far more comfortable life physically than do the local people, the struggle for them was not about basic needs but how to live in communion with one another in spite of the traditional tensions between their diverse religious, national, racial and class backgrounds.

More interior yet was the struggle in the third sphere, in the heart of the rector of Tantur. For a rector of Tantur's position will inevitably act as a prism which intensifies the hopes and hatreds from all sides to which he is exposed and which will burn his heart.

Since it is possible to distinguish clearly the three spheres named above it would have been convenient both for the author and for the reader if the book were divided into three separate sections. What decided me against such a format was a conversation I once had with the late Sir Maurice Powicke. Sir Maurice was speaking rather sadly, and with some irritation, at the failure of certain reviewers to understand his recently published book, *Thirteenth Century England*. He said that what many reviewers seemed to have anticipated from his pen was a series of chapters, each of which would have neatly summed up a particular aspect of English life during that century – one chapter on home policy, for instance, and another on foreign policy, followed by others on social movements and religious life; completing the book would have been a chapter on art, architecture and literature. But, Sir Maurice said,

The only snag with that format is that life is not like that. On the day, for example, when King Henry III was dealing with the architects responsible for rebuilding Westminster Abbey, he was also attending to the troubles in France, making decisions about ecclesiastical appointments and the raising of armies. As historians we do, of course, have to draw out certain threads so that their significance is not obscured by mere chronology. But we must never leave the impression that they were not interwoven with everything else. That would be a falsification. Life is not like that.

Sir Maurice's words kept coming back to me when I began to think of writing a book focused upon the years that my wife and I had spent in the Holy Land. The easiest plan would have been to have developed a series of reflections under such headings as 'community', 'Eucharist', 'encounters with Arabs and Jews', 'peace spirituality', and the like. Yet to have done so would have left a false impression since it was precisely the concatenation of events, their density, which constituted the peculiar flavour of our life at Tantur.

What I mean may be illustrated by just one example that is to be found in its chronological order.

On a certain afternoon I had invited a German biblical scholar, Professor Jeremias, to come to my apartment to discuss matters of mutual interest over a cup of tea. We had not long entered upon our discussion when we heard a noisy argument taking place in the corridor outside the apartment door. On opening the door I found myself facing two angry Arab shepherds who were shouting at each other, disputing which of them was entitled to pasture his sheep on our land and appealing to me to judge between them. I realised immediately that the best way to prevent mayhem around the Institute was to invite them into the apartment and to sit them down, in the hope that the unfamiliar surroundings would awe them into silence. No sooner had I done so, however, than a message came from our reception desk to say that the cardinal archbishop of Toulouse had just arrived, unannounced, with his secretary; and he would like to come down straightaway to introduce himself.

Ringing the changes upon a German biblical scholar, a French cardinal and Arab shepherds, as I then had to do, was not, admittedly, an everyday occurrence; but something of the kind

3

certainly was. Which is why I decided that the most authentic way to give an account conveying the lessons of those years would be to base it upon the detailed journal which I kept throughout the period. The phrase 'base it upon' needs stressing, since my original journal contains many entries so brief as to be unintelligible to anyone but myself without some elaboration; and there are other entries, naturally, which are of no interest to anyone but myself.

It was, nevertheless, only with considerable hesitation that I eventually opted for the journal form, since experience has shown that it has many disadvantages and often gives rise to deep misunderstanding. One need only call to mind, for instance, the shock and even outrage expressed by many Swedes upon the publication of Dag Hammarskjöld's *Wägmarken* in 1963. Many of them felt betrayed at discovering in *Wägmarken* that their much-admired representative of Sweden before world opinion, the secretary general of the United Nations himself, had all the time been leading a hidden life of self-scrutiny based upon the teaching of medieval mystics, who in the minds of modern secularised Swedes symbolised Dark-Age ignorance and neurosis.

Yet that reaction on the part of many Swedes ought not to have surprised anyone who remembered the storm provoked in England by the publication in 1838–9 of Hurrell Froude's *Remains*. These were in large part extracts from the young Froude's private diaries, and recorded spiritual and ascetic practices undertaken by him such as even his close friends had not suspected to lie behind his handsome appearance and lively manner. As with *Wägmarken*, so with *Remains*: its publication led many to deem its author a neurotic, pious prig. Yet anyone who tries, as Froude did, to record honestly the testing that he and his companions had been undergoing will inevitably concentrate on their struggles and failures from which they hoped to learn. They will leave it to others to list whatever triumphs there may have been.

And though I am not quite so unbalanced as to suggest comparison with either Hammarskjöld or Froude, nevertheless I do realise that by choosing the same journal form as they employed I run the danger of similar incomprehension.

One example may explain that danger, especially as it illustrates incomprehension on the part even of the journal writer – that is, myself.

Being the *episcopus* (the Greek word *episkopein* means

'to oversee') of the Ecumenical Institute, part of my duty was to keep an eye upon all the members of the community so as to detect early any signs of unhappiness or dissatisfaction. And towards the end of one term I did, in fact, imagine that distinct signs of dissatisfaction were appearing in several members. The first was a Jesuit priest who had spent many years in various of his Society's houses; and among the others was a Protestant married couple. After detecting the signs of their dissatisfaction, I began to worry over what to do about the matter before the term came to an end. However, several days before the term did end, both the Jesuit in question and the married couple made a point of coming to tell me that their stay at Tantur had proved to be 'the best experience of community' that they had ever enjoyed in the whole of their lives. That such a comment might have been made upon Tantur at that time would have been quite incomprehensible to any reader of my journal, including myself, since it was full of forebodings, problems and failures.

However, there is one great advantage about a journal which is quite irreplaceable. The advantage is that the entries in it, far from being 'emotions recollected in tranquillity', do record the feelings and thoughts experienced in the actual turmoil of making decisions, facing obstacles and encountering joy and truth. The turmoil is very similar to that experienced by a married couple during those hectic years when they are still struggling with their own sexual relationship, with earning a living for themselves and trying to control their turbulent children, as compared with that period years later when they can look back with some detachment upon their middle years and can afford to describe them as being much more smooth than they were in reality.

A further advantage of the journal form is that it makes demands of readers which, if the writing is reasonably well done, are legitimate in the sense that they help them to unearth truths which they could not have discovered had they not been subjected to those demands. In this Introduction, for example, it would have been simple to have provided a brief biography of the writer with an account of his interest, of how he came to find himself in the Holy Land and what subjects readers may expect to learn about. Instead I have paid heed to the admonition given by Eduardo Galeano when he said, 'Reading should not be an act of consumption. The reader is the creator and completes what is written. The act of reading completes the act of writing.' In the light of

Galeano's admonition, a Prelude to the years in the Holy Land has been given which contains a few extracts from my journal previous to my going to Jerusalem in 1981, and which may be seen, in an oblique, unwitting manner, to foreshadow some of the testing that was to come.

One further remark. Nearly all descriptions that I have read of Christian communities – or, indeed, of other kinds of community, if it comes to that – fall into one of two categories. Either they reflect the disillusionment of the author, whose unreal expectations of his companions have been compounded by his own lack of self-criticism; or else they are cosmeticised descriptions intended to advertise the virtues of a specifically Christian community, to say nothing of the wisdom and tolerance of the author. What I miss in virtually all descriptions of community are the nitty-gritty details, those irritations over seemingly small matters which are often more difficult to deal with than big ideological differences. I hope that at least some sense of the nitty-gritty emerges from the following pages.

In order for that to happen, of course, an honest journal must record certain conflicts; but when it has been essential to do so I have disguised the identities of people involved as well as I could – though the identity and character of the journalist himself is obviously beyond disguise.

I.

Prelude
1979–1980

⋴ Prelude

⋴ 7 February 1979

Claremount, West Riding of Yorkshire

'I must not turn this into poetry.' That is the sentence which has been dinning itself into my mind as I have sat by the bedside of my dying father for the past several days. He has lain there, propped up against the pillows, his eyes closed, his strong frame shaking as his whole being has panted for breath. Even when we change the catheter attached to his penis, or turn him to ease the pain from his sores, he gives no sign of consciousness, apart from occasionally emitting a deep groan.

Those groans are so deep that each of them sounds as though it must be the final one, all the breath available to him on this earth expended. They warn me that if anything is to be saved from this wreckage of a man, it cannot come from outside this room; it cannot come from any subsequent poetry that glosses over the fearful fact that death is now bringing to an end the 80 years of my father's struggle for light against darkness.

And what a struggle that has been throughout the years – the constant effort to survive on this bleak Pennine hilltop where tonight the snow is swirling against the windows and the freezing wind outside is blowing it into deep drifts, leaving the road along the village to the moors impassable. And how typical it is that in my father's involuntary groans no trace of self-pity is to be heard, any more than there was in his last words to me before he drifted down the road into oblivion.

We did manage to speak a few halting sentences to one another the day after I arrived back from California. Late on Monday evening he said very clearly and firmly, his voice full of that lilting wonder with which he has always greeted life, 'The human frame, lad! Isn't it a marvel?' In view of the fact that his own strong frame was at that very moment breaking up, I could

9

not help reflecting how generous and noble was Dad's response. Nor could I help smiling at his words, so characteristic of one who had always been given to philosophising. He continued to philosophise even to the end, when a few minutes later he pronounced his last upon this world: 'It's all a great mystery. Nobody can fathom it.'

ᏍᎦ *10 February 1979*

Claremount

Tonight the wind is fiercer than ever, and one can readily believe what people say: there is no high ground between the Ural mountains in Russia and this bare Pennine ridge that might shelter us against the bone-chilling blasts from Siberia. So it demanded a real effort on the part of the young Anglican vicar this evening to struggle through the deep snowdrifts from his warm home to this barely-heated house. Sometimes it feels as if the wind is wuthering through the walls as though they are made of nothing but rice paper.

All the same, we, every one of us – the vicar, my mother, my sister and myself – felt a real glow of warmth as we knelt together around Dad's bed and said the 'Our Father'. And we were grateful when the young vicar said he hoped to come again tomorrow and celebrate Holy Communion here, in this tiny bedroom. For a moment, as he was promising to come, the vicar hesitated when he turned towards me, knowing that I am a Roman Catholic and that it is not customary for Roman Catholics to receive the Eucharist from an Anglican priest.

But he need not worry. The man lying there on his death bed – though still thirsting for breath and for life – who is my father, has taught me the meaning of Eucharist more certainly than have any of the theologians whose books I have read or whose sermons I have listened to.

That happened almost 50 years ago, when we lived in an even smaller house, actually inside the yard of the brickyard, opposite the kilns where the workers fired the clay to make drain pipes and toilets – an ironic circumstance, in view of the fact that none of the back-to-back houses on our row themselves had toilets! We had to make do with the earth closets at the end of the row, some 20 yards distant from our own house. That must have made life even harder for Mum and Dad at that time, when it was already hard enough for them, with Dad out of work, because they had to try to nurse me through a bout of pneumonia which was threatening to put an end to me, their seven-year-old son. In fact, I clearly remember one day saying to them, quite calmly, 'I think I'm going to die'. What distress they must have suffered then and subsequently in that tiny bedroom, shared by all four of us, as they listened to me struggling for breath week after week.

But my school teacher, Miss Clayton, sent me a gift of a bunch of grapes, the first I had ever tasted. And from that moment I never looked back. Nor do I ever forget to bless Miss Clayton each time I taste grapes.

Five weeks later I was able to go downstairs. And soon I began to take walks with Dad to get my strength back. Happily it was blackberry time. So Mum sent us off one sunny morning to collect blackberries which would help to feed us for a period when there was little food to be had. As Dad and I were setting out across the flagstones from the brickyard, she also gave us an apple apiece for our lunch.

It is not generally known that though the tops of the hills in the Pennines are mostly bare and daunting, nevertheless our valleys in between are often beautifully wooded with oak and elm, ash, elderberry and blackberries. My father made quick pencil sketches of all these trees in the pauses we took to sit down on grassy banks, as we walked first towards the upper end of the valley in order to be able to work our return way southwards and finish near to home by late afternoon.

It was a heavenly day, and Dad and I were quick to share our delight with one another as first one then the other would come upon a further fresh cluster of the bright black beauties. And I myself was bathed not only in the warmth of the sun but also in the warmth and tenderness of my father, whose heart was visibly rejoicing that his son was now restored to him. All the same, my strength had not yet fully returned. So by midday it was a tired boy who agreed to his father's suggestion that we should put down our brimming carrier bags and sit on the railway embankment to eat our lunch.

No sooner were we sitting on the coarse grass than I took out my apple and with scarcely a pause for breath proceeded to eat it, every bit of it apart from the pips. All the while I was

11

doing so my father sat watching me, an amused smile on his lips, as he unhurriedly polished his own apple on his shirt.

When he saw that I had spat out the last of the pips he said to me, 'You were right hungry, lad!' 'Yes I was', I heartily agreed. Whereupon my father said, 'Well, would you like half of my apple as well?' 'No, Dad,' I answered, almost indignantly, 'You're hungry as well'. My father looked at me, his fine honest eyes filled with love; and speaking in a deep, contented voice he assured me, 'No. I'm not really.'

Of course, I knew that he was. But I also sensed that he had long since mastered his hunger. Strong man that he was, he then took the apple into his hands, which had become cut and calloused over the years through his work, and he very deliberately broke the apple in two. And even now, before my mind's eye, I can see the shining white flesh of the halves of that broken apple, each half resting between the thick muscles of my father's thumb and forefinger. He placed one half into my hands and we ate in silence. This time I ate slowly and deliberately. Something had changed as a result of which the whole world had become a different place: it could never be the same again.

In those days, only a child of seven, I could clearly not have ventured any explanation of that sacred action in which my father had served as the priest. But the course of life since has made me realise how, on that abandoned-looking railway embankment, I had been touched at the centre of my being, in my very substance, at a level far deeper than the consciousness of a seven-year-old could fathom. And nothing would be the same again. That is the effect of communion.

Fifty years later, our roles now reversed, it was I who was serving my father as his body was breaking. And so the young Anglican priest need not worry lest I, a Roman Catholic, might not feel free to share in the Eucharist tomorrow evening. Could anything, in fact, show more clearly how far astray Christians have gone, that even the slightest shadow of doubt could be cast on the rightness of my doing so?

For here we are gathered, the four of us: my dying father, my mother brimming with love for him, and my sister solicitous for them both, as well as myself, back home from the far ends of the earth. All their lives the three of them have been devout Christians in the Anglican tradition, faithful in receiving communion each week, saying their prayers at the beginning and at

12

the end of the day, generous in giving from their meagre wages. We four have shared everything with one another for more than 50 years, in sickness and in health, in joy and in sorrow, and now we have reached the moment to share with my father in the breaking of bread on the last stage of his journey.

Could you conceive of anything more monstrous than the suggestion that on this sacred occasion I should stand back from the Lord's Table, separate myself from my beloved family and make a division between us at the very moment when our hearts, my father's especially, are aching for union, for communion? If any such suggestion were to come to me, whether from pope, bishop or priest, I should not hesitate to tell him, 'If you say I should stand back at this moment, then let me tell you, pope, that you are far indeed from the mind of our Lord and Saviour, Jesus Christ.'

ᏚᏩ *14 February 1979*

Heathrow airport, 6 a.m.

Just before I left home, my sister said that she could not understand how I had managed to go on sitting beside my father all the day long and into the night in that cold bedroom and then sleeping for only a few hours on the floor of the room below. There is nothing surprising in that, because you feel you can manage anything when you are serving someone whom you love with all your heart. Nevertheless, sitting as I am now on a bench in this almost deserted airport, I have begun to feel utterly bereft and comfortless as I go over in my mind again and again the events of these last weeks, and try to discover some meaning in them. Perhaps that is what poetry does for us, and maybe we *are* meant, after all, to try to transform our experience into poetry?

But how can you transform the unrelenting cold, the cold outside on the moors, and within 'a heart cold under a breast of pitiful fear'? You can't run away from it because then it will only pursue you the more relentlessly and bite into you deeper than before. So last Sunday I made a seemingly strange decision that arose unexpectedly from some instinctive source. I determined to go out into the bitter wind through the deep snowdrifts and climb Beacon Hill to the hamlet where, as a young man, Dad had lived for some years with Grandma Nicholl after his elder brothers had left for the war. From that high point I could look out over Halifax and survey almost all the places where he had spent his life – the school, the mill, the brickyard, the football field, the church and the surrounding streets; and, on the steep slope of the hill, the graveyard where Grandma and the rest of the family are now buried.

As soon as I had made the decision to climb the hill I realised that I was doing so as an act of thanksgiving towards Dad and all my ancestors and relatives for the courage that they had shown in living such good lives in the midst of these grim surroundings. Also, I was intent on affirming their faith, and Dad's faith in particular, that beyond the grimness and the cold and the temptation to despair, there lies a meaning in life which even death cannot eliminate.

My mother, I think, did understand at some instinctive level why I was choosing to go out for a few hours on this threatening afternoon when no other human being seemed to be stirring. I'm not sure that the others did. But they nevertheless wished me well when I opened the door and stepped over the threshold as a blast of wind swept down the path and nearly blew me back into the house. They shut the door and hurried back to the warmth of the hearth.

Even though it was quite early afternoon, still the sky was so unbrokenly leaden no one could possibly imagine that, somewhere above and beyond that heavy covering, there might stand a sun which actually gives out light and warmth. And within a few minutes, after I had walked no more than 300–400 yards through the village and across the bridge to the bottom of the hill, my feet were wet with snow that had melted inside my boots, and I could feel the cold biting into my hands and fingers sending freezing shock waves throughout every bone in my body. That is how it has always been for me ever since my childhood in my native Pennines with winter upon us – the cold wind picking on my bones so remorselessly as to leave imprinted on my brain an image of my own skeleton, accurately and clearly defined. And now when I have grown to a height of six feet and six inches, and even thinner – if that were possible – with my blood also thinned out from years in warmer climes, the chill wind has still less difficulty in searching out my bones and striking an imprint of my skeleton.

As I made my way up the hill I kept stumbling and

falling into the drifts which were so deep that it would have been useless to seek for the path. Instead, for almost an hour, I kept heading for where I knew the top of the hill to be. It was as well that I did know because several times it was completely obscured by thick curtains of snow.

I kept thinking to myself that if anyone down in Halifax looks up to Beacon Hill and sees this tiny figure dark against the snow, they will conclude there is a madman at large, or a criminal taking advantage of the storm to escape.

Eventually, however, I did reach the very summit of the hill and turned towards the town below so as to face the wind and say farewell to the place on behalf of Dad, who now lay helpless in one of those houses whose shape I could just make out in the white expanse below High Sunderland: never again would he look upon this grim landscape of worn-out industries that had been his life's arena. And as if the place itself was intent upon my not escaping its unrelenting demands, the wind blew fiercer than ever as I turned towards the town. It so numbed my brain that I was incapable of making the proper farewell I had intended.

Instead my mind was taken over by one image that sustained itself for the short space of time my face was able to bear the lashing of the wind.

That image was of Grandma Nicholl and Dad on a winter's morning, while it was still dark, making their way on foot together down the bank towards the mill at Dean Clough where they both worked. She must have been in her fifties already, several years a widow. Left to bring up four boys on her own in the notorious slum of Charlestown, she had managed it by the simple expedient of working in the mill from six in the morning until five in the evening, and then serving as a barmaid in the pub at night. Dad had begun work as a half-timer, also in the mill, at the age of 12. In later years he would reminisce to me about those early morning journeys with Grandma, remarking what a blessing it was for them to walk together and grow close to one another, whether through talking as they went along or through just being silent with one another. Often they had to struggle along holding each other by the arm because of the strength of the wind.

It was the same wind which now drove me to seek some relief on the lee side of the hill. For a while, as I tramped along, the snow became deeper, and nowhere did I see any tracks to indicate that either man or beast had passed this way. But soon I came to a pair of standing stones that I remembered as marking the beginning of Dark Lane, which leads down into the valley. Dark Lane provided some respite from the freezing wind, but since almost no one uses it these days it also provides pot-holes, broken fences and stray lengths of barbed wire which were now concealed by the snow, as a result of which I several times pitched full length into the drifts.

After about an hour I passed the pit (where Dad's brother, Uncle Isaac, had once worked), and then went up past the derelict industrial school where boys used to be sent who had got into trouble. The windows these days have all been smashed, and the tiles in the old swimming bath lie scattered around. However, by this time I was beginning to feel warm, not only because of the strenuous plunging around in the snow but also through the warmth that comes from knowing that one has carried out the proper ritual, an act which makes some sense out of an apparently meaningless situation, meaningless beyond redemption. Nor did it take me long, once I was on the paved road, to walk the remaining two miles, again without meeting another soul, that brought me home, where there was a hot meal waiting for me.

That night, at 9.30, I was due to set out on my journey back to California, and we had been hoping that my eldest daughter, Mary, might be able to drive up from Shropshire so as to take over from me at my father's bedside. Yet with every hour it was getting more and more unlikely that she would do so, in view of the warnings on the radio that even the main roads over the Pennines were virtually impassable and should only be attempted in extreme emergencies. The news saddened me because it would have been a great comfort to me to have seen Mary just then, not having seen her for a long time. But what will be, will be. And by 9.30 she had still not arrived, while the snow was coming down in thicker flakes than ever. So I said my last goodbye to Dad; and then to Mum and the rest, and I set out alongside the garden wall leading to the village street. There, through the curtain of white flakes, I saw the approaching head-lights of a car which was moving ever so slowly, as if trying to find a grip upon the shifting snow.

When I came abreast of the car it stopped, and suddenly my beloved Mary's face became visible through the car window. 'Hello, Dad', she said in her soft voice as she stepped out into the

16

storm, and she put her arms around me and kissed me. For a minute we stood there holding one another, knowing that there was no time to go back to the house and talk. With the wind screaming around us, the snow gathering on Mary's fur cap and the car engine throbbing away, the world seemed to have become a wild nightmare of a place in which the two of us were left orphaned, exposed to every force of terror known to man or demons.

Within a minute we had parted, and already as I struggled on against the wind, my meeting with Mary had acquired a fictional quality, as if it were a scene from Pasternak's novel *Dr Zhivago*, as if our desolate hilltop had become another Varykino with a different sort of wolf howling around us.

But the railway station in Halifax, when I finally reached it, was real enough, in all conscience – or surreal enough – to drive every hint of poetry out of my head. It was like the house of the dead – no human being to be seen, only ghosts of what had once been the junction for a prosperous community. The grimy signboards, the broken benches, the platform lamps of which only half gave light, the waiting room with its dead cinders in the fireplace and gaps in the door through which the wind whistled – all of these once shining artefacts now witnessed to the neglect and despair which had overtaken the culture of this Pennine township.

And the same message of despair was spelled out to me once more as I sat almost alone in a scruffy carriage while the train made its way slowly through the frozen countryside, past chapels that had once been centres of life but were now empty shells, past factories and warehouses that were now neither dead nor alive, not standing up yet only half fallen down.

So it was in accordance with all these silent messages that in Leeds, when the train for London drew in, it turned out that only those carriages fitted with sleepers were heated. The handful of us without sleeper bookings at this midnight hour would be spending the night shivering in the semi-darkness.

And yet by comparison our discomfort seemed as nothing when a few hours later, stretching our stiffened limbs, we stumbled across King's Cross Station, because there, dozing on benches or hanging around the public lavatories, some of them seeking solace in cigarettes and others in strange contortions with each other, was such a haunting group of derelicts as you would rarely come across by day. Most of them looked starved, their eyes bulging with hunger; their clothes were worn thin, no protection against the winter's night; and whenever they moved, their limbs seemed to be sighing that they had long since come to the end – and beyond the end – of the road.

So if my daughter Mary and I had seemed to be characters in the story of Zhivago, these poor wretches appeared rather to have come out of the storm scene in *King Lear*. As I travelled on the first tube train of the morning towards Heathrow airport the image of them before my mind's eye was all I needed to push me into a state of frozen despair. And that is how I felt as I wandered around the halls of Heathrow, which were almost entirely empty and echoing hollowly at the sound of my footsteps. Where I was supposed to go to wait for a stand-by place on a Pan Am flight to San Francisco, I had no idea. Nor was there anyone of whom I might enquire. And if it came to that, I was so tired from all those nights by my father's side, whom I would never see again, that I felt too disorientated to search for anyone.

That was when I saw a young woman come round a corner some 30 yards away. She was a rather dumpy person, bespectacled, with short hair of a nondescript brown colour. But as she approached, that undistinguished appearance of hers mattered less to me than the fact that she was wearing a uniform, a uniform that held promise that its wearer knew about airways.

So I moved over to my left to intercept her, and I asked her if she knew where I was supposed to go in order to secure a stand-by place on a Pan Am flight to San Francisco. Though she was clearly in a hurry she stopped to listen to me, and then looked kindly at me as she answered that she was sorry but she didn't know.

And then something happened. Whether it was some note of sadness in my voice that she picked up or whether she saw something in my face that moved her – whatever it was, she had been touched. Perhaps that is why she in turn touched my sleeve and said, 'Wait a minute, my love. I think I may be able to help you. Please come with me.' And at that she led me across the hall towards a window on which she tapped. Soon a man appeared to whom she explained my need, and he straightaway assured me that if I were to wait outside his window for a quarter of an hour he would assign me a place on the flight to San Francisco.

The young woman who had come to my aid turned

towards me and smiled. 'There you are', she said. 'Have a safe journey.' I bowed towards her and thanked her for her kindness.

✑ *1 September 1985*

Betley, Staffordshire
It is never easy to convey in writing the significance which certain seemingly trivial events or actions assume in a person's life. To an outsider, that casual encounter in a deserted Heathrow airport between an unusually tall, bearded man wearing a dufflecoat and a dumpy woman airport worker could hardly have seemed of any importance in the life of either the man or the woman. They had never met before and they have never met since – not knowingly, at least, since neither knew the other's name and almost certainly would not recognise the other's face. Indeed, it is doubtful whether the woman even remembers the incident, since she has probably dealt with thousands of such passengers subsequently who are no more than a blur in her mind.

But the man, myself, will never forget how his numbed heart was melted by the warmth in the woman's voice when, though a total stranger to him, she said, 'my love'. I have wondered since if she often says 'my love' to total strangers, or whether it was the Spirit of God which inspired her to do so that winter morning. And is she a believer? The answer to that I shall never know, any more than she can have the remotest idea what significance her generous, though modest, gesture has come to assume in my own life.

What further fascinates me about the whole incident is the hint it provides of how the web of human relationships may well be more determined by such small deeds, accomplished each day by millions of unknown people, rather than by the decisions and acts of those who imagine themselves to be the controllers of human destiny.

The great virtue of such deeds, small in the eyes of the world but great in the sight of God, is that they cannot be contrived. They cannot be planned; for if they were planned they would be no more than exercises in manipulating other people. And none of us can have the faintest idea of the reverberations for good that they may produce throughout the world wherever the good news of hope is being spread. It always fills me with wonder, for instance, when I think of those words spoken to Jesus by the centurion at Capernaum, 'Lord, I am not worthy that you should enter under my roof but only say the word and my servant will be healed.' When he pronounced those words the centurion cannot have known that they would reverberate in the hearts of millions of human beings over the centuries and over the face of the whole earth at the most sacred moments of their lives, when they receive the sacrament of communion – in their childhood, at their marriages and in their last moments as death approaches.

Nor again can that peasant serf on the Dostoevsky estate, Marei, have ever imagined that he would be remembered and blessed throughout the world for that moment of *umilenie*, that melting of his heart by grace of the Holy Spirit which the great Russian novelist has recorded for all time.

Dostoevsky tells us how, on Easter Day, 1852, when he was serving as a political prisoner in Siberia, he was so disgusted by the drunkenness and violence of his fellow-prisoners that he climbed on to his bunk and turned his back upon the hell of a barrack room. For a long time he nursed his loathing of the other prisoners, until there suddenly arose within him the memory of an incident which he had completely forgotten from 20 years past.

As a child of nine he had one day been wandering alone across an open field on their estate when he thought he heard a wolf approaching. In his terror he ran towards the lonely figure of Marei, the serf who was ploughing the field. Marei quickly comforted the boy, stroking him on the cheek and murmuring, 'Don't be frightened, my dear. Christ be with thee. Cross thyself.' Dostoevsky recalled:

> But I did not cross myself. The corners of my lips quivered; and, I believe, that was what impressed him most. Slowly he stretched out his thick thumb, with the black nail soiled with earth, and gently touched my trembling lips . . . and he looked at me with a long motherly smile.

And now, 20 years later, it was Marei's soil-blackened thumb that Dostoevsky particularly remembered:

> And if I had been his own son he could not have bestowed upon me a glance full of a more serene love. And yet, who had prompted him? He was a peasant serf, while I was a nobleman's son. No one would find out how he had caressed

me and no one would reward him. The meeting was a solitary one, in an open field; and only God, maybe, perceived from above what a profound and enlightened human feeling, what delicate, almost womanly tenderness may fill the heart of some ignorant Russian peasant serf.

And when I climbed down off my bunk and gazed around I felt I could behold these unfortunate men with a wholly different outlook, for suddenly, by some miracle, all the hatred and anger had completely vanished from my heart.

৺ *27 March 1980*

The Hermitage, Big Sur, California

Monks and nuns often seem to establish themselves in quiet, beautiful places, which can lead one to ask them, 'Out of the moiling street with its swelter and its sin, who has given you this sweet and given your brothers dust to eat? When does their wage come in?' And yet, however critical I sometimes feel about monasteries and hermitages, I have to recognise, whenever I spend a few days here, that I am glad there are such places as this – an oasis of sanity and peace to remind us that the world of noise and words and money and power and sex can never satisfy the longings of the human heart.

It is quite remarkable how soon after arriving here I always feel the whole of my being to be changing – even within only a few hours. I sit on a bench at the edge of the tiny garden fronting my small cell and look out over the Pacific Ocean some 2000 feet below. Behind me the wooded mountain rises to a height of 5000 feet. And everywhere there is a profound silence which seems all the easier to breathe in by virtue of the regular songs and cries of the birds which nest in the steep gulches on either side. The warm sun relaxes all the muscles in my body, and my lungs take in deeper draughts of air than they ever imagined possible. And it is pure air, so sparkling that one understands why air is sometimes said to be like wine. The whole of my being, my body, my mind and my spirit, slips into a rhythm so perfect that if only I could sustain it for ever I would be in paradise.

For there is something paradisal about those of the hermits who have not allowed the rhythm of monastic life to put them to sleep. That is what also endows them with such unusual sensitivity to the feelings of their fellow creatures. One such person is Father Bede, the 80-year-old Englishman who entered the hermitage almost 40 years ago. He is now incredibly bent but still manages faithfully to cultivate the garden and to celebrate Mass with complete absorption. Yesterday he moved me to tears by unexpectedly coming over to me and saying that he had heard of my father's death; and would I allow him to celebrate Mass this morning for my father's sake? What moved me so deeply is that he and I have never spoken more than a few words to one another. But at some very deep level he has been exquisitely aware of me and my needs. And during the Mass at which he presided, I was made aware of a need within myself so deep down that only a touch of God could have brought it to light.

I need to go home, to return to England and live there so as to be with my mother when she is dying. The grace of being with my father in his last days now makes clear to me that there is nothing more important for a son or daughter than to be present at the dying of their mother and father. In the strictest sense of the word that is a unique occasion. It can never be repeated, and if one fails to be present at it through choice or through heedlessness, then the burden of that failure can never be lifted.

⫸ 22 July 1980

Santa Cruz, California

What a blessed release, and relief, it would be if a messenger from the Lord were to appear and say to me, 'Once you are back in England, for the rest of your life, you are not required to utter any word of criticism of any institution or any individual. You need rebuke no one. You are henceforth relieved of that obligation. From now on you may live as Father Sergius lived, who gave his name to Tolstoy's novella: doing menial tasks, teaching Scripture to children, eating simple food, in quietness and peace.'

But that is not what the messengers are saying. They have been saying, 'Don't imagine that you are meant, like a *sannyasi*, to "get beyond" all earthly tasks while you are still in the body. Your longing for utter purity, simplicity and peace itself needs to be purified by the tensions of finding shelter, earning your bread and your clothing and raising your voice on behalf of the dumb. Not until the very end will you be relieved of those tensions.'

II.

Tantur
1981–1985

ᏋᎧ 1981

Betley

Often I have to laugh at myself for my habit of wanting to communicate with virtually everyone under the sun when I read what they say or watch the way they are behaving. But sometimes my impulsiveness can surprisingly turn out to be rewarding, as it did today in the Israeli embassy in London.

On the surface, my impulse to write to the Israeli ambassador on account of his letter to *The Times* of December 24 last year was strange. After all, his letter contained no arguments that one has not already heard thousands of times from Israeli propagandists; but there was something about it that moved me. Perhaps it was the fact that the letter appeared on the eve of Christmas, and I was saddened to think that our Jewish brothers and sisters are excluded from the joyous celebration of the birth of the Jew, Jesus. Even more significant, I think, was an echo that could be heard beneath the ambassador's argumentative sentences – a cry from the heart lest the fears of Jews should once more go unheeded.

For several weeks I looked in *The Times* for some response to Shlomo Argov's letter, but none appeared. So after three or four months I myself decided to write in order to assure the good man that his *cri de cœur* had not gone entirely unheard; but also to ask him to explain to those of us who feel committed to the Jewish people, how we may yet be free to criticise the policy of the state of Israel (just as we criticise other states, especially our own) without fear that we shall be condemned as anti-Semites.

Unfortunately from my point of view, the ambassador has been subjected to a terrible grilling by the British media in recent weeks, so when we met today he was too excitable to deal calmly with my question. In fact, I never raised it during our hour-

25

long meeting. Instead he poured out torrents of words denouncing a British television programme about Israel entitled *Hanging Fire*. Much of his criticism was justified, though I demurred at his demand that the producers of the programme should be put in jail. But one thing he said about Israel was so fundamental that anyone venturing an opinion on that state should never forget it.

His own family not being a particularly religious one, he said, their longing to escape from exile and persecution and live in a state of their own had not been inspired by religious tradition. Rather, what his family had hoped for, above all, was to live in a country of their own, like all other human beings, in order that gradually the memory of all those thousands of years of persecution would be eroded and the ancient wounds would be healed. Whereas instead, he continued in an agonised voice, just the opposite had happened. 'When we started living in the Land we discovered that absolutely everyone else there, everyone whom we met, had a similar history to our own; so that far from the dreadful memories being eroded and the ancient wounds healed, everything reminded us of our terrible past and every encounter called attention to our wounds.'

When I heard those words from Shlomo Argov's lips, I recognised on the basis of my own sojourns in Israel how true and fundamental his words were. The ingathering of the Jewish people has heightened their sense of isolation, and for them the state of Israel has acted like a burning prism, intensifying the remembrance of their suffering.

My interview with the ambassador left me puzzling over another conundrum as I walked away from the embassy down Kensington High Street. How is it that there are certain people you cannot take to, although they are altogether polite and correct in their behaviour, and their viewpoint is close to your own; while there are other people of whom you can hardly say the same, and yet you like them – even sometimes when they are rogues? Well, Shlomo Argov is anything but a rogue; all the same he is explosive and unreasonable on some questions, but I really did take to the man. He has a good heart.

☙ *10 July*

Betley

'I would never go there now', said a friend of mine when I met her for the first time in many years and told her that I was going to live in Jerusalem. 'It would be like going to live in Naboth's vineyard.' In spite of being slow on the uptake even I realised that by Naboth's vineyard she was referring to the land of Palestine, and that she was casting present-day Israel for the role of Ahab. My friend was carrying out a typical rabbinic exegetical practice by taking a biblical story as paradigmatic for the state of contemporary relations between Arabs and Jews.

For my own part I do not find that particular exegetical practice to be very illuminating generally; indeed, on many occasions its use has proved positively dangerous, having been invoked to justify robbery and slaughter on a large scale. All the same my friend's remark brought me up sharply and set me wondering what my own precise role might be in the drama of Naboth's vineyard. I could never, for instance, imagine any event that would convince me to don the mantle of Elijah the Tishbite who went to the king of Israel and declared, 'Yahweh says this: you have committed murder; now you usurp as well. For this – and Yahweh says this – in the place where the dogs licked the blood of Naboth, the dogs will lick your blood too.' And I fervently hoped, of course, that I was not destined to share the fate of Ahab's son, Jehoram – he upon whom Jehu drew his bow and sent an arrow between his shoulder blades which came out through his heart; then Jehu had his body thrown into the field of Naboth, at the same time calling upon the blood of Naboth and the blood of his sons. In all conscience, I thought, there has been altogether far too much blood spilt already in this neck of the woods, from the day of Cain and Abel until today, without any sojourner adding to it, whether by thought or by word or by deed.

So now, in my third sojourn in the land, I thank God for the instruction that he gave me years ago, before I arrived for the first time. And it is significant, I believe, that he gave the instruction, not through the Peoples of the Book, but through the peaceable and tolerant Taoists.

My instruction came in the form of a story which tells of a scholar who was about to leave his native town on a journey

27

of many years. Before setting out he went along to say farewell to his friend, the town butcher; and in the course of doing so he noticed the butcher's chopper. It was shining and spotless, its blade incredibly sharp. After admiring it at some length, the scholar bade his friend farewell and then set out on his travels, which were to take him all of 25 years. Upon returning once more to his native town and settling in at home again, the scholar went to visit his butcher friend. After they had greeted one another with due ceremony, the scholar chanced to notice a chopper on the butcher's bench, just as shining and spotless as the one he had noticed 25 years previously. And when he tested the blade it was just as incredibly sharp. 'It amazes me', he said to his friend, 'that you are able to secure a supply of such wonderful choppers, year after year, and that you can keep the blade so sharp in spite of all the meat that you chop with them.' 'It is quite simple', the butcher replied. 'That chopper is none other than the same chopper which you saw 25 years ago, and I have never needed to sharpen it since then, in spite of all the meat that I chop with it each day. You see, in every piece of meat, in between the various parts, there is always an infinitely small space, a way (*tao*), and if the blade is sufficiently fine, the chopper can actually go along that way between the parts, without spilling any blood or getting stained or becoming blunt.'

In the Taoist story God was saying, 'Go through it all without harming anyone, without spilling blood or yourself becoming stained or blunt.' And I continue to think that the Taoist story offers a better paradigm than the Naboth story for anyone who is going to spend some time in the Holy Land.

But even my Taoist story cannot be regarded as a completely satisfactory paradigm. Certainly it brings out the need for detachment in a memorable fashion, but it does not do justice to the demand for commitment asked of one in Jerusalem.

And 'demand' is the right word to use here, because Jerusalem is the most demanding of cities to live in – not in the same way as Calcutta or New York, but in the much more subtle sense that here you are called upon to exercise the virtue of justice every minute of the day, or so it seems. Nor is this exercise of justice required of you simply in your deeds or in your words. In deeds or in words it is comparatively easy. Far more demanding is the fact that you are called to make a secure dwelling for justice in the deepest point of your heart, in the *guha*, as the Hindu sacred scriptures name it, 'the cave of the heart'. For in this mysterious city of Jerusalem you can not only see people's deeds and hear their words, you can actually feel their heartbeats and sense what is going on in their hearts – and they in yours. Which is why, perhaps, this is the city of lies: people pile one lie upon another in a desperate, futile attempt to heap lies so thick that the truth relentlessly demanded of them by this holy city shall remain hidden.

How then can one reveal to oneself those lies that, in this city, prevent justice from securing a dwelling in the cave of one's heart? Is there any sign available to indicate when one's heart is becoming corrupted? These were questions that I anxiously put to myself during the months when I was preparing to live once more in Jerusalem. And an answer was given more apposite than that of Naboth's vineyard or even of the Taoist chopper.

It is simple. If your immediate spontaneous reaction – if the movement of your heart – upon hearing of some tragedy, is an ideological rather than a human one, then your heart has become corrupted, and you should leave straightaway and go on pilgrimage until it is cleansed. Suppose you hear, for instance, that scores of civilians have been killed in an air raid upon PLO headquarters in Beirut, and your immediate reaction is, 'Well, what else do they expect if they share quarters with terrorists?' In that case, your reaction is not a human one but an ideological one. Your ideology may even be correct; but if it is primary, then you have lost your heart of flesh and set up in its place an idol of stone.

I quoted this example to a high-placed Israeli official, and when I noticed how his facial muscles twitched I realised that he was grieved by what had been revealed to him in the cave of his heart. A good man, nevertheless; and he grieved. More saddening was my encounter with a Marxist whom I know. After describing to him the sign of discernment that I had been given, I proposed a different illustration as a test, an incident in Haifa bus station. There, a bomb planted by the PLO killed a number of innocent citizens. Again, I said, if one's instant reaction is to sigh, 'Well, such things are only to be expected if they are oppressing another people', then an ideology has turned one's heart to stone. However, my Marxist brother seemed not to be grieved, as my Israeli brother had been, by what had revealed itself in the cave of his own heart. Instead he attacked me sharply for being obscurantist, for not recognising that ideas also 'have life'.

Granted that ideas have life in a metaphorical sense; but it is also true that they can kill compassion, and when compassion dies, what is there left in the cave of the heart except an idol of stone? And though such petrifaction is saddening when it happens to people in any city of the world, whether in Belfast or San Salvador or Washington, there seems something peculiarly tragic about its happening in Jerusalem, this holy city so improbably situated high in the hill country of Judaea, a provincial city which nevertheless remains the cave in the heart of the world. It is a cave full of stone idols.

๛ *26 August*

Betley

Packing up once again! How many scores of times Dorothy and I have done this in the last 15 years. Every time it is like a little death, especially the task of putting my books into cardboard boxes once more. As I was doing so today it was like seeing my life pass before me all over again in my books, which represent various aspects of my life's journey: 1935, *Stalky and Co.*, my first school prize; 1940, another school prize, *The Destiny of Man* by the Russian thinker, Nicolas Berdyaev; 1944, *The Complete Works of St John of the Cross*, given to me by Dorothy for my birthday. Oh, the fragility of human life and aspirations! Seeing and handling those series of Celtic books and Russian books and books about church history and many others also made me feel miserably how little I have to show for all those years of learning and reading – *Holiness* (published in 1981), for instance, seems very small fruit for all that endeavour. Also, how quickly it seems empty as soon as it is brought face to face with suffering. Suffering strips away all our pretentiousness.

'How long must this go on, archpriest?', Dorothy said to me this morning in a self-mocking voice as she painfully straightened up after filling yet another cardboard box. She was referring to our in-joke that our destiny is duplicating the story of the seventeenth-century Russian priest Avvakum and his wife Markovna who, with their children, spent many years being dragged around Siberia in the train of the soldier-adventurer, Pashkov. One day, as they were tramping along the icy roads, Dame Avvakum – and not for the first time – stumbled and fell. This time, almost too weary to get up again, she cried out to her husband, 'How long must this go on, archpriest?' He answered, 'Until our very death, Markovna!' And she replied, with a sigh, 'Let us, then, plod on, Petrovich'.

So to Dorothy's similar question I gave Avvakum's reply, 'Until our very death, Markovna!' To which she replied with feigned resignation, 'Let us, then, plod on, archpriest.'

৫৭ *30 August**

Letter to the Tablet

Yesterday sunrise was more splendid than ever. Usually these days, when the sun rises beyond the mountains of Moab east of us, it instantly appears like a clean disk, clearly outlined over the sharp horizon of the mountains. It can be quite literally breathtaking. You hold your breath as you see the sun slowly rise – first the brilliant tip of light and then the rest of that golden ball. Some days ago, when only half of it was visible, yet all golden, it seemed for a moment as though the very Dome of the Rock had been lifted by the hand of God from the Temple Mount in Jerusalem, five miles north of us, and gently set down upon that mountain range in Moab, just beyond the Dead Sea. But then the rest of the sun's globe ascended, and you realised that the Dome of the Rock upon the mountain was just a mirage. Except that for a moment, yet enduring still in one's memory, it was not just a mirage. In such moments one begins to understand how in this land people can believe that everything is possible.

Yesterday, however, was different again because lying upon the mountains was a low bank of purple clouds, and the first rays of the sun lit up the clouds' edges in hues of red and gold and silver – until eventually the sun emerged fully above the purple bank. And for an instant, from where I stood on the roof of Tantur, looking through a gap between the bare hills of the

---

* The following articles and journal entries were all written at Tantur, unless otherwise stated.

Judaean desert, I could just make out a sliver of light which I knew to be the waters of the Dead Sea.

What more beautiful spot could you dream of as a place to practise your morning yoga than the high, flat and spacious roof of this Ecumenical Institute, with its superlative views. Eastwards, as I have said, lies the Judaean desert, where Bishop Pike of San Francisco perished ten years ago. South-eastwards the Herodian is visible, unnaturally flat-topped, the mound within which Herod the Great built his palace and to which his body was later transported with such pomp and ceremony across the desert from Jericho. As your eyes scan towards the south, towards the Shepherds' Fields at Beit Sahur and the Church of the Nativity at Bethlehem you can hardly avoid the contrast between the worldly and successful Herod and the underprivileged child of Bethlehem, who finished up on the gallows. The world never learns. Perhaps, indeed, that is the very definition of the world: that which never learns.

Somehow Herod seems very remote now and Jesus very close, since in the clear morning air you feel as if you could stretch out your hand and touch Bethlehem with its endless jumble of churches and convents and bell towers that nestle in the hills around. To say nothing of the mosques that have sprung up in recent years, especially in the ancient town of Beit Jala, which for centuries was wholly Christian but which today houses many Muslim refugees with their numerous children. As to the nature of their faith I can hardly remain in doubt, because every morning at about 4.15 the voice of the muezzin, many times amplified by loudspeakers, comes billowing in through our apartment window to assure us that God is great, that he is one, that he has no son and that prayer is better than sleep.

Beit Jala lies south and west of Tantur, leaving the western and northern bowl of the hills to the dominating, fortress-like stretch of apartment blocks which is the modern Israeli settlement of Gilo, where many Jews from the Soviet Union are now housed and where no one seems to know what the population will eventually number – some say 10,000, some even more.

I have never heard anyone describe Gilo as beautiful, and yet from our magic roof I have even experienced the beauty of Gilo. That was on the day of Yom Kippur, the Jewish Day of Atonement, when this present Jerusalem took on a touch of the heavenly Jerusalem. Across all the roads around the city hurdles were put up in order to stop traffic going into and out of the holy city on that day of awe. They were set up outside our own enclosure walls, since we are just at the point where the Bethlehem road crosses the boundary of Jerusalem. By the dawn of Yom Kippur all traffic within Jerusalem had stopped; Israeli radio and television had gone silent; the air itself was uncannily still that day. Something unique in the modern world had happened: the noise and bustle and tension of a great modern city had been stilled, not because of a disaster such as war or an earthquake, but simply in obedience to the command of God. It was truly awesome – a touch of the eternal sabbath of God. And Gilo also took on a look of great peace, its stone apartments no longer forbidding, but mellow and quiet in the early morning sun – beautiful.

The air was so still that a few minutes later, when the muezzin was calling to the Muslim faithful of the Temple Mount in Jerusalem, I could hear not only his cry but, very faintly, the deep groan of the answering faithful, like the swell of the sea. Soon they were followed by the gentle, modest sound of the Christian church bells in Bethlehem, Beit Jala and Beit Sahur.

Lastly, but most important of all, came the birds. Every morning one hears the smaller ones chattering in the pine trees that sway above the four-foot-high wall encompassing our roof. They sustain their chatter for about a quarter of an hour and then suddenly, as if in obedience to some great conductor, they all go silent on the instant. Afterwards, within a few minutes, one hears the whirring of the wings of bigger birds – wild pigeons, I think – which fly past in formations of 40 and 50. Winging in from Jerusalem in the north, they head for the hills towards Hebron in the south and then swing eastwards round the bowl of the hills before turning north to speed a second time over our roof.

In a land beset by political divisions and strident theological quarrels those birds are such a blessing: in their flight they pass with ease over the boundaries between Arab and Israeli territory. Amidst the often wearisome talk of God which is my lot they witness to his presence not by words but by their simple existence.

∝ 7 *September*

Though this is not the first time in my life that I have
succeeded to an office in some institution and had to spend many
hours working through the files so as to familiarise myself with its
operation, yet never before have I come across records, memoranda and letters so fissiparous as those deposited here. The
impression they are leaving upon me is that, from its very beginning, this Institute has served as an almost perfect screen upon
which men and women from far and near have been enabled
freely to project their own schemes, desires and dreams. And then,
when those schemes and desires have proved impossible to fulfil
in the actual Tantur, as opposed to their dreamland Tantur, it
seems that their positive projections have suddenly got switched
on to the negative and consequently appear upon the screen in
the form of frustrations and criticisms.

Sadly, and not for the first time in Christian history, it is
precisely the act by which it is hoped to create the perfect community that seems to have precipitated most division here at
Tantur. Communion/community is the *raison d'être* of the Institute,
and if we slacken our efforts towards communion/community then
nothing else we achieve will be of any lasting significance. So it is
essential for me to get my own head as clear as possible on this
issue of Eucharist before the scholars arrive and the arguments
begin.

Here is how I see things as a result both of reading the
files and of speaking with those who have been living here of
recent years.

It is painful merely to listen to people as they give vent
to their pain at having been expected to attend a Eucharist in
which not all those present were permitted to receive the sacrament of the altar. This pain, which is felt on all sides, suffuses the
atmosphere of the Institute – not always very perceptibly, of
course, but nevertheless it is apt to surface quite suddenly at the
most unexpected moments – at meal times, for example, or in
the children's playground or the laundry. In the expression of pain
which I hear there is often, as I recognise, an egotistic note: my
pain is greater than his pain, and therefore he should concede
that my theological position is more genuine than his theological
position. All the same, these good people are for the most part

giving expression not merely to personal pain but even more to a common agony that is felt by the whole Christian community throughout the world. What intensifies both the pain and the agony is that here Orthodox, Baptists, Quakers, Mennonites, Lutherans, Anglicans, Melkites, Methodists, Congregationalists, Presbyterians, members of the Church of Christ and Roman Catholics are all living next to one another, skin to skin, as it were, sharing everything, minute by minute, hour by hour, day by day, for a long period. There is no escape! And this, I imagine, makes the experience at Tantur different from the ecumenical experience anywhere else in the wide world: nowhere else does such a wide variety of Christians live so much on top of one another and for such a sustained period.

There is a further source of the pain being experienced here, of which the sufferers themselves may not be aware – or, at least, they may be aware of it at some level of their being below consciousness, but they are suppressing it. That element is one of anger against the guidelines for eucharistic practice at Tantur, laid down by our international advisory council. What, in particular, causes the anger is the guidelines' insistence that there shall never be more than one Eucharist celebrated at Tantur on any day, and that all scholars are expected to attend the one and only Eucharist on a Sunday, the celebrant to be nominated each week by the rector, whose duty it is to give each ordained minister the opportunity to celebrate in turn. It is further specified that the celebrant is expected to adhere to the rubrics of his own tradition (with the implication, presumably, that he is not to start fashioning a liturgy according to his own personal whims or according to what he takes to be the special circumstances of Tantur).

In my own judgement these guidelines are perfectly sensible, but I can understand why they have got under the skin of so many members of the community. As always when communication is attempted, one can hardly exaggerate the crucial importance of words, of idiom, of language. And the language of our guidelines is sober, measured, precise English, the idiom of the Anglican tradition. I could hardly have foreseen that it would be criticised as 'cold and juridical', but since that same criticism is urged by both Baptists and Catholics we must pay attention to it. And I think that I have found the clue to this unusual accord among Baptists and Catholics: the Baptists and Catholics in question are all Americans, and it is the American in them which looks for more warmth and emotion when speaking of the Lord's Supper; their national idiom, being more rhetorical, demands something of a *fervorino*.

I must try to explain to the dissidents that it was precisely on account of the passions and hot words generated between Protestants and Catholics by the Eucharist that the advisory council devised such a sober and measured statement, in the hope that the very choice of language might help to cool passions. The upshot, perhaps, will persuade the council to accept an axiom that is fundamental to this enterprise; that is, *you can't win*. You can't win quite simply because the contradictions within Christianity over Eucharist have arisen from the history of the whole Christian Church and cannot be resolved except by the whole Church. Only a reckless fantasy could claim that this Institute is capable of resolving those contradictions. To demand that we should do so is plain foolish.

The members of the advisory council themselves need also to recognise the presence of suppressed anger against them for the way in which they fly in here once a year for two or three days, lay down laws that the scholars have to observe and then fly out again, not to appear for another year. The reaction of the scholars reminds me of our reactions as young soldiers during the war, when we were confronted with orders drawn up by pundits in Delhi which we would have to carry out but the demands of which, we believed, made no impact upon the pundits' own lives.

The soldiers in this case are the four or five Benedictine monks of Montserrat who have been living here for ten years already, ever since the foundation of the place. And, as is the fate of common soldiers, they bear the burden and heat of the day while others are giving orders and making grand speeches, oblivious of what pains the common soldier has to bear in silence. No one, for instance, seems to realise the quite elementary fact that every Sunday when a Protestant is the chosen celebrant here, the Benedictines obey the advisory council guidelines by attending the celebration, thereby missing the Mass to which they are obligated as Roman Catholics. At the same time they follow the rubrics of the Catholic Church by not receiving communion at the hands of a Protestant minister. In doing so they seem constantly to incur the wrath of many Protestants who attribute the monks' abstention to personal narrow-mindedness.

The mutual pain is all the more acute on account of the fact that these monks, being Catalan, speak little English, and so their position is never fully explained. Moreover they are all blessed with the monastic virtue of discretion and are therefore reticent about the restraints from all sides under which they live. Whether they could ever satisfactorily explain the weightiest of these restraints to the scholars who come here I very much doubt. Even the most sensitive and perceptive of the scholars are hardly here long enough to appreciate the weight which attaches hereabouts to the Orthodox Church and, supremely, to the Orthodox patriarch of Jerusalem. Yet it is above all in view of unity with the Orthodox that the Benedictines were called to Tantur. Our monks are constantly working, in season and out of season, to assuage the traditional hostility felt by the Orthodox towards the other Churches whom they regard as invaders. In spite of the warm personal friendship that the monks have steadily cultivated with both Orthodox clergy and laity, we at Tantur need only put one foot wrong in Orthodox eyes for years of patient work by the monks to be brought to nought. The Orthodox hierarchy are particularly suspicious of the Free Churches, whom they accuse of proselytising, of stealing members from the Orthodox flock. And their suspicions are returned in good measure by a number of Western scholars who do not conceal their contempt for a Church which they regard as superstitious, priest-ridden, archaic and unevangelical.

When currents of suspicion are running so strongly and so deeply, almost any issue can give rise to open polemics and even serve as a pretext for holy warfare; and the Lord's Supper in Christian history is not just any issue: it is *the* issue. Predictably, therefore, soon after the establishment of the Institute the rumour ran around Jerusalem that Tantur fostered the practice of intercommunion, by which all members of the community, no matter what their ecclesiastical tradition, whether Quaker or Anglican, Lutheran or Roman Catholic, were urged to partake of the Eucharist, even though their beliefs about what is happening at the Eucharist are quite irreconcilable. That was enough for the Orthodox patriarch to forbid Orthodox to come to Tantur, a prohibition to which some Tantur supporters responded with a shrug of *je m'en fiche*, but which for the Benedictines was a body blow – their hope of a reconciliation with the Orthodox seemed to have been dashed from the beginning by the heedlessness of others. No wonder that they have cringed whenever the issue of intercommunion has been approached in a cavalier fashion, or that they have discreetly let it be known they will leave Tantur if any rector practises intercommunion.

Nor, as may be imagined, did it please the Vatican some time later when an article written by an Anglican who had stayed at Tantur was published in a prominent Roman Catholic journal praising the Institute for its policy of 'open communion'. The Vatican riposte arrived during the period years ago when I was myself a scholar here. Which of us, indeed, who were present in chapel that Sunday morning when it was read out will ever forget it? As the reader droned on through one severe paragraph after another, each couched in Vatican jargon, you could feel a chill wind blowing through the chapel and the bones and hearts of all the worshippers freezing.

I had always considered that an indispensable quality of every living body is warmth, and I concluded that any community which claims to be the body of Christ must likewise be characterised by warmth: the relations between the members have to be warm. If that is true then we were not the body of Christ when that bone-chilling Vatican statment was read out.

Yet in the end it is perhaps neither the Vatican nor the Orthodox nor the advisory council which has laid the heaviest burden on our Eucharistic gatherings, but certain Americans. At least you know where you stand with the former three authorities, but the lack of consistency, the unpredictability, among American priests and ministers inevitably sets certain other people's teeth on edge. One week, for instance, a celebrant priest or minister will announce that all those are invited to receive communion who are baptised Christians, and then a week later another priest or minister from the same tradition as the first will issue a much more restrictive invitation. This is particularly true of the Roman Catholic priests. Many of them come from American university campuses which are often genuinely liberal and enlightened, but where sometimes it seems as though 'anything goes'. They, in the eyes of our Protestant scholars, tend to be good guys, whereas those who stick to the official guidelines are classed as reactionary and narrow-minded. The impact which this inconsistency has upon priests from the Third World is particularly grievous. Granted the condition of their countries and their own training, they are bewildered and pained at being pilloried as unenlightened and reactionary.

It is certainly not going to be easy disentangling all these issues so that we can live together at peace, especially since I suspect that one of the main difficulties is rooted so deeply in such a sensitive area that it is hidden by taboo. For just as Catholicism in, say, Scotland is strongly Calvinist and in Latin America strongly Indian, so in the USA it is markedly Protestant: US Catholics do not spontaneously think of the Church as a divinely established organ of salvation with a hierarchy that must be obeyed and a tradition that must be revered. In accordance with good democratic traditions, they have a tendency to think of the Church as a continuing town meeting at which the members present can at any given moment change everything that has been decided in the past. That is a perfectly defensible concept of a Church – but it happens not to be the Catholic one, according to which it is the Church which makes its members and not the members who make the Church. Confusion results when Catholics act upon one concept while professing something different.

Reading about these matters in the files, and listening to the permanent residents discussing them, convinces me that on the first Sunday of our year we must not attempt to celebrate the Eucharist. Before doing so everyone must have the opportunity to say, in a leisurely atmosphere and at full length, what Eucharist means to them, as well as to listen and discover what it means to the others who are to constitute our community. When we do eventually enter the chapel to celebrate, there must be no debates going on inside our heads. Rather we must enter with clean hearts – hearts turned towards God, not towards our own arguments.

❧ *26 September*

This evening I am feeling very happy with the mood that the community has achieved as a result of many hours spent in discussing the Eucharist – or the Lord's Supper, to adopt the usage of our Baptist friends, who pertinently reminded us that to them the very word 'Eucharist' has a strange sound. Even in our language we must be careful not to impose our own habits upon others.

What has struck all of us, I think, is how near the mark Karl Rahner is when he says that 'faith as it is actually experienced today is the same in the different churches among average Christians', and that 'the major Christian Churches of today could unite, even institutionally: their sense of faith presents no insuperable obstacle.'

At the same time we all recognise that only a minority of people in the various Churches have so far realised the truth of Rahner's statement. And so it would be irresponsible of us at Tantur to say, 'The people who do not agree with Rahner and us are just ignorant and reactionary. We who constitute the community at Tantur will go ahead and act as though the Churches are institutionally united and will thereby advance the cause of Christian unity. The rest will have to catch up with us.' On the contrary, we are here as *representatives* of the different Christian Churches; if we turn Tantur into an *ecclesiola*, a little Church on its own, we thereby turn ourselves into members of a tiny new sect and cease to have any influence within our own Churches, because we no longer represent them.

It is at this point that St Paul's admonition to the Corinthians is most appropriate: 'You say, "Is my freedom to be called into question by another man's conscience? We are free to do anything." Yes, but is everything good for us? Does everything help the building up of the community?'

These words of St Paul must constantly guide our behaviour, especially in view of our Orthodox brothers and sisters whose whole historical experience has been different from that of the West. Until now, the Reformation, the Renaissance and the Industrial Revolution, which have so shaped Western theology, have scarcely had any influence upon Orthodox theology, and so their theologians come to these questions with a very different mind-set from our own, and it is both wrong and foolish of us when we dismiss their hesitations as 'anachronistic'. They may, in this instance, be the 'weaker brethren' whom St Paul is constantly urging us not to offend with our 'liberalism'. And perhaps we should even ask ourselves whether we may not have something to learn from them, since 'God has chosen the weak ones' to teach the clever ones.

Yet when all is said and done, we do not want to remain stuck in our present positions, and so today we decided to emphasise certain aspects of the Eucharistic liturgy which will to some extent assuage the pain of division and symbolise our longing for full communion.

In the course of our discussion, for instance, someone pointed out that it is a symptom of superstition and of a mind given to magic to imagine that the Eucharist 'takes place' in the very split second when the priest pronounces the words of consecration over the bread and wine on the altar. So we should not fall into the habit, induced by such a misconception, of treating all the other rituals of the Eucharistic ceremony as secondary. After all, Jesus said that what he leaves to us is peace and that peace comes to us in many ways which are symbolised in the ritual kiss of peace. We resolved, therefore, to accord the ritual kiss of peace the devotion which it requires, and not to perform it perfunctorily, as happens in so many churches. Since our congregation usually numbers no more than 50 it is easy enough for each of us to give the kiss of peace to every other member of the congregation, and to do it in an unhurried fashion. Which means that the celebrant must not start any subsequent prayer until everyone has greeted everyone else.

That resolve about our Sunday celebration seemed to be wholeheartedly accepted, but I am not so confident that the same is true of my own suggestion. Though it was accepted eventually, that may have been, I fear, because it was the rector who proposed it. In an attempt to temper the sense of being excluded which must afflict all of us at one time or another when we cannot receive the sacrament of the altar, I proposed that we adopt an Orthodox practice which I have found consoling when I have attended the Russian Orthodox liturgy at which, obviously, I am not permitted to receive the sacred species. But on those occasions I have received the *prosphora*, the blessed bread which is distributed to everyone present. In taking the *prosphora*, not only have I been brought closer to all my fellow worshippers but I have done so in the faith that Christ does not need permission from anyone to be truly present in any form he chooses, and if he chooses to be so present in the form of the *prosphora* then I am doubly grateful.

In future, therefore, at the end of our Eucharist here there will be *prosphora* for everyone as they are leaving the chapel.

Yet on reflection I am beginning to get slightly queasy about what I have done. Remembering the facial expressions and

41

body movements of one or two scholars during the discussion, I fear that some of them are going to regard the *prosphora* as a rather contrived device to try to conceal the truth that they are being treated as second-class citizens. We can only hope and pray that it will come right!

And I think it may do so, because you really could sense that we are all of one heart in believing that it is nonsense for Christians to keep insisting on the importance in our lives of the Eucharist, the *koinonia*, and then to spend the rest of the week in petty quarrels and egotistic tantrums that undermine community, that very *koinonia* about which we make such a fuss on Sundays. Our lives throughout the week should manifest the *koinonia* which we enjoyed on Sunday, the first day of the week, and they should in that way prepare us for yet deeper *koinonia* on the coming Sunday.

Just when chair legs were being scraped on the floor as a sign that everyone thought our discussion had finished, I introduced a rule about which I had consulted nobody. I left it until last because I wanted to emphasise that there are certain matters beyond discussion. The rule is that nobody is to raise for discussion, or to gossip about, the reason why anyone did or did not go to receive communion. If someone chooses to explain why they did or did not, that is a different matter; but it is quite intolerable that the most intimate relationship of any creature, their relationship with their Creator, should be subject to speculation on the part of anyone.

ॐ *29 October*

At last I have done what I have intended to do from almost the first day that I arrived at Tantur. That day was the very last of the year 1976, when I came here as a scholar. The rector at that time, Dr Walter Wegner, very kindly gave me a tour of the Institute, in the course of which we walked together on our open, flat roof. As we were examining the landscape westwards, my eye lit upon a stone shack situated beside an old quarry, some 50 yards outside the high, protective walls of Tantur.

'Is there someone living there?', I asked Dr Wegner 'Yes,' he said, 'an Arab woman and her children.' At which reply there came into my head, unbidden and spontaneous, the words 'Dives and Lazarus'. Already, at a subliminal level of my mind, I must have been troubled at the contrast between the triumphalist style of Tantur and the poverty at our very gate; and I must have further felt in my bones the parallel between our position and that of the rich man, Dives, gazing down on poor Lazarus, symbolised by our Arab neighbour.

Having previously read a list of the projects that Tantur scholars were engaged upon, I was in a position to enquire, 'Is there not one of this year's scholars working on the meaning of the Beatitudes?' 'Yes, there is, a Benedictine sister', replied the rector. His reply left me musing to myself, 'I wonder if she has ever gone over to the Arab woman in order to find out from someone who is poor what it feels like to be in the Kingdom, as is promised in the Beatitude, "Blessed are the poor"?'

My question on the roof has pointed itself at me ever since we came back to Tantur two months ago. So I was very happy this morning when my Arab friend, Geries Khoury, agreed to accompany Dorothy and me over to our feminine Lazarus in order to act as translator for us. Since today is the Muslim feast, *Id al ras al sena al hegira*, we hoped it would not seem patronising for us to take sweets and fruit across to the lady in the shack whom, from the vantage point of our roof, I had observed hanging out her washing and doing her cooking at an outside oven in all kinds of weather.

I need not have worried about seeming to patronise her. There are some people so strong that you could come a cropper if you tried to do so. After all, as her sister-in-law who happened to be visiting her explained, our Lazarus had lived in that shack for 25 years and for the last 14 years she had been a widow, her husband having been blown to pieces in 1967 by an Israeli land mine as he was tending his sheep on the adjacent land. Since that date she has brought up four boys and two girls in that one-roomed shack where there is neither electricity nor running water. Having heard these stories, I then noticed our neighbour's bare feet, gripping the earth so confidently, each of her toes regularly spaced, as she prepared for us cups of coffee so strong and so highly sugared that I felt as though they were knocking my brain against the top of my skull.

Women such as these, I mused to myself, could eat pompous Western men of position and power for breakfast, partly because they have endured so much but partly also because of

43

their Islamic formation – witness the sister-in-law's unhesitating words this morning as soon as she understood why we had come. With no preliminaries whatsoever she simply said, 'When we die – and we shall all be brought to death soon – the only thing that will count for anything will be our good deeds.' That instant reference to life beyond death and to the day of judgement is so typically Muslim. For a Muslim, the path is straight.

ૡ *6 November*

God is a great puzzler. Today's puzzle left me quite incapable of working out in what way our meeting with Mother Teresa has changed my attitude towards her.

I truly don't think that I have idolised her in the past, though certainly she has proved a tremendous influence on my life as she has on the lives of millions of other people. Nevertheless, I have sensed a karmic connection between us ever since our first meeting 15 years ago. On that occasion, in Southall, she was being introduced to four or five of us in a quiet drawing room. Coming to me last of all, she paused, looked at me with those all-encompassing eyes of hers and then said, 'We have met before, haven't we?' When I said not, she thought for a moment as if searching in her memory, and then said, 'I seem to recognise your face'.

Granted my temperament, her remark was enough to make me believe that, in some dimension of time and space, we had indeed met, and that she, being more sensitive than me, was recognising me from a previous existence. It also stilled at source any hesitations I might have conjured up as reason for refusing when she suggested that I might teach her novices church history. When I agreed to do so, she calmly accepted my offer without bothering to discover that it would mean travelling down from northern England one Saturday each month just for a two-hour session!

In Jerusalem today Mother Teresa once again filled me with wonder. She did something apparently trivial, but her manner of doing it provided an unforgettable lesson. Dorothy and I were standing on the cobbled street in the Old City which leads to the Bab el Jadid. We had just spent an hour or so with Mother Teresa and two of her sisters, all three of whom were now beside us waiting for their van to pick them up and take them to Gaza. Up the street there came wandering in twos and threes a group of pilgrims – Italians, I would guess from their appearance and gestures. When they came to within a few yards of us, one of the pilgrims looked up, immediately recognised Mother Teresa and quickly started nudging her companions, drawing their attention to this world-famous figure.

At first the pilgrims, caught unawares, were rather confused, not knowing quite how to respond to this occasion – whether to pass by as if they had not recognised her or to fall on their knees and ask her blessing. However, one of their number relieved the confusion by going up to Mother Teresa and handing her some money for her work – a gesture that was followed by the others before they all went on their way in wonderment.

What remains quite unforgettable was the manner in which Mother Teresa received the pilgrims' offerings. It was perfectly done – such an act as persuades devout Jews to cry, 'I go to my teacher not in order to learn Torah from him but to see how he laces and unlaces his felt boots', or 'I learn Torah from the very limbs of my teacher'. Mother Teresa's action was perfect in the sense that she simply took each offering, thanked the pilgrim and then, not even looking at the money that had been pressed into her hand, she passed it on straightaway to the sister beside her. If her manner had been in the very slightest degree more casual, it could have seemed brusque, even ungracious. On the other hand, if she had responded any whit more fulsomely she might well have left the pilgrim filled with pride at having made an offering to this holy woman. As it was, Mother Teresa's action struck a perfect line between brusqueness and fulsomeness, much as a great singer strikes the perfect note – or a great cricketer hits the ball absolutely in the centre.

Another aspect of that incident which made a powerful impression on me as I reflected on it was the realisation that you cannot act in that fashion by taking thought, by deliberately intending at a particular moment, for instance, to strike a perfect line or a perfect note. An action, if it is to be perfect, has to be spontaneous. It can only come about in a human being as a result of unremitting training directed towards some other end, beyond the immediate one. In this case, it was Mother Teresa's lifelong struggle towards the love of Christ which gave birth to that action which taught me so much.

Nevertheless, what I find so intriguing about our encounter with Mother Teresa today was that, far from dazzling me, it had the opposite effect. Because during the hour of conversation before we had emerged into the street, not only had she said a number of things which I realised to be uninformed or simplistic, but I also noticed that none of her sisters uttered a single word spontaneously in her presence. As a result, I have to recognise that our encounter today 'demythologised' Mother Teresa for me. That does not mean I am disillusioned in the bad sense of the word, because I feel that my respect for her is even deeper and more real than before. In a sense, I feel more at ease in her presence – but I can't quite work out why that is so, beyond saying that my encounter with Mother Teresa today demythologised her to me.

❧ 24 November

There must be many lessons about community to be derived from the ups and downs in the mood of the *piccolo mondo* of Tantur this day.

Soon after breakfast I received pouting protests against the notice I had posted which announced that Father Carlos Alvarez's colloquium, 'Healing in St Matthew's Gospel', would be given in Spanish, since Carlos speaks very little English. Spanish, admittedly, is not one of the three official languages of the Institute, and so my notice afforded one or two scholars the opportunity to wax indignant about such a departure from the rules of the Institute. I was not altogether surprised, knowing that in any group of academics in any part of the world, one always comes across certain characters who at the drop of a hat will draw themselves up in indignation, adopt a wise mien and announce that they 'foresee difficulties' – as though foreseeing difficulties is their speciality and a sign of their superior wisdom. The difficulty, said today's protesters, is that 'We are thereby setting a precedent.' And then, 'What is to happen when, say, some Polish scholar wishes to give his colloquium in Polish? Shall we all be expected to listen to Polish for an hour?'

On reflection, I realise that I should not have treated the protests as cavalierly as I did. After pointing out that we had already agreed to translate Carlos' Spanish into English as best we could, I added, rather casually and impishly, that no doubt we could probably manage to translate Polish if necessary, or even Serbo-Croat at a pinch. (Will I never learn that the English habit of teasing should be strictly confined to transactions among English people? – and not with all of them, either!)

In the event, however, Carlos' colloquium proved to be a memorable occasion which no one enjoyed more than the protesters from earlier in the day.

What happened was that Carlos would speak a phrase, or a sentence, or even sometimes a whole paragraph in Spanish, and would then look towards Brother Bartomeu or myself to translate. One or the other of us would do so, though quite often we both began at the same time and collided with each other in mid-sentence, and sometimes certain of the scholars would break in with their unsolicited suggestions, hoping, presumably, that their knowledge of English might make up for their ignorance of Spanish. As a result, the conduct of Carlos' symposium was not such as would have commended itself to a session of the American Academy of Sciences. At times it was hilarious, and at times it was riotous, especially when everyone in the room seemed to be prompting Bartomeu and myself, or when he and I concertinaed our sentences. Yet it proved to be a wonderful couple of hours; because no one was pretending to an expertise which he did not possess, and because everyone in the room was drawn into a common task. So no one got huffy or stood on their dignity when their proposed translations were queried or criticised or even laughed out of court. In fact, an atmosphere of celebration was generated which grew more exhilarating as the scholars came to realise that, with good will, a group of human beings can accomplish much more when working together than they ever imagined possible.

At the same time, what saved the day was the quality of Carlos' presentation at both the academic and the human level. His rare combination of academic rigour and human feeling must surely be due to the fact that he spends half his days as the inspirer of a base community in one of the poorest areas of Bogotá, and for the rest of his time teaches in the university – and due also to the fact that he leads an extremely disciplined life of prayer and austerity. That is why he was able to take us through those texts of St Matthew which are centred on healing, in a rigorous scholarly fashion yet with such conviction that we began to feel ourselves being healed in some extraordinary way by the very texts which we were meticulously analysing. As a result, when Carlos brought his presentation to a close, everyone sat for quite a time in silence, the atmosphere of the seminar room being permeated by a deep sense of peace.

And then something happened which I found really strange and disconcerting. As if at the tap of a conductor's wand, all of the scholars simultaneously closed their Bibles, shut their notebooks, pushed back their chairs and stood up to leave the room. It was as though they were saying in unison, 'That was an excellent seminar. I now have it filed away in my notebook, ready to take out again when next I have to lecture on Matthew. Now, what is the next item on the programme?'

I found such a pattern of behaviour on the part of the scholars to be really amazing: its implicit message seemed to be that nothing remarkable had occurred during the two preceding hours which might give us pause for thought before we carried on with our various routines. This reaction – or rather, lack of it – is so symptomatic of the professional deformation endemic in academic communities that I asked them all please to come back and sit down, and then to discuss whether it was good enough, after such an extraordinary experience, simply to sidle off as though nothing had happened. Had we not just learnt how the Gospel, according to St Matthew, had healed both individuals and communities in centuries gone by? And had we ourselves not now received a touch of that healing? Ought we not to respond to that touch by seeking healing for whatever wounds there might be within our own community at Tantur, here and now?

Happily, the scholars immediately realised what I was getting at, and they urged me to call a gathering for healing which would include not only scholars but also their spouses and other adult members of the community. Though they maintained that it was my responsibility to preside over such an occasion, they also agreed that Carlos should be invited to initiate and lead our search for healing. We were all of one accord, moreover, that we should direct our attention to what St Paul calls 'the deep things of God', and not upon surface issues such as the preferred time for dinner or the cost of field trips and so forth.

෫ *28 November*

Talk about sailing between the rock of Charybdis and the monster Scylla – or perhaps, more exactly, between Martin Luther and Ronald Reagan!

That is a bit hard on Martin Luther, because Lutheran Pastor Wehrmann's invitation to deliver a sermon in Jerusalem's Erlöserkirche was wholly prompted by motives of friendship, and in the end proved to be 'a happy fault'. After all, it was quite reasonable of him to assume that, since all previous rectors of Tantur had been ordained ministers, then I must also be ordained; and since he knew that I am married, then I could not be a Roman Catholic, because all ordained Roman Catholics are unmarried. Hence there was no obstacle in his mind when he asked me if I could preach a sermon in German at the Erlöserkirche on 1 November.

He asked me out of friendship and I agreed out of friendship; but neither of us realised at the time what we were letting ourselves in for – not, that is, until some weeks later, when he asked me what Scripture readings I had chosen for that day – so that he could then announce them in the church bulletin. As soon as I pointed out to him the scriptural passages I had chosen, his brow furrowed and he enquired further, in some puzzlement, 'Then what is to be the theme of your sermon, Donald?' 'What else', I replied, 'would a Roman Catholic preach about on All Saints' Day other than reverence for the saints?'

At which his puzzlement turned to alarm and he said, 'That would be a very strange sermon for a Lutheran congregation on Reformation Sunday! I didn't know that you were a Roman Catholic.' And then it was my turn to be embarrassed as he continued, 'I had hoped you would concelebrate with me, and would take round the chalice at communion.'

Once more I was back in the labyrinth which Christians have constructed for one another around the issue of Eucharist. Certainly I could not concelebrate since I was not ordained, but would it not offend my Lutheran friend if I said that, in obedience to Catholic discipline, I could not take round the chalice at communion and – even more offensive – I could not receive communion at a Lutheran Eucharist?

For several days after our conversation, and for some sleepless nights as well, I wrestled with these issues, knowing that if I chose a way that would not offend the Lutherans, I would thereby offend others – Jerusalem is such a gossipy place; and Reformation Sunday is a big occasion at which non-Lutherans are present, and church people are such a gossipy crowd that some of them were bound to take scandal no matter what I did.

How I wished that those ecclesiastics who formulate the disciplinary rules were themselves more frequently thrust into exposed positions, and did not spend their lives like army generals, issuing commands to the troops while they themselves are protected by whole phalanxes of subordinates who dare not say boo to a goose.

In the end, it was not as bad as I had feared because my Lutheran friends turned out to be a most sympathetic congregation. But the Reaganite Scylla a few days later proved a different kettle of fish, if I may use such a mixture of metaphor for such a monster.

Why I should have again been asked to preach in the Erlöserkirche within three weeks of Reformation Sunday I can hardly guess. Since the occasion was American Thanksgiving Day, the reason may again have been a case of mistaken identity: rectors of Tantur have been Americans, so the present rector is American: therefore he is eligible to speak on Thanksgiving. Or perhaps it is simply that I am fated to confront Reagan, albeit indirectly, since I had already found myself publicly opposing his policies twice during my time in California when he was governor.

'Third time unlucky', I thought to myself, as I sat in one of the seats of honour, and listened to the US consul general in Jerusalem reading out President Reagan's Thanksgiving message to the packed congregation in the Erlöserkirche, a congregation composed not only of Christians but also of American Jews and American atheists, indeed of all sorts of Americans, apart from blacks.

From where I was sitting during the address, I could see that many of the congregation were very content with Reagan's message, chauvinistic though it may have sounded to alien ears. And for the opening ten minutes of my own address, I could sense the same contentment with what I was saying. I was speaking about how much the world owes, and how much I personally owe, to the American people in their pilgrimage as a nation. In particular, I declared my conviction that if democracy were to go under in the US, then democracy would perish throughout the rest of the world.

For the same reason, I continued, all who look to the US for democratic leadership are distressed at having to recall that the United States has also taken the lead in the development and deployment of nuclear weapons which threaten to destroy the whole of the human family and possibly all other living creatures as well. Moreover, when we proclaim the danger to the world of a 'Communist bomb' or an 'Islamic bomb', we should always bear in mind that there has already been a 'Christian bomb', the one dropped on Hiroshima by a country which claims to be Christian. Nor should we forget that those airmen taking part in the mission also took part, before they did so, in a service of worship conducted by a Lutheran pastor.

By this time, the atmosphere in certain areas of the Erlöserkirche had changed from the earlier mood of contentment with my praise of the US to one of hostility towards me for reminding them of matters that they wished to forget. In particular, there was one lady sitting only a few yards in front of me, very fat and lavishly dressed, from whose shoulders I could almost see the steam rising, so angry was she at what I was saying.

No sooner was the service over than she strode up to me looking like thunder, and castigated me for speaking about politics at a time when people had come together 'to praise the Lord'. That phrase, 'praise the Lord', confirmed my intuition about her: she is, indeed, a very rich charismatic, one of those who constantly use the phrase as a thought-stopper, as a pious way of avoiding disturbing thoughts – which they usually describe as 'politics'!

She was not the only one, of course. From a similar stable there came a Protestant minister who felt that I had abused the hospitality of Americans by speaking harshly of America on a day that was meant for rejoicing and not for dwelling upon the troubles of the world. When the American consul general himself accosted me at the reception afterwards, he was more genial and diplomatic – though as a good diplomat, he knows how to make double-edged remarks. He said, 'We will not take your green card away from you'; and then, after a pause, 'At least, not yet'.

↝ *1 December*

Doesn't it bring you up with a jolt sometimes when an incident or a remark reveals to you how you appear to other people?

This morning I called together the senior permanent members of the Institute and reminded them that, for several months now, on Tuesday mornings, I had left myself free of engagements so that any of them who wished could come to my office and talk to me about their worries, hopes and needs. 'Today', I said, 'having listened to all of you for three months, I myself now wish to say a word. It will not take long – no more than 20 minutes.' And so for 20 minutes I outlined what I took to be the virtues and defects of everyday life in the Institute, with some indications of changes that need to be made.

Later in the day I learnt that one of those present, an Arab, had whispered to another Arab as soon as they had left my office, 'We are back again under the British Mandate'. Amusing as others may have found the observation, I have to confess that it brought me up with a jolt. Can it really be true that I give the appearance of belonging to the same stable as those colonialists from whom I have always tried to distance myself?

↝ *4 December*

How grateful I am to Carlos for the skilful manner (not only spiritually but also psychologically) in which he conducted the healing meeting for the community this evening. Probably such skill in psychological dealings is anyhow a function of spiritual sensitivity – I am thinking of how Carlos quietly but authoritatively ensured that our meeting began at the time arranged, and how he impressed upon us all, without actually saying anything, that we were going to finish in good time and that we were not going to drift on and on into what Americans call a 'bull-session'. The effect of his quiet insistence was to make everyone alert, concentrating on the matter in hand; they were on their best behaviour, not slouching around as people everywhere tend to do at evening meetings. This in turn produced a sense of common purpose in which each of us was listening for the needs of others, and showing our readiness to bear one another's burdens. I do believe that many misunderstandings were overcome, and I could see the dawning of relief on many faces as one knot after another of pain and anxiety within the community was unravelled. Indeed, you could see something more than relief: you could on many faces see radiant peace by the time I brought the meeting to an end with Bishop Appleton's beautiful prayer:

> Grant, O Lord, that each day before we enter the little death of sleep, we may undergo the little judgment of the past day, so that every wrong deed may be forgiven and every unholy thought set right. Let nothing go down into the depths of our being which has not been forgiven and sanctified. Then we shall be ready for our final birth into eternity and look forward with love and hope to standing before thee, who art both judge and saviour, holy judge and loving saviour. (*Journey for a Soul, p. 229.*)

❧ 5 December

Carlos surprised me this morning, when I spoke to him about last night's meeting, by being much less sanguine over it than I had been. In particular he said that, in spite of some good things that had emerged, it was obvious to him that many of those present at the meeting had come to Tantur with much heavy matter of unforgiveness and resentment lodged inside them from previous experience. That heavy matter is now blocking the flow of life and love within the community; and the worst of it is that it is precisely those who talk most about community-building who block the flow, because they are the ones least aware of the matter of unforgiveness that they are carrying around with them, like a lead ball attached to their waists.

I have great respect for Carlos' insight, which reminded me of the observation made by Dietrich Bonhoeffer, that whenever someone came along full of talk about the need to 'build community', then he could be pretty sure that such a person would prove disruptive of whatever community (not ideal but real) had already been established.

Those comments by Carlos and Bonhoeffer certainly accord with my own experience both here and in the USA. So many of those in California who preached the 'need for community' had themselves failed to live at peace in the basic community of their own family, and went around trailing their failure behind them. But because it was behind them, they never turned round and noticed it. In consequence, they took no responsibility for their own feelings of discontent but instead blamed them on others. Perhaps there is an essential connection between the refusal of responsibility and the tendency to blame other people.

Also, in the light of what Carlos said, I can clearly see the answer to a puzzle that has been nagging at my mind for some time about this community at Tantur. That is, how do you account for the difference – which anyone with even half an eye can recognise – between the quality of the presence here of the Benedictine monks and that of all the rest of us? For long enough I have been conscious of such a difference, but have never been able to put my finger on it.

The answer has to be that the Benedictines came here out of 100 per cent obedience to their community in Montserrat, and so they brought with them no hidden agenda – not, at least, in their relation to Tantur. In contrast, all the rest of us have come here with some hidden agenda; for some of us it may only constitute about 5 per cent of our motivation for coming, while for others it may represent almost 100 per cent. But no matter how small the percentage may be in any of our cases, still it does to some degree flaw our presence here and constantly gives rise to difficulties: it makes members of the community frustrated and angry with one another, when the hidden agenda of one person clashes with the hidden agenda of another person. Not surprisingly, therefore, the people who are for ever causing dissension are precisely those who have hidden their agendas so deeply that they no longer believe they have any.

ॐ *9 December*

What a character Mother Teresa is! The story told to us this morning by Sister Damien is so typical.

Because she is nowadays in such great demand, Mother Teresa no longer has the time to write letters to the sisters in every one of their houses across the globe, so instead she speaks her messages on to a cassette, copies of which are then sent to all their many houses. But in the Gaza house, because they did not possess a cassette player nor money enough to buy one, they were unable for many months to discover what Mother Teresa was saying to them. Eventually, however, some friends in Jerusalem bought them a cassette player so that they could listen to Mother's messages.

Unfortunately for them, Mother Teresa came to visit Gaza soon afterwards and noticed the gleaming cassette player on a table. She asked whose it was and when the sisters said it was theirs, a gift, Mother Teresa grew stern: 'Then you must give it back', she said. 'To own a cassette player is contrary to our vow of poverty.' When it was timorously pointed out to her that the player was only used for listening to her message (with the implication, presumably, that they did not go in for pop music), she put an end to all discussion by saying, 'Our vow of poverty is more important than my messages'.

And when later the donors of the offending cassette player protested that there was no need to be so literal-minded, Mother Teresa countered by saying, 'If they will do that while I am still alive, what will they get up to when I am dead?'

It is also the case, probably, that Mother Teresa was offended by the very slightest contrast, however innocent, between the lifestyle of the sisters and that of their Arab neighbours in Gaza. Because one of the sisters has told us that in many ways there is even deeper misery in Gaza than in Calcutta. And I can believe it after having visited a number of Arab houses today. One such house will haunt me, I am sure, for the rest of my life.

The house is at the very end of a long dirt-track and consists of one room. At least half of the room is taken up by a heap of straw, apparently for feeding the family donkey which was standing patiently in a corner. The family consisted of father, mother and their daughter, some 20 years old, though she might well have been their granddaughter, so aged-looking were the parents. Until six weeks ago there had been a second daughter, but she had died from skin cancer which may well have been caused by the miserable state of the house. And judging from the eyes of the surviving sister, shining with unnatural brilliance, it will not be long before she follows along the way of death. Although that event will undoubtedly be a tragedy for the household, I was left with the strange feeling that it would be an equal tragedy if the donkey were to die, because the donkey is for them more essential to the household than the daughter. Harsh as that thought may seem, it is at least plausible in view of the fact that the only water available to them for all their needs (washing, cooking and watering their little vegetable patch) has to be carried a distance of one kilometre – and that task belongs to the donkey. We were told by the father that there is no prospect of a more convenient water supply because the Israeli occupying authorities here, as on the West Bank, refuse to allow Arabs to sink wells.

What shattered me, however, really making my bones shake, was the moment when the mother declared that she was going to kill one of their five chickens in order to provide a meal for us. Luckily we all agreed, spontaneously and immediately, on a white lie that we had already eaten. But as we came away my mind was still trembling at encountering such a depth of hospitality from these utterly poor people: they have absolutely nothing in this world save some straw, a donkey and five chickens; and yet they would gladly have presented us with one of those precious chickens.

೫ 1982

೫ *14 January*

It was late in the afternoon by the time I made my way into the new church, which is now nearing completion. It is most majestic, a whole cosmos of finished stone. There was no one else in the church except that, in one of the far chapels, almost camouflaged in stone dust which floated in the atmosphere and lay like a grey blanket upon him, there sat an aged Arab stonemason. Holding the heavy mallet, his arm was rising and falling in a mechanical fashion, almost as though it no longer belonged to him but had been hired out. As I walked slowly around the numerous chapels, noticing the fine mosaics, I kept watching him at his work; the mallet seemed to be getting heavier all the time and his arm wearier. I felt nigh on frantic for him as I thought of all that dust getting into his lungs and mouth and ears and nose every day of his life. When eventually I came to his chapel, I said to him in Arabic, 'You seem tired'; he replied by placing his mallet down and raising his hands towards heaven, as if calling Allah to witness; he whispered hoarsely, 'I am very tired'. Like many Arab workers, he has a lot of dependants to support.

As I moved on I began to examine the hundreds of chisel marks on each of those thousands of magnificent stones that make up the church. Running my fingers along the grooves left by the chisels, I saw in each of them the stroke of the mallet made by poor, weary men such as my friend in the corner. Then I thought, as I was going along the corridor where the tourists were buying their picture postcards and souvenirs, 'Things can't go on like this much longer. This order of things must soon pass away, under which rich visitors like ourselves have these magnificent spaces adorned for our contemplation by those who have to work from dawn until dusk simply in order to put bread into their mouths and the mouths of their children.' Because you always know, whatever land you are in, who it is in that land who bears the burden of history. All you need to do is to travel on the buses between five and six o'clock in the morning and look at your fellow passengers. They are the ones who are carrying society on their backs, whether you are in Rotherham or Pittsburg or Bombay. Here in the Holy Land it is the Arabs. And they are in no way 'romantic'. Take away their keffiyehs from around their heads and you can see quite clearly that, by middle age, their bodies are just as broken as the bodies of those being jolted along in the first buses in Rotherham, Pittsburgh or Bombay.

↩ *10 February*

Where angels fear to tread it is precisely fools who will rush in. On Friday afternoon, during the colloquium, a Protestant minister suddenly broke the rule which has until now done so much to keep clear the atmosphere around our eucharistic discussions. In open session he not only challenged Ned Jackson, a Roman Catholic priest, to explain why he does not go to communion if a Protestant is the celebrant, but when Ned sent out many signals to indicate that he did not wish to discuss the matter in the presence of 20 people, the Protestant scholar kept pressing his question. For a moment I thought I should be forced to intervene with a really stern rebuke, but fortunately Ned, whose neck by this time was rapidly turning red, did the job for me by exclaiming angrily, 'You are out of order'.

That put a stop to the unpleasantness for the moment; and I gather that many of the scholars afterwards gave Ned a word of support. But I was not altogether surprised this morning when he came into my office and asked me to remove his name from the list of those who have accepted the invitation to celebrate the community Eucharist on a pre-arranged Sunday this term. 'I couldn't celebrate', he said, 'knowing that there are people present who are so critical of my eucharistic practice.'

Though not surprised at Ned's request, I was saddened, not only because he is such a kindly fellow, but because I am not at all sure what to do about his inquisitor.

◄€ *23 February*

Yesterday morning I came across an article in the *National Catholic Reporter* for 26 November 1981, which troubled me greatly. The author of the article asserted that a lot of the money which makes the University of Notre Dame so wealthy comes from the coffers of a billionaire called Ludwig, and that Ludwig makes his money by exploiting Indians of the Amazon and destroying the land upon which they depend for their livelihood. Since, in turn, much of the money for Tantur comes from Notre Dame, we are now faced with a serious moral dilemma: are all of us here, so comfortably established, living on the backs and on the skins of Amazonian Indians? And if so, should we not leave as soon as possible?

Throughout the whole of yesterday that question was running through my mind, in spite of the day being so busy as seeming not to permit even one chink of space for the question to pop through. But it did so continuously.

In the morning Dorothy and I went to visit the stricken Romanian Archimandrite Vasileus in the hospital on French Hill, taking him a cake which Dorothy had baked for his birthday. Vasileus' room was bathed in a wonderful sense of peace which both Dorothy and I remarked upon afterwards. It was due, we did not doubt, to the two beautiful Romanian nuns who are nursing Vasileus, night and day. One or other of them is present in the room at every minute, usually sitting in a corner, quiet, still and radiant with prayer, watching all the time for any sign of need on Vasileus' part, ready to move across to his bed calmly and completely composed. These two nuns have imbued me with a quite different awareness of what nursing is really supposed to be.

At lunch-time we were plunged into a completely other world. We were entertaining as our guests at Tantur about 100 members of the Jerusalem Committee, an international group of wealthy and influential figures assembled by Teddy Kollek in order to help him make Jerusalem into the beautiful city of his dreams. I also suspect that Kollek, wily politician that he is, finds that the Jerusalem Committee's standing comes in useful for him sometimes when he faces opposition from the central government people, who are not as enlightened as he is.

Many of the Committee are what the Americans call 'fat

cats'. One of them was sitting next to me at lunch, a millionaire socialist. Through misinterpreting one of my remarks he obviously concluded that I am by background a member of the British establishment, for which reason he gave me a lecture on the sufferings of the English poor in the 1930s. I thought of my native village in the 1930s, looked at the suit he was wearing which must have cost as much as my monthly salary, and said nothing. However, I did permit myself a wry smile as I stood watching him drive away, the sole passenger in an extraordinarily luxurious chauffeur-driven car.

By contrast, I had a pleasant chat with Conor Cruise O'Brien, who was surprised and delighted to discover that I had read some of the poems in Irish written by his wife, Maire Mhac an tSaoi. He was so taken by the attractions of Tantur that he suggested he might like to come and stay here in order to write his next book. Knowing his reputation hereabouts as a scourge of the Arabs, I was a bit alarmed at the thought of what effect his presence might have. However, when I earnestly enquired what kind of theological research he was engaged upon he dropped the matter.

No sooner had the Jerusalem Committee departed than I found myself presiding over a colloquium given by one of our scholars, Daniel Philipps. He was extremely crotchety during the discussion.

From the colloquium we went immediately and thankfully to evening prayers. Waiting for us outside our chapel were some 40 Yugoslav priests who were on pilgrimage. They were such a wonderful tonic. Everything about them – their open faces, their rough dress, their manly voices and ready smiles, their complete unpretentiousness – all these characteristics told you that these men were worker priests, not as a result of some theory or experiment but by nature and through the situation of the Church in their homeland. And their singing seemed to come from another world, especially when those deep, masculine voices were joined in tender, traditional folk hymns to the Mother of God. After the last of the hymns, all of us continued standing in silence, immersed in the beauty of the occasion.

Then, suddenly, the silence was broken by the leader of the Yugoslav group, a professor of theology, who stepped to the centre of the chapel and began to speak. I was expecting him simply to say a few words of thanks to us for inviting them to join us in our evening prayers. But instead he launched at full throttle into an astonishing lecture, delivered in excellent French, on the theme of unity and its relationship to *différentiation, non-identité, diversité* and *altérité*. It was a scintillating *tour de force* which led us though Parmenides, Plato, Plotinus, Scotus Erigena, Nicholas of Cusa, Hegel and Heidegger. There was no reason for him not to speak in French since French is one of the official languages of the Institute; nor was he to know that in practice the Institute is becoming monoglot through the predominance of language-lazy Anglo-Saxons. But by plunging *in medias res* the good professor had caught us all on the wrong foot.

However, our people quickly recovered their balance and composed themselves, self-consciously reverent, ready to endure two or three minutes of incomprehension and bewilderment. But as the minutes passed by, with no pause in the breathless flow of erudite philosophy in a foreign language, you could see the bodies beginning to sag, their eyes growing wider in disbelief. Since I was standing facing them all and could notice how the expressions on their faces and their knees pleaded that this torture might end soon, I almost disgraced myself by bursting into laughter.

At least the professor's long discourse did give me an excuse to make my own reply very brief and to thank him sincerely for an address which did, in fact, explicate the philosophical concept of unity so expertly as to make it unexpectedly relevant to the task of Christian unity.

Nevertheless, below all these diverse and demanding tasks which engaged my attention through the day, there murmured an undercurrent of worry: are all of us at Tantur, and particularly myself as rector, living on the backs of exploited Amazonian Indians?

So in spite of feeling distinctly weary I was actually looking forward to the Carlos* that we were due to hold after supper because it held out to me the hope that I could share my worry and seek the help of my brothers and sisters.

In the event, what happened at the Carlos was both revealing and symbolic. For although I do believe that most of the community take seriously the injunction 'bear ye one another's burdens and so fulfil the law of Christ', I am afraid that their

---

* The name attached by this time to any healing gathering, after Father Carlos Alvarez.

voices were never heard. Because no sooner had I expressed my concern over the Ludwig story than one scholar jumped into the discussion and told me, in the flip-sided manner of a Job's comforter, that it is really misguided of me to go on worrying about such matters. 'Even if the *National Catholic Reporter* story is true', he said, 'you cannot possibly be so scrupulous about where money is coming from – in the modern world each of us is involved in similar financial networks every day of our lives.' (As a matter of fact, I later pursued some enquiries and came to the conclusion that the story was untrue.)

On the surface, the man seemed to be consoling me, and even, so to speak, absolving me. But that was only on the surface. In fact he came near to mocking me for my naïveté. And he certainly was making light of my burden. And once he had dismissed that matter in such a cavalier fashion there was no way that anyone else could then bring the Carlos round to centring upon trying to heal wounds in the community.

The course of the evening was fittingly symbolised in the one decision taken: each Wednesday evening we are to lay on a 'happy hour'. The happy hour is a rite of academia according to which members of the university faculty gather during the period preceding the evening meal in order to drink and gossip. 'Happy' it usually is not.

❧ 28 February

For more than a week now I have been trying to discover the root, or roots, of the impurity within me that caused me to behave so badly towards Antoine Foucauld. It is a sign, perhaps, of how very deeply the impurity is rooted that I was quite unaware of having offended him until he came to see me. As soon as he began to speak, I realised that this good man was having to exert himself strenuously in order to control the anger that he felt towards me. He accused me of having 'banalised' the talk he gave two weeks ago by the way I had presided over it, and he felt that I owed him an apology. What saddened me even more was that he interpreted my behaviour as a sign that I have little personal regard for him and his intellectual work. Since the opposite is true, and I respect him highly, I have to ask myself: How does one manage to give such a false impression?

The surface reason is obvious enough: my mind was preoccupied by the expectation of a telephone call from the US, from HQ, as a result of which I would learn whether money was going to be made available to pay our staff this month, next Friday being the pay day. The adrenalin had therefore been flowing fast all day as I prepared for a possible showdown with HQ over the issue, so when the call did come some ten minutes into Antoine's talk, I was on a real high of aggression. Then, as it happened, there was no battle with HQ. They were sad that we are spending so much but realise that if there is no money for the Arab staff next week, I may have a rebellion on my hands.

My expectation of battle having been frustrated, when I returned once more to the lecture room to preside over the discussion, the adrenalin in my system was still bubbling yet I was at the same time sighing with relief. So I let it all out in provocative questions, ill-considered parallels and wisecracks which must have both mystified and infuriated Antoine.

But below that surface explanation there is a deeper and, I imagine, a complex series of reasons, for my offensive behaviour.

Strictly speaking, of course, one ought always to be able to switch one's attention from one subject to another, or from one person to another, with no emotional carry-over from one subject or person into the realm of the other. Certainly that is an ideal to be worked towards, but, to be realistic, one has to acknowledge that almost no one achieves such a blessed ideal. And while working towards the ideal, one has to pinpoint other possible changes in behaviour patterns that may at least mitigate one's failures.

But if I have to make a guess at the root cause of my behaviour, I would put it down to my constant desire to protect people, a desire which is itself rooted in a reluctance to share my concerns and anxieties with them, a reluctance which in its turn is rooted in a lack of trust. In other words, if only I had told the scholars about the looming money shortage, then I would not have felt so isolated, tense and embattled. And they might well have suggested to me that I had no obligation to preside over the lecture in the afternoon, and should feel free to deal with the thorny question of the money. Then this unpleasant episode would never have occurred.

On the other hand, knowing what gossips some of the scholars are, I am pretty sure that within a few days rumours would be circulating in Jerusalem that Tantur is on the verge of bankruptcy. After which, tradesmen would start to demand immediate payment for their goods, intending scholars would be writing to ask if the Institute is going to be open next year, and so on. That would be much more disastrous than my contretemps with Antoine, which we were able to clear up within the confines of my office without involving people in Jerusalem, Chicago, London and Rome!

There is here a real problem about institutions. For institutions to be real communities there needs to be the very widest possible sharing of information and feelings. In an ideal community everyone completely trusts every other member. In fact, there has never been such a community. Even in the honeymoon period of the Christian Church, for instance, we know that 'there was grumbling on the part of those who spoke Greek against those who spoke Hebrew'. And, unfortunately, the barrier against complete trust is fixed and located according to the capacity for trust of the least trustworthy member of the institution or community. That is why monasteries tend to be good communities capable of lasting for centuries, while hotels are non-communities which spring up and vanish like mushrooms: monasteries examine carefully the trustworthiness of those wishing to enter, whereas hotels only ask for your credit card.

Tantur is a monster of an institution, something between a monastery and a hotel. In trying to form a community within it, you are bound to win some and to lose some. But I must learn to push the barrier of trust as far out as possible, and at least a little bit further than is strictly advised by my 'loner' temperament.

ঙ্গ *6 March*

Letter to the **Tablet**, *after visiting Tiberias and Galilee*

It was still night when I went out on to the high balcony. The air was almost motionless as though nature itself recognised that today was sabbath. And the very stillness of the air and the darkness of the night meant that the lapping of the water on the edges of the lake sounded all the more clearly, even on our balcony. I have never heard any lapping of waters so musical and magical as of these waters. 'From all the seas which God created,

he chose for him only the Sea of Kinneret. Why is it called
Kinneret? Because the voice of its waves is pleasant as the voice
of the harp.' (The word *kinnor* in Hebrew means harp.)

For a full hour I gazed over the waters of this Sea of
Galilee, waiting for dawn to break – though the word 'break' is
inappropriate to describe the slow, silent way in which the dawn
came over the lake and the steep slopes opposite, the Golan
Heights. Inevitably I thought of the beginnings of our Lord's
ministry beside those very waters. As the dark shape of the Golan
Heights emerged, and the lake grew pale in the early light, a
gentle breeze sprang up and I felt again, as I always do in this
place, the breath of the Holy Spirit over the face of the deep and
the freshness of the message that Jesus brought to humankind.
What a contrast between those fresh beginnings, hidden in this
remote corner of the Roman empire, and the noise and strife that
has accompanied the spread of the message to the far corners of
the earth, to Anchorage in Alaska and Dunedin in New Zealand,
to Santiago in Chile and Kyoto in Japan. What a strange, improb-
able story! Jesus came to reveal things hidden since before the
foundation of the world and what the world does is to shout as
loud as it can in order to keep his revelation hidden.

In this quiet spot from which I could now see Mount
Hermon rising serenely to the north, snow-covered, as well as the
bare heights of Golan to the east, the contrast was striking between
the peace, the stillness, the hiddenness of this dawn and all the
noise that I knew was being made throughout the world over
Golan. Whereas the real Golan was at peace, there was another
'Golan' on the lips of radio and television announcers and in the
minds of millions of listeners and readers throughout the world,
from Manila to Frankfurt and back. This second Golan was like
a black, thunderous cloud in the lives of those millions, threatening
them with nuclear destruction. This second Golan was a product
of their fears and ambitions and lies. The real Golan, which they
had never seen, stood peaceful before me.

Why does the world shout so loud about strife and hide
the things that make for peace? This question has exercised me
greatly since the day – or rather, the night – when Israeli troops
blew up three houses of our neighbours in Beit Sahur just before
Christmas. That incident was spoken about and written about in
the world press and on television and radio – quite rightly. But
there was an incident within the incident that no one has thought

to describe, which should perhaps be known. It occurred just as the soldiers were preparing to carry out the demolition. A young man who lived in one of the houses, a Christian, spoke courageously and calmly to the soldiers, asking them to consider whether there was not a better way, the way of peace revealed by Jesus whose birth in neighbouring Bethlehem was soon to be celebrated. The young man was gently taken aside by one of the soldiers who whispered to him, 'I agree with you, but don't go on like that or else you will get arrested for trying to convert Jews'. I like to think of that whispered conversation between two young men. It redeemed the bankruptcy of the night.

The reason why it is only 'perhaps' that such an incident should be known, however, is on account of the delicate mystery of hiddenness: do you inevitably destroy the hidden things by revealing them? Certainly there can be enormous virtue in keeping things hidden. This was illustrated by yet another incident that arose from the happenings of that night in Beit Sahur.

Soon after the demolitions had taken place, I was present when a Jewish professor was being given a rough time about them by some Christian scholars. Though he answered their questions very honestly and bravely, nevertheless his defence of the Israeli action seemed lame to them and left them unconvinced. But the next week, by chance, I discovered another side to the story. I happened to be in the company of some friends of that same professor and learnt quite incidentally that, in 1948, the professor's whole village had been razed to the ground by Arab soldiers. When I heard that story I could not help thinking that only one person in a thousand, under the barrage of questioning that my professor friend had endured, would have kept silent about that even greater tragedy in his own young life. And I admired the austerity, and what I can only think of as a certain mental chastity, that enabled him to keep that sadness in his life hidden. The professor certainly knows the wonderful Jewish legend according to which our universe depends for its continued existence upon the presence in it of 36 just men. But they are hidden. No one knows who they are; they themselves do not know who they are. Yet they are the secret pillars of the universe: without even one of them, the universe itself would collapse.

At the same time, Jewish tradition does allow that there are certain rare moments when one has a sense of having not so much encountered as glimpsed one of these just men, indirectly –

seen his shadow, heard his footfall, felt his breath upon one. We can never be sure; but even the chance that it may be so can redeem a dark situation.

So it was with me when I drove from the lake in the company of two Arab friends, Boulos and Butros. We drove first up the steep, endlessly winding road into upper Galilee, towards the holy city of Tsefat. I think of it as the holy city because of all the places in the Holy Land it is the one that for years I most longed to see. Situated more than 3,000 feet above the lake, Tsefat is the city where the great Jewish mystics congregated in the sixteenth century after fleeing from their Christian persecutors in Spain. When I first saw it from a distance, its white stone houses glistening upon the mountain top, it was utterly ecstatic, and in that brilliant sunshine and pure air it was not difficult to believe that in its streets I might actually meet Rabbi Izhak Luria or Josef Caro or some other of those inspired holy men of the past. Even today, when a swirling mist hid much of the old city and the only holy man around was a meditation teacher from Santa Clara, California, one could still feel the magic of the place. But this morning we were heading beyond Tsefat, to those parts of upper Galilee from which my Arab Christian friends originated.

I was not prepared for the bitterness of the experience. Previously no one had ever told me the story of how, in 1948, Israeli troops had cleared the inhabitants out of these Christian villages, allegedly because of the danger from Lebanon – at the same time assuring them that they would soon be allowed to return. Since 1948, however, the villagers' lands have been given to Jewish immigrants and the Christians have not been allowed to return to their homes. So, as we drove by one stretch of beautiful hill country after another, my companions would mutter, 'This is the land of my village', or, 'That is my mother's field', or, 'Here is my uncle's land' – all of it now in the possession of Jewish settlements. The longer this went on, the more hopeless the world began to appear in my mind's eye. Being an old-fashioned Roman Catholic, I did not need reminding of the dictum, *audietur et altera pars* – don't make a judgement until you have heard the other side of the story. Even so, there was no mistaking the bitter wound which my companions had suffered. And it seemed to get worse as we drew near to the ancient Christian village of Kafar Bir'im. You will not find the village marked on your map, and in Zev Vilnay's *Guide to Israel* it is only mentioned (a 'deserted village') in order to call your attention to the ruin of an ancient synagogue of the second or third century. Certainly, the ruin is wonderfully preserved, and nearby is situated what is said to be the grave of Queen Esther. Here was also found the inscription in Hebrew: 'May there be peace in this place, and in all the places of Israel'.

However, after parking our car we did not direct our footsteps along the official path towards the synagogue mentioned in the guidebook. Instead, we turned left through the wood surrounding the hill-top until we came to a church hidden in the trees.

That was when I felt the presence of one of the 36 just men, at the threshold of the church. Still weary with the misery of the last few hours, I was about to step inside what I thought to be an abandoned church, when all at once I looked into the face of an old man whose white moustache glistened, even as a welcoming smile lit up his face and his eyes glowed with happiness. 'Welcome! welcome', he said, and led us into the church, a Maronite church of which he has constituted himself the guardian. He stays there night and day, sleeping at night on a camp bed in the porch, as if to assure his dear church that it is not after all abandoned.

There were so many of that old man's little gestures which edified me – the grace with which he offered all of us Turkish coffee, the yet greater grace with which he indicated that the money we offered him should go into the church box and not into his pocket; the unfeigned delight that he showed when I revered the picture he had pinned up of St Charbel Maklouf. But what edified me most of all was the courtesy with which he treated two young Jews who stumbled upon the church while we were there. They looked pleasant enough young men, but they had not the faintest notion of how to behave in a church. They smoked away, talking loudly, and laughed at various of their own observations. If the old guardian had become incensed with them one could scarcely have blamed him. On the contrary, however, he showed them round the church and offered them Turkish coffee (which they accepted) with exactly the same courtesy he had shown to us, his fellow Christians.

My heart, as I was leaving the church, felt much lighter and the world a better place. After we had said goodbye to the old man, I turned round again as though by a quick backward glance I might discover his secret. But all I saw still was that glistening white moustache, the unfeigned smile and the kindly eyes.

Our next place of call was to be the church belonging to the village of Iqrit, also forcibly evacuated in 1948. My friend Butros especially wished to say some prayers in it, out of piety towards his ancestors who had worshipped there. We caught sight of the church when we were already at a distance; and a heart-warming sight it was. Small but beautifully proportioned, it stood on a knoll just above what had once been the village, and it seemed to beckon to us to go there and recite some prayers.

But as we drove up the road we realised that, where once the village had been, there was now an Israeli military camp encircling the knoll on which the church stood. Nevertheless, we were still hopeful of being able at least to visit the church, until we were stopped at the guard post. The soldier on guard with his machine gun was only a young man and he looked frozen, because it was a cold day. He seemed to be glad to see us and even switched off the pop music on his transistor with which he was trying to beguile the hours. At first he seemed puzzled by our request to visit the church, but then said he would phone his commanding officer, and he expected it would be all right. Again and again he kept calling on his field telephone to try to secure permission for us, but he seemed never to have any luck. Occasionally he turned to us and explained that he would go on trying, so 'just hang on'. Then he suddenly looked startled as a figure eventually emerged from the unit HQ about 200 yards away, violently waving its arms and jumping up and down like a dancing dervish. We got the message. And he, poor soul, got the message even more explicitly over his intercom. Sadly he came over to us and explained that our visit was forbidden; and there was a look on his chilled face as if to say, 'Sorry, chums. It's a crazy world'.

We thanked him for his efforts and drove away. Butros and Boulos remained silent. They did not even say anything 200 yards further down the road, when two Israeli soldiers tried to thumb a lift.

That night I slept in their village. I was awakened around 5 a.m. by the tramp of men's boots along the village street. The men of the village were all going to catch the buses which take them each morning to work many miles away on construction projects for Jewish settlements. They would return only at night-fall. Meanwhile another people would be cultivating the fields across the valley which had been theirs and their ancestors' for generation upon generation. I thought of their tragedy. And I thought of the tragedy of thousands in the settlements, Jews who had survived the Holocaust or been driven from Morocco or Egypt or Iraq. And I could not sleep.

Then I remembered the young Jewish soldier and his good, innocent face, his warmth and goodwill towards us. And the happy thought struck me that he is one of the 36 just men. And that other one, the old Maronite at Kafar Bir'im? He also may be one of the 36. Or perhaps our Jewish friends would rather describe him as 'a just among the Gentiles'. And the other one, the young soldier? We shall call him 'a just among the Jews'!

Then I was able to sleep. The 36 are still there. The universe will not be destroyed.

ଏଟ *9 March*

The trouble with proclaiming ringing truths is that they are likely to fly round like a misguided boomerang, and strike you on the back of your head.

For years now I have been going on about the Lord's injunction that if we come to the altar knowing that one of our brothers has something against us, then we must leave our gift at the altar and go and first be reconciled with our brother. In the light of that injunction I have repeatedly underlined the question put by Vincent Donovan, 'One wonders, how often do we really achieve Eucharist in our lives?'

That question has now become a burning one for me. Truly it has been burning me up since last Wednesday. Because late on Wednesday evening an almighty, violent quarrel sprang up between two of the scholars, known here as Olaf and Canute. I will not describe the gory details of what took place but simply record that, by Thursday morning, they were at daggers drawn and each of them was trying to convince their fellow scholars of the justice of their own case.

I think I made a mistake by going to each of them separately on Thursday afternoon, too confident that, as good Christians, they would quickly forgive one another and be reconciled. That did not allow them a long enough cooling-off period, with the result that when I expressed even a muted plea for a sign of forgiveness, the explosive reply I received from each of them said, in effect, 'So you are accusing me of being the guilty one?'

Of course I was not attempting to apportion blame. Yet on looking back, I can see why my approaches to Olaf must have irritated and angered him. He interpreted my hunch that he was the one more ready to seek reconciliation as a sign that I thought the obligation to do so was his because he was the more guilty. And I made matters worse two days ago by saying to him, 'How can we in this community celebrate Easter when you two are at enmity with one another?' At which point he went through the ceiling with rage and shouted at me, 'So you are saying that because of me this whole community will be unable to celebrate Easter?'

Although I withdrew at this juncture, I have since been going about my duties in something of a daze, wondering what on earth I am to do. All the same Olaf is fundamentally a generous fellow, and I believe that my question did lodge in him at some hidden level. Still, I cannot imagine what the rest of the community, and the monks especially, are going to say if I announce that I do not believe this community here can properly celebrate Easter Eucharist while two of our members are in a condition of such unforgiveness towards one another.

One thing about which I must be particularly careful: that is, not to fall into my lonely-man-on-the-bridge syndrome. As rector of this place, acquainted with many factors of which almost everyone else is unaware, it is always tempting for me to follow my ingrained habit when facing a difficult decision. That is, I worry about it on my own for a long time and then suddenly announce to all and sundry that I have made up my mind – and that's that!

There are positive gains to be had from that pattern of behaviour which, on looking back, I can see was ingrained in me from my childhood and then reinforced by the British army's stern and quite justified warning against 'raising alarm and despondency among the troops'. That warning echoed the more drastic rule observed by the fierce Vikings, that anyone guilty of spreading rumours calculated to cause despondency must be executed. Both Viking and British commanders realised that alarm and despondency is death to a community – and that, in any case, most of our fears eventually prove to be baseless.

On the other hand, if I do follow my natural inclination and gnaw away at the problem on my own for a few weeks, and then suddenly tell Father Adalbert, the Benedictine prior, that we cannot in good conscience celebrate Easter in this place, then I fear he may suffer a heart attack.

◌ɜ *14 March, Sunday*

One advantage, at least, of living in community is that one's estimates of various members of the community are constantly revealed to have been mistaken. Or perhaps it would be more accurate to say that I am for ever being surprised at encountering sides of my colleagues' characters to which I had been blind. My surprise springs from having taken one aspect of a colleague with which I had become familiar to be his overall character when, in fact, it was just one minor facet of his personality.

Sometimes, of course, the surprising revelation may turn out to be unpleasant, as when you are being driven for the first time by a highly cultured, gentle friend and discover that at the wheel of a car he behaves like a berserker, roaring along at 80 m.p.h. and issuing a chorus of curses against every other driver he meets. But this morning provided a most pleasant surprise when we went to the neighbouring Orthodox village of Beit Jala for our Sunday Eucharist, as we do fairly regularly at the invitation of the villagers.

I am sorry to have to record that invariably, before we are due to go, the word seems to pass around mysteriously among Free Church members that the experience of visiting the Beit Jala Orthodox is not specially edifying. From a Free Church point of view I can understand, of course, that they find the Orthodox service extremely disconcerting. At one level it is highly formal and liturgical, with much bowing and kneeling and crossing of oneself to accompany the processions led by priests, who keep vanishing behind the iconostasis and reappearing again to bless the congregation. All the same I was disappointed to discover this morning what a small number of our community had assembled to go to Beit Jala. After all, we had been invited, and I would have thought that anyone who is serious about Christian unity could put up with being a bit disconcerted.

However, my disappointment was completely dispelled by the Millers. The word that had formed in my mind to characterise them is 'dumpish'. The two of them look just like the caricature of an American tourist couple beloved of the cartoonists. They look heavy in build, in gait, in speech and in thought. I had never heard either of them utter any sentiment that was not conventional; and the comments they make on theological issues are predictable once you know the particular ecclesiastical tradition out of which they come.

But in spite of the word of discouragement that had gone around previously, they both turned up this morning for our Beit Jala visit and really entered into the spirit of it. For instance, whenever we came to a point of the service at which worshippers sit down, I noticed that Anne Miller would very deliberately make sure not to sit with her legs crossed, faithfully remembering my warning that to sit in church with one's legs crossed is regarded by our Beit Jala friends as deeply offensive. Indeed, I have known them come across on occasion and slap offending crossed legs. And then, when it came to distribution of the *prosphora*, both Anne and Joe eagerly took the bread and chewed away vigorously – undeterred by the example of their proper English neighbour who declined the *prosphora* rather primly, as if she feared that by eating it she might be turned into an Arab!

The revelation of the day, however, came when I joined Anne and Joe as they were tucking into cakes and coffee in the mayor's parlour after the service. For some obscure reason, I felt that I had to apologise to them on behalf of the Orthodox for the fact that out of the whole congregation in the church no more than three members, all of them old ladies, had gone up to the altar steps to receive the sacrament. In the Orthodox Church, I explained, contrary to the practice in their own tradition, it is not customary for virtually all members of the congregation to receive communion.

'That didn't worry me at all', Joe replied. 'In fact, you know, I got the feeling that somehow everyone present received the risen Lord. I mean, those old stagers, and the young men beside them gathered round their big books, stationed under the pulpit, singing away for a couple of hours and knowing every twist and turn of the liturgy. And then the kids running around with the *prosphora* and the collection bag. No! St Nicholas' really is a people's church. And I believe the risen Lord came and dwelt in the whole people.'

Ruminating on Joe's words since this morning, I realise

73

how that good 'conventional' Protestant has opened my eyes. He is right. The eucharistic current of grace – of the Lord – permeated the whole of the church this morning, and not just those three who went up to communion! So though I don't claim to be able to provide a theologically satisfactory account of how it happens, I see more clearly how the Eucharist is not just for one's personal sanctification, nor even for the sanctification of those present in a particular church. The Eucharist is a *cosmic* act, an act by which the redemptive love of Jesus permeates the whole cosmos.

'And in order to know that', as one of my Yiddish friends might exclaim in different circumstances, 'you needed to go to Beit Jala? Oi! Oi!' But it is true, and it took a Protestant to open my eyes.

What is more, not only has Joe Miller opened my eyes; he has also lifted a weight off my shoulders – the burden, that is, of not knowing what path I myself should follow towards receiving communion at our own Sunday Eucharist here in the Institute.

In the first few weeks of my period as rector, I adhered to the practice customary among Roman Catholics at ecumenical conferences; that is to say, I received communion when a Catholic celebrated but abstained from doing so when a non-Catholic was the celebrant. But living out that practice, week after week, in spite of its theological rectitude, made me aware that it only heightened the sense of division within the community and gave rise to feelings of anger that you could sense in the chapel as unmistakeably as a foul wind. You could also sense the feeling of relief on the part of some people when they emerged from the chapel after the Eucharist, as if to say, 'Thank God that's over'.

Under the burden of that awareness, I decided to follow a different practice. In union with my Protestant friends I would not receive communion when a Catholic priest was the celebrant; neither would I do so when the celebrant was a Protestant, thereby adhering to the discipline of my own Church. This produced the strange situation, therefore, whereby the rector of an ecumenical institute never received communion at the Sunday Eucharist in the Institute's own chapel!

This evidence of bankruptcy led to a further twist in the labyrinth of paths around the Eucharist. One of the very sweetest members of our community, extremely Protestant and anti-Catholic by background, came to my office recently and very hesitatingly asked if I would mind her raising a matter which was troubling her. No, I assured her, I did not mind. Whereupon she said she had been upset at noticing that I never went to communion, and she was wondering whether I was abstaining as a protest against the reactionary stance of the Benedictine monks!

Since my feelings towards her are warm and affectionate, I managed not to react by displaying my distress at the suggestion that anyone would treat the Eucharist as a means of protesting against some policy one disagrees with. But it also became clear, subsequently, that some other members of the community had entertained the same suggestion. Which means that I need to convey obliquely to them my sense of distress at the notion of the Eucharist as an occasion for protest. At the same time I shall be able to pass on Joe Miller's revelation to me that receiving communion is not merely for the good of an individual or even a particular ecclesiastical group, but is participation in a cosmic act which benefits the whole of creation. Therefore in receiving communion, one is a representative of all creation; and so if one is in a position to receive communion while one's friends are for some reason excluded, then, apart from anything else, it is an act of friendship to partake on their behalf. No longer need I abstain.

❧ *17 March*

Although I am very exhausted, emotionally drained, by the events surrounding Father Lane's death, I feel that I must put some account of those events into my journal so that the memory of him will remain vivid in the years to come.

Having known for some time how sick Father Lane was, I had been negotiating with his superiors to have him recalled either to the US or to Rome, or to some place where he might be better cared for than we can manage here. So I was saddened when it became clear, even to Lane himself, that he would have to go immediately into hospital. At first I tried to persuade him to go to the Hadassah in Jerusalem, where they have the very latest medical equipment. But he pleaded with me not to have him sent there – as it is 'cold and soulless' – but to the hospital in Bethlehem. Bethlehem had become home to him by this time, and he wanted, above all, to be near his friends, the Christian Brothers, as well as to all his Arab friends. And they would have been nervous about travelling to an Israeli hospital to visit him.

And once he was settled in his room in the French Hospital in Bethlehem, Lane was indeed wrapped in consolation as one group of Arabs after another flocked into his room to show their affection for this gentle American priest, and to wish him a speedy recovery. On the other hand, and not for the first time, I found myself having to read the Riot Act to those Arab friends in order to protect Lane, to prevent them from killing the patient through kindness. They crowded along the corridor outside Lane's room in large numbers, men, women and children, sitting and standing around, loudly chattering – except when a hospital official appeared, at which point they would become obediently silent, each hoping to be the one allowed in to see Lane. There is something very touching in the way that Arabs will crowd around a sick person, as though the mere presence of a group of warm human beings will somehow ward off the cold hand of death.

At Tantur, meanwhile, the crisis brought about by Lane's illness generated a wave of generosity and unselfishness fit to melt your heart. There was an immediate response when I proposed to the community that we should set up a 24-hour rota to ensure that at least one of us should be present with Lane all the time, whether by his bedside itself or on stand-by outside his room in case the nurses or doctors ministering to him needed any help.

There was no lack of volunteers for the rota. Nor was there any lack of them to give the blood which he needed in considerable quantities. And just as one discovered during the war that sometimes it was the most surprising people who came good in an emergency, so now various lesser lights among the scholars rose to the occasion marvellously, even anticipating my needs and coming to my aid when they saw me getting exhausted. Also interesting was the fact that Adam and Basil, two of our most grumbly scholars, suddenly seemed to find themselves. They came alive and grew quite cheerful, as though the drama of Lane's illness had provided them with a role in the community which they had previously lacked. Perhaps grumbling is the way in which some quite good people get through life.

The other side of the coin was the undoubted, though scarcely perceptible, dragging of feet on the part of two of the best organised and genuinely research-minded of our scholars. Although those two have actually been the most co-operative in routine administrative matters – their minds being so clear about their goals and their schedules – it may precisely be their capacity for organising their lives neatly around their own egos which makes them reluctant to get involved in anything that seems a threat to their fixed goals. By contrast, some of the scholars who used to spend an inordinate amount of time hanging around the coffee room, and constantly grumbling, became exemplary members of the community. I expect it is the usual case of swings and roundabouts: you have loss and gain with every type of human being.

Not that the saying about swings and roundabouts can be treated as a general law, because there are some people who are just generous and dependable at all times and seasons. This was proved true of Sister Maria and Brother Maur. In spite of doing her teaching during the day at Bethlehem University, this Maryknoll nursing sister, Maria, somehow or other managed as well to tend to Lane throughout the night. Besides keeping us all cheerful, she also prevented us clumsy helpers from making any fearful mistakes. In the same way our Benedictine brother, Maur, unobtrusively took on the dead shifts in the middle of the long nights, and yet emerged in time for early Mass in our chapel, showing no signs of strain or tiredness. The example of Maria and Maur has again set me racking my brain trying to sort out my attitude towards professed religious. Perhaps the truth about pro- fessed religious is best conveyed by applying to them what Mary McCarthy once said about Roman Catholicism: 'A very good religion for those who take it seriously, but a very bad one for those who are half-hearted about it'. When members of religious orders are good, they are marvellous; but when they are anything less, they are a pain in the neck.

I certainly felt this to be true on the Thursday evening as I was standing in our kitchen handling kettles and cups, pre- paring coffee for a whole company of scholars and guests whom we had invited to our apartment. In burst an American sister, uninvited, who accused me of failing to secure the best medical attention for Lane and then shrieked that if he died I would be responsible.

In fact, that very day and the next day Lane had seemed much better, and was himself talking about coming out of hospital soon. But it was not to be.

Saturday was as wild a day as you are ever likely to encounter. The winds blew at gale force from every direction; the dark grey clouds scudded across the stark hill-tops in endless

77

succession, and the rain lashed mercilessly against the windows and walls of the Institute until there were streams running down over the walls, washing them startlingly clean. Then towards evening, the weather became more fearsome still, so that now you could no longer see the hills because sheet upon sheet of rain was blotting out everything more than a few yards distant. It was one of those evenings when every creature, both man and beast, seeks a dry corner in which to huddle until the storm passes over. So when I said to Dorothy that I thought I might drive along to the hospital in Bethlehem, just to make sure that Lane was maintaining his improvement, she told me not to be crazy but to wait until morning.

However, my instinct told me that I was meant to go. And so I did. When I drew up at the roadside opposite the hospital, the rain was sheeting down so heavily that by the time I had run from the car to the hospital entrance my duffle-coat was soaked through. Yet all thought of how wet I had got was driven from my mind as soon as I entered Lane's room, where I found him in a state of wild delirium, with Brother Joe at his side desperately trying to calm him down.

The next few hours were extremely painful since Lane kept demanding to go home and kept attempting to pull out the various tubes attached to him so that he could indeed walk out of the hospital. Knowing that would be fatal, Brother Joe and I tried everything we could think of to humour him. At one point we agreed to push Lane along the corridor in his wheelchair, each of us pushing with one hand and with the other holding various pieces of his life-support system. To crown it all, we had the bright idea of capitalising on Lane's love of music: we would distract him from his escape plans by singing as we guided his wheelchair up and down the corridors. The only snag in that stratagem was that we knew so few songs in common. As a result, we were reduced to singing the first verse of 'The Battle Hymn of the Republic' over and over again, until Lane got fed up of our singing and we all burst into laughter at the thought of what an absurd sight the three of us made – Lane sitting in his wheelchair, like some Eastern potentate, and the two of us, wet through, trundling him up and down the corridor, like a couple of incompetent slaves, stumbling over the words of the Battle Hymn.

But the laughter came to an end. After several hours Lane did manage to detach the tubes, not in the event enabling him to walk home but ensuring that his next destination would be the grave.

As I left Lane, who was now sedated, and climbed into my car, I suddenly realised that for four hours I had been wearing my soaked duffle-coat; but so absorbed had I been in the night's drama that I had not managed to take it off or even been aware of it.

The rest of the story – or, at least, the glimmerings of redemption that make the story worth recording – belongs to the Arabs, beginning soon after 5 a.m. on Monday, when I reached the hospital and learned that Lane had died just a few minutes earlier. There arrived at the same time Um Ibrahim, the bent old Arab lady whose job it is to clean the rooms in the Institute but who, in fact, manages to clean very few since she is now very old and frail, and moves painfully slowly, shuffling along as though her feet are held to the ground by an invisible magnet. She followed after Dorothy and myself, Sister Maria and Father David Burrell (a Holy Cross priest, like Father Lane) as we bundled the trolley bearing Lane's body along to the hospital chapel. There we stood by the body, and from our prayer books recited the prayers for the dead and the appropriate psalms. We did everything according to the rubrics and with proper dignity, each of us awed in the presence of death.

But then, without seeking anyone's permission and seemingly unconcerned with the judgement of any human being, Um Ibrahim moved forward to a position opposite Lane's feet; and gazing towards a point just above his head, she began to sing a most moving hymn in Arabic, singing not from a book or according to any rubric, but freely and spontaneously from her heart. Scant though my Arabic may be, I needed no telling that the hymn, which went on and on and on, was to the Mother of God, asking her to intercede for eternal blessing upon our dear brother who had just crossed the threshold of death. Um Ibrahim's love for Lane, for Mary, the Mother of God, and for all suffering creatures seemed to fill the chapel as one refrain followed another, her voice eventually becoming quieter and quieter until eventually she stopped singing. After a pause she crossed herself, turned round slowly and shuffled out of the chapel, extraordinarily self-contained, as if she knew something beyond the reach of us Westerners. We, for our part, were aware, without any sense of resentment, that the priest in the early hour of that day had been an unlettered Arab woman.

Not that all Westerners found it easy to bow to Arab sensibility in these ultimate matters. No sooner was Lane dead than I found myself being bombarded with advice by Westerners who flatter themselves on knowing the appropriate Jerusalem manner of burying the dead. One person maintained very firmly that the coffin should be closed, because in this climate the body begins to decay so quickly. Another egregious character recited for me a list of the representatives of local churches and associations who positively must be invited to act as pall-bearers – by the time he had finished I felt as though we would need a computer to work out who should be asked first and how long each should carry the coffin, and so on.

I did notice that no Arabs figured on his list. However, I need not have worried. Our Arab staff, in their affection for Lane, really took over the whole ritual without any fuss. They made it clear to me that it would be more than my life was worth if the coffin were not open in the church, since that would make it impossible to say goodbye to Lane in Arab fashion. And then, when it came to carrying the coffin from the Dormition Abbey to the cemetery half a mile away, the Arab menfolk simply moved in and took the coffin up without any instructions from anyone. Christians and Muslims, they seemed to know instinctively when to change as bearers – one of them walking behind the coffin would simply move up and tap the shoulder of one of the pall-bearers who would then release his burden to the new bearer. And so the ritual went on, smoothly and quietly, until we entered the cemetery.

At that moment, completely unexpectedly, we heard the most heavenly sound – the sound of a human voice singing, tender and clear, which seemed to pierce the vault of the blue sky above our heads. For a brief space I could not make out where the voice was coming from and whose voice it was. And then I turned round and saw that the singer who had begun to sing Psalm 130 ('Out of the depths have I cried to thee, O Lord') in Arabic was our own cook, Issa. The gentlest and most self-effacing of men, Issa, the leader of the choir in the Nativity Church at Bethlehem, had timed his cry for God's mercy upon Lane to perfection, and was now exercising his authority as liturgist with unwavering confidence.

There is a note of longing in the liturgical singing of all the religious communities of the Middle East which touches you at the very core of your being, whether the tradition be Jewish or Muslim, Armenian or Melkite. The sound of it, sustained over and over again, brings you into touch with the Absolute. Issa's inspired singing this afternoon lifted us into that absolute dimension where we all became present to Lane.

❧ *20 March*

Whenever someone close to you dies before their time, you nearly always start wondering whether you have done enough for them while they were still alive. Certainly I have been asking myself whether I had shown sufficient affection to Lane during our time together. The pain of that thought was intensified for me today as I spent many hours going through the articles left in his room to decide what should be done with them. As always on such occasions, the whole of the dead person's life is revealed to you at an unexpected depth, and a well of compassion is opened in your heart at the knowledge of our fragile hopes.

Had I done enough for Lane? Then, as I was sorting out various articles on his bedside table, I came across a copy of my own book *Holiness*. There was a book-marker placed between pages 60 and 61.

That discovery was a great consolation to me, a sign from Lane that we had become friends during these months together.

❧ *21 March*

'Whew!' as they used to say in the school storybooks. 'That was a close-run thing.'

At Mass this morning I was still worrying – more than ever, I expect – about how we can possibly celebrate Easter in good conscience while Olaf and Canute are engaged in cold warfare against one another. Moreover, I realised I had left it very late to share my concern about Easter with the community – perhaps it was already too late to do so. And tension was heightened this morning by the presence of both Olaf and Canute in chapel for the first time in several weeks, which set me wondering whether they would avoid one another when the moment came to exchange the kiss of peace.

What happened, in fact, was a miracle. As soon as the priest had announced the peace, dear Olaf (bless his heart) shouted from the side of the chapel where he was standing to the other side, where Canute had stationed himself, 'I forgive you, Canute, and I ask your forgiveness!' And as he spoke he strode across the centre of the chapel towards Canute, who then came to meet him. The two of them embraced in the midst of the astonished congregation.

Everyone began to smile as the Holy Breath swept through the chapel and cleansed all our hearts.

I doubt whether anyone quite realises what relief the incident brought to me. It felt as though a heavy weight had literally been lifted off my heart, enabling me to breathe freely and deeply once more. 'Breathe on me, Breath of God', for sure! My very lungs declared their thanks.

ເຈ *23 March*

No wonder that this journal contains nothing for this past week except cryptic abbreviations, times of engagements, names and exclamation marks! Leaving aside all the internal disputes among Arabs, scholars and staff, it seems as though external relations have entered a delicate stage.

I knew that something was brewing, of course, when Ezer telephoned me ten days ago to invite me for lunch at the Hilton. Never having so far darkened the doors of a Hilton hotel, I was very happy to accept, even though I realised that his Ministry was up to something, and that I was not being invited simply by virtue of my scintillating conversation! In any case I like Ezer very much; he is far too nice a person to be in that particular job and would, as they say, 'have risen higher' in officialdom if he had not been such a gentleman.

Working out on the basis of the invited company what is afoot nearly always defeats me. The other five at table were three Israelis, a German Lutheran and a visiting Anglican dignitary. This last one baffled me entirely. We had hardly sat down before he told me that he supported Mrs Thatcher's Falklands War, and then looked towards me quizzically in that peculiarly

English manner as if to say that I, presumably, was not one of those outsiders who disapproved of her policy. What provokes me is the bland assumption of the English establishment that we are all 'decent fellows who belong to the same club'. So I simply said that it would be surprising if I did support Mrs Thatcher now, since I had never previously agreed with anything she has done. Maybe this, in turn, provoked him, because soon after learning that I am a Catholic he commented that 'Basil Hume is very good, of course, but who knows . . . he might be succeeded by an Irishman!' Strangely enough his comment did not so much annoy me as amuse me – it was so damned pompous. I thought to myself, 'Goodness! An Irishman in Westminster Cathedral! A fate worse than death!', and I was tempted to say that a similar remark about a Jew would undoubtedly have brought upon his reverend head the charge of anti-Semitism.

But I let the remark pass out of respect for Ezer, who, in any case, was now burrowing away about his own business, which turned out to be my business. His opening gambit consisted of a very appreciative and quite detailed survey of the articles on life in the Holy Land which I have regularly been publishing in the *Tablet* under the heading 'Letter from Jerusalem'. And then suddenly, in a tone of detached curiosity, he looked at me and said, 'By the way, Donald, did you write that unsigned leader on Israel in the *Tablet* of last month?' So that was what it was all about! The leader, I remembered, was sharply critical of certain Israeli policies.

With a little smile at Ezer in which he (bless him) joined, I said quietly, 'No, Ezer, I did not. And if I ever do publish anything unsigned, rest assured that I shall personally send you a copy – signed!', which was not a bad way of bringing our Hilton lunch to a close.

But that was only the beginning of my encounter with Israeli officialdom this week. On Wednesday I spent several hours, at their request, in a 'getting to know one another' session with two officials, a man and a woman, from a different Ministry. Ostensibly their visit was part of an annual tour of Christian institutions, but as I sat at the desk in my office being grilled – in a civilised manner, admittedly, but grilled none the less – I realised what was worrying them: our recent proposal to hold a Muslim–Christian Dialogue Conference. They did not say that in so many words, of course, but their concern was clear; and it saddened me that any sign of friendship between Christians and Muslims is immediately interpreted as a sign of hostility, and even conspiracy, against Jews.

They kept asking when we were going to hold a Jewish–Christian Dialogue Conference here, not seeming to understand that there is no need to put on a special meeting for that purpose, since a dialogue of Jews and Christians is going on here the whole time, day in and day out. I wish they could see it as a healthy sign that we do not need to contrive any such a meeting, considering that so many Jews come into the Institute all the time, either to work in the library or to give seminars or simply to have meals with us. And all this happens spontaneously because of our personal friendships with Jews – who in many cases studied at the same schools and universities as ourselves and share the same Western Enlightenment background.

By contrast, our Muslim friends come from a world quite unfamiliar to most of us. We speak almost no Arabic, have not travelled much in Muslim lands nor hitherto lived side by side with Muslims; and so we have to undertake quite a campaign to enjoy any sort of communication with them beyond the superficial level.

Contrary to what I would at one time have anticipated, my third encounter with Israeli officialdom this week went much more smoothly. I describe that smoothness as contrary to my earlier expectations because the Israeli official who came in on Thursday was an army colonel, and I was brought up with a suspicion of all soldiers above the rank of sergeant. Colonel Nissim is the 'civil' governor of Bethlehem whom I had really warmed to at two previous short meetings – but I couldn't help being a bit taken aback, as well as amused, at the process by which he now turned up for lunch with his second-in-command, his Arab adviser, a couple of other spare soldiers, all with their guns, and two very attractive women soldiers who are, I imagine, secretaries. Did I invite him? Or did he invite himself?

The answer seems to be neither: I did not precisely invite him, nor did he precisely invite himself; but he and his caravanserai simply appeared at our table through a process of osmosis. The truth behind that seemingly fanciful answer is actually a source of hope for the Middle East, because the osmosis in question was achieved by the silent collaboration of our Jewish accountant, Yehuda, and our incomparable Arab business manager, Yusuf

Sa'ad. Their collaboration often makes me think that if only the Yehudas and Yusufs who dwell in this land were left unmolested by the Great Powers and external busybodies in general, then they would certainly manage to live together in peace. The arrangements they made would not be up to the standards demanded by the hypocrites of the West, but at least they would be of a kind that the human beings hereabouts can live with.

The fact of the matter is that Colonel Nissim, as governor of Bethlehem, obviously needs to keep an eye on what is going on in this Institute so strategically situated on the hill of Tantur. And I need to have a good line of communication with the governor for those occasions when members of our staff get arrested, in which case I have to try to make sure that they are not unjustly treated or do not simply vanish for a few weeks, causing heartbreak in their families. And what better way is there of fulfilling both our needs than over a good meal, a glass of wine – and, in the case of the Israelis, endless cigarettes which they light up regularly at the meal table without any by-your-leave? Interestingly enough, I find I do not resent that bad habit in these Israeli soldiers as I would in most people. My explanation to myself is that the habit is just one trait out of the many rough traits characteristic of an army that I think of as genuinely democratic. At least once, in talking to Colonel Nissim and commenting on the easy, informal relations between all ranks in the Israeli army, I had described it as a 'democratic' army – but he had immediately and sagaciously corrected me. 'No! You cannot have a *democratic* army. An army is inevitably hierarchical. What we have is a popular army, a people's army, and that is why we are so much less formal than other armies.'

There was something else he said today which I shall always treasure. The two of us were standing alone in our library discussing controversial issues very freely when he said, 'It seems to me, professor, that you try, as rector of Tantur, to be neutral as regards Arabs and Jews, neither on one side nor the other'; to which I answered, 'No! I dislike the word "neutral"! It carries a connotation of being unconcerned. What we try to do is to be on both sides, never to lose our sense of compassion for either Arabs or Jews, who are both caught in a situation which is largely not of their own making.'

The vehemence of his reaction surprised me. Vigorously slapping his thigh he exclaimed, 'You are absolutely right! We are

all in an *impossible* situation which is not of our own making.'
Suddenly I had a glimpse of the man's heart, and an inkling of
what it must cost a sensitive man to exercise high office in an
occupying force: trying to carry out as humanely as possible a
policy which is inevitably oppressive.

⇜ 8 April

A meditation

Yad Vashem* is a touchstone for all time. You cannot
prevent this monument from searching out your impurities either
by refusing to go near it or, in contrast, by constantly going
there. You may try to avoid the self-questioning that Yad Vashem
demands of you by staying away from it; or, if you are Jewish, by
using it to induce guilt in Gentiles. However, no formula, no
matter how brilliant, can settle anyone's account with Yad Vashem,
not even that of the Spanish abbot who said, 'Yad Vashem is a
place which all Gentiles should visit, but no Jews'. He meant much
the same, of course, as Gladstone did when he declared, 'Let
England remember and Ireland forget'. But both the abbot and
Gladstone were asking too much of the Jews and Irish respectively
in requiring them to forget their people's sufferings. Similarly
my friend Emmanuel Littmann, himself a concentration camp
survivor, is misreading the possibilities for Israel when he maintains that the Israeli government should at least abandon the
practice of making it compulsory for all Israeli schoolchildren to
visit Yad Vashem. He is right when he points to the danger that the
practice will leave generations of Israelis with the self-destructive
conviction that the whole world is against them and wishes to
destroy them. Nevertheless, Jewish children, and maybe even Arab
children in Israel, need to encounter some memorial of the annihilation of six million Jews.

There is not, nor could there be, any completely satisfactory way of remembering such an unimaginable catastrophe. But
we can all at least be alive to the impurities in us which are
unearthed by the attempt to remember it. At the moment I am
thinking especially of the danger at Yad Vashem of legitimising
the pornography of suffering. The danger of succumbing to por-

---

* The memorial to the Holocaust, in Jerusalem.

nography in the form of suffering revealed itself to me more than 20 years ago when I used to teach a course on the Holocaust. Surprising as I found it, the fact is that human beings may find surreptitious fascination and pleasure in the depiction of suffering.

And it was at Yad Vashem that I came face to face with that surreptitious pleasure. The occasion was a visit to the memorial, which I had arranged for Tantur scholars. As they were slowly and reverently processing through the museum of the Holocaust, I wandered away in advance of them, not only because I have visited their museum many times but, even more, because I do not believe that one should go through Yad Vashem as a group. One needs to be alone in that searching examination, unrelieved by the distractions and vulgarity of a crowd.

So I found myself waiting at a corner of the corridor, obliquely opposite to where there hangs a greatly enlarged photograph of a town square in Poland, showing the bodies of some half a dozen Jews dangling from a gallows on which, in 1943, they had been hanged by the German occupation forces. One feature of this photograph had always sickened me, and that is the expressions on the faces of the Polish townsfolk and peasants who had come to witness the execution: they were fascinated by the spectacle, and thrilled by it.

Just as I was ruminating on these matters a group of American Jews walked round the corner and began to look at the photograph under the instruction of a verbose guide. As I was observing their reactions to the photograph, an awful, eerie realisation dawned upon me: the expressions on the faces of those American Jews constituted a mirror image of the expressions on the faces of the Poles in the original photograph. The pornography of suffering is not confined to any one people, any more than is suffering itself.

Yet maybe there is an area of ourselves which is even more corrupt than the one which allows us surreptitious pleasure in suffering; and that is the area which permits us to use the sufferings of other people for our own nefarious purposes. I shall never forget the disgust that overcame me once when I was walking through Mea Shearim, the area dominated by the Orthodox Jews of Jerusalem, and came across graffiti on a wall proclaiming 'The state of Israel is a betrayal of our six million brethren'. What sort of people have the brazenness to claim for their own ideology the sufferings of millions of their fellows, many of whom were socialists or atheists, some even Christians, and who would never have been accepted in their lifetimes by the Orthodox Jews?

This morning I again felt the same disgust as I had previously experienced at the sight of the graffiti in Mea Shearim – though this time the source was very different, not an Orthodox Jew but a very secularised America Jewess who, moreover, had been comfortably ensconced in the US throughout the war. She is a clever woman, as she has shown both by taking possession of a fine house that once belonged to rich Arabs, and by the skilful way in which she took advantage of our conventional English manners. She cleverly put us into a position where it would have seemed rude on our part to refuse the invitation to visit Yad Vashem with her, although we had mildly indicated that we had already been there.

It was no use. She bundled us out there in a Volkswagen (the irony of which I did not refer to), and then, to my utter astonishment, she left us at the entrance to the museum, saying that she had been round the museum many times, and so would go round to the exit and read a book while she waited for us. Once I had recovered from the shock of such *hutzpah*, I told Dorothy that I was going to walk quickly through the museum and arrive at the exit before our persecutor got there and see how she reacted. Fortunately Dorothy restrained me and we took a reasonable amount of time going through the museum, though we went rather too quickly according to the subsequent estimation of our unsought guide.

And yet no visit to Yad Vashem is ever superfluous. After my anger at the attempt to manipulate us into feeling guilty, as Christians, for the Holocaust, I said I wanted to spend some time in the Hall of Remembrance, which is incredibly moving and powerful because of the silence, and because of those eternal flames burning before the memorials inscribed with those terrible names: Maidanek, Treblinka, Auschwitz, Sobibor, Belzec, and all the others. The unpretentiousness of that Hall, the simple names, the pure flames and, above all, the silence . . . that silence, above all – above all. What, if anything, does God say to us out of that silence?

I don't know if God says anything in the Hall of Remembrance, and, if he does, I cannot understand it. But what I do hear through the silence, the simple names and the pure flames, are the voices of those who died in Maidanek. Treblinka, Auschwitz and all those other places of evil. And in the presence of those whose voices out of eternity were now echoing in my heart, even in my very bones, all anger against our guide dissolved and I was able to behave courteously towards her without any sense of strain.

☙ *10 April*

Letter to the Tablet

'We could do with more Anglicans around here!' These words, addressed in mock exasperation to my companions at the lunch table, were occasioned by the fact none of us had an Anglican prayer book handy, and I wanted quickly to locate an Anglican collect. But, as happens so often with one's spontaneous and light-hearted words, they began, some hours later, to take on a really deep significance for me. In this instance they bore upon the future of the ecumene. Because as my words continued to echo in my mind, I realised that I have no desire to see a Great Church of the future that is without Anglicans – and faithful Anglicans at that. And then I realised further that neither would I feel completely at home in the Great Church of the future that did not contain my Baptist friends. Moreover, if I single out Baptists that is not in order to exclude Methodist friends, Presbyterians and others. It is simply that, by a strange turn of events at Tantur during last semester, we were almost all either Roman Catholics or Baptists, in more or less equal numbers; and during those four months of living, working and praying together, day in and day out, I came to appreciate Baptist qualities as never before.

But at first it was something of a shock for me to realise, and then to accept, that my vision of the ecumenical future had changed so irreversibly. There always is considerable shock, of course, when one recognises that one has been changed at a very deep level of one's being, not by taking thought but imperceptibly, through the reality of God's demands upon one in the struggles of day-to-day living. At one time (that is to say, some 25 years ago), I envisaged the shape of the Great Church being more or less the same as that of our post-Tridentine Church. There would be a Latin Mass, identical in words throughout the world. All priests of the Great Church would be celibate. All its members would subscribe faithfully to the social encyclicals. Everybody would go to Mass on Sunday and to confession about once a month. There would be no Protestant hymns, and the Church of England would return the cathedrals and monasteries which they had stolen at the time of the Reformation.

But if I were to see such a Church emerging now it would undoubtedly send my heart down into my boots: because it would imply a denial and rejection of all those traditions among Methodists, Quakers, Orthodox, Baptists, Anglicans, Presbyterians, Lutherans, Copts and many others, which are manifestly due to the inspiration of God. Somehow or other the Great Church will acknowledge and celebrate that inspiration of God and will rejoice at the manifold and diverse ways in which God has spoken to us.

Not, however, that it all becomes easy and smooth once you begin to rejoice in the Baptistness of your Baptist friends or the Orthodoxy of your Orthodox friends. Even within the emerging Great Church, there is no doubt that we will continue to suffer unexpected shocks. Take, for instance, my innocent announcement that the seminar theme for the Fall semester at Tantur is to be 'Eucharist and human liberation'. Not for a minute did it occur to me that such a title would prove immediately unattractive to certain scholars who might be considering coming to study at the Ecumenical Institute. Soon, however, my Baptist and Presbyterian friends gently pointed out to me that the very word 'Eucharist' sounds strange to their ears, and they assured me that if I continued to use it, many worthy Protestants throughout the world would decide that the seminars were not for them.

Such a difference in terms could, I imagine, have led at one time to strife and enmity. But in these happier days I just said, 'Oops! Sorry!', or words to that effect, and provided an alternative title – 'Worship and politics'. Not a bad solution, all things considered, when I remember that our seminar leader, Rafael Avila, wrote a book, entitled *La eucaristia y sus implicaciones sociopoliticos*, which was translated by a Baptist minister under the title *Worship and Politics* and published by a Catholic publishing house. It is through such incidents, which crop up every day in an ecumenical community, that we are drawn ever closer to one another in our hearts. Though sometimes these incidents also reveal how far apart we are in other respects. During the course of our discussion of the term 'Eucharist', for example, two of my Protestant friends told me: 'You attach much more importance to Eucharist, or communion, than we do. For us it is not central.' When some other Protestants agreed with them, I then realised with a certain consternation that whatever else may be true, one thing is certainly true: those for whom the Eucharist is not central can scarcely believe the same as we do regarding what is going on at the altar (Lord's Table); if they did believe the same as we do, then what goes on at the Lord's Table would be central for them.

This issue of what is central uncovers a further reality about our ecumenical situation, which many of us tend to ignore but which the Roman authorities have adhered to firmly. It is that there can be no umbrella formula at the moment to draw all of us into full communion: for some time, at least, Christians from one tradition will have to commune with Christians from a second tradition in a somewhat different way from that in which they commune with Christians from a third tradition, but without those differences in any sense implying that one tradition is superior to the other – because the fact is that each has unique, irreplaceable traditions which it is called upon to hand on to the others.

The influx of Anglicans into Tantur this semester, for instance, has suddenly made the lack of full communion between Catholics and Anglicans appear not simply as scandalous and sad, but also as quite literally beyond belief. Here we have a group of Christians who are really in *koinonia* one with another. They share their meals together; they share their aspirations and their fears and their intellectual work with one another. They share their very lives. When they pray to God night and morning they use precisely the same words. When a Catholic celebrates the Eucharist, they use the same words as he does in proclaiming their faith; likewise when an Anglican celebrates, they all use the same words as him; they all believe in the real presence of Christ in the sacrament of the altar. So, on the Lord's day, all of us, Anglicans and Roman Catholics, come together in order to celebrate the Lord's victory over death and division; we repeat his words, praying that we all may be one as Father, Son and Holy Spirit are one; we all bow as one at the consecration in acknowledgment of his real presence. And then, when the Lord commands us, 'Take, eat; this is my body', something strange happens. A number of us do what he tells us to do one week, but others do not; whereas the next week, those who last week did take and eat do not now do so. It will surprise no one, therefore, to be told that such a pattern of behaviour seems to become more and more incredible with every week that passes, until it is quite literally beyond belief. In fact, I doubt whether even one single person standing there at that moment can believe in his or her heart of hearts that our behaviour is in accordance with the will of our Lord and Saviour Jesus Christ.

In the light of that heart-rending experience we may perhaps understand better the *cri de cœur* of our present pope, when he said: 'It seems to me that the question we must ask ourselves is not so much whether we can re-establish full communion, but rather whether we still have the right to remain separated'. It is true that when he said those words he was speaking to Patriarch Diodorus; but was he not also voicing a wider longing of the whole people of God? Did the pope not show himself to be one of those church members of whom Karl Rahner has written: 'the official doctrine of the church may sometimes have to adjust itself to what actually on goes in the heads and hearts of church members'? Because what the people of God actually believe is always somewhat ahead of the official doctrine.

ᵉᶾ *17 May*

I cannot imagine, being on the verge of my sixtieth year, that I shall ever now get over my astonishment at the capacity of human beings to deceive themselves.

Ten days ago we discovered who the Institute thief was; and we dismissed him. There was a sigh of relief all round, as if to say, 'Well, that little drama is now over'. But, so it seemed to me, that was not good enough; the episode did not end with the thief's dismissal, because a lot of other people had incurred guilt through pointing an accusing finger at individuals whom events have revealed to be innocent of the crime.

I thought it might be heavy-handed on my part to remind the community of the Talmudic teaching that one who speaks evil of others loses his share in the world to come unless he repents, and that a part of such repentance is to inform the maligned person of what you said, even if he is unaware of it. Since we are living in a community with a highly Christian profile, I thought it would be sufficient for me to put up a simple notice on our information board announcing that the thief had been dismissed, from which it was clear that innocent people had been falsely accused. I reminded everyone who had pointed the finger of suspicion at the innocent that we are each of us obliged to make reparation for such actions.

Though the notice was posted ten days ago, Yaser assures me that no one has come to him and apologised for having wrongly suspected him. And he tells me that none of the other common suspects have received any apologies either. That does not altogether surprise me, but what absolutely astonishes me is the number of people whom I heard voicing their suspicions soon after the robbery, but who are now talking as though they never said a word against Yaser and others.

It is enough to make you wonder whether the words we speak in chapel, in the hymns, prayers and readings, mean anything at all, or whether they are not a form of religious muzak, analogous to the background noises in a supermarket.

∞ 30 September

Letter to the Tablet

I am so grateful for having been trained as a historian. It really does help you to put into perspective events which could easily lead you to make rash judgements if you didn't have such a training.

Take the other day, for instance, when I was standing on the tarmac at Ben-Gurion airport, having just alighted from the charter plane from Luton. Most of my fellow-passengers had departed in buses for the airport terminal, and I was gazing rather dreamily at the Israeli Defence Force soldier stationed some 15 yards away. Both his green beret and his Uzi machine gun spoke of uncompromising power. My daydreams, however, were suddenly interrupted when someone from behind tapped my elbow and announced, 'Security'. It was a security officer who told me to go with him over to the security van for questioning. As I did so I saw my fellow passengers looking at me suspiciously.

For the next quarter of an hour the security officer and his aides questioned me in the politely menacing manner which is second nature to those in their trade. After a time they seemed to get bored with my answers to their questions, and the officer said, 'OK. We'll take you to the terminal.'

Knowing how essential security precautions are for Israel, I did not attach great importance to the incident. Rather, I smiled to myself as I thought, 'Well, since I am six feet six inches tall and have blond hair, at least they could hardly have taken me for an Arab!' Nevertheless, I did begin to wonder whether I may not look sinister and subversive when, a few days later, I was walking along the road to Jerusalem and found myself brusquely accosted by two Israeli policemen on a motorbike who also interrogated me – though much less politely this time than the airport security officers had done.

These incidents would hardly be worth recording were it not for the fact that so many visitors to Israel, and even long-term foreign residents, are prepared to make sweeping judgements about this country merely on the basis of such small, everyday incidents which have affected them personally. I am sure that we should, on the contrary, try to keep such small incidents in perspective by seeing them against the background of the long history of the Jewish people and their struggle to establish a state.

Israel will continue to be misunderstood unless one fundamental truth is recognised and never for a moment lost sight of. This fundamental truth is that the Jews of Israel are still in a state of traumatic shock as a result of one of the most terrible deeds in all human history, the so-called Holocaust. When one states that truth to Gentiles nowadays, their reaction invariably shows their feeling that they have heard the same story so may times already that they automatically switch off, having long ago dismissed the Holocaust to the distant realms of history. In so doing they make a terrible mistake. Because for Jews, especially for the Jews of Israel, the Holocaust is as present a reality as their daily bread.

As a Sephardic Jew from France has written:

Affliction dies away in time, but shame and humiliation ever renew themselves. A shock psychologically dominated is called a trauma. People afflicted with a trauma are mentally diseased. Every psychiatrist knows that a person afflicted with a trauma unconsciously strives to recreate the situation that is at its source, in order to be given a 'second chance' to act differently. Ashkenazi leadership in Israel unconsciously tends to provoke a new holocaust – a holocaust when Jews will die not 'like vermin' but as heroes and in a way commanding admiration. I claim that this alone is capable of explaining Israeli behaviour. (Gustav Kars, *New Outlook*, January/February, 1982)

Whether or not this insight alone can explain Israeli behaviour, there can be little doubt that it does help somewhat. How otherwise can one understand Menachem Begin's letter to President Reagan on his sixty-ninth birthday, when he wrote concerning the Israeli encirclement of Beirut: 'I feel empowered as prime minister to instruct a valiant army facing "Berlin" where, among innocent civilians, Hitler and his henchmen hide in a bunker deep beneath the surface'?

Mr Begin's statement confirms what we know about him from his own writings and from the evidence of many of his contemporaries and colleagues: he is still struggling to live out, to outlive, that trauma, that nightmare into which he was plunged by the unbearable cruelty inflicted years ago upon his closest and dearest ones simply because they were Jews. In order to succeed, as Gustav Kars says, Begin needs to 'recreate' that dreadful situation in which every *goy* in the world, every single one of them, was against the Jews. But this time he, Menachem Begin, will not allow his people to be humiliated but, like a true hero, will lead them to victory against the whole world. He will establish 'for ever' *eretz Israel*, the land promised by God to the Jewish people for ever, where they can be safe from the cruelties and humiliations that the *goyim* have inflicted upon Jews for as long as the human memory runs.

It hardly needs emphasising that the nightmare just described is not peculiar to Menachem Begin. In one measure or another every Jew is plunged into it – especially, as I have said already, the Jews of Israel. One needs also to bear in mind a further effect of being in a state of traumatic shock: that is, you simply do not hear what is being said to you by other people. Not that this failure to hear is due to ill will or obstinacy. It is simply that the noise produced in your head by the soundtrack of your nightmare drowns all other sounds.

Nor is it merely that Israel as a whole does not take in what the rest of the world is saying, but that even within Israeli society no one seems to listen to anyone else. That, presumably, is why most people here shout so loudly, in the vain hope of compelling some other one to listen to the story which they are ceaselessly telling themselves inside their own heads. This observation, I hasten to add, is by no means original and was expressed to me in almost identical terms on separate occasions by two professors at Hebrew University. In comparing notes about teaching in California, each of them said to me what a pleasure it had been to have had students who actually listened to what you were saying, since 'in Hebrew University the students don't listen to you at all. They just wait until you finish, then they immediately explain to you why you are wrong and they are right.' After which one of my professor friends added very sadly, 'This is the root of our parlous condition: there is no communication here – not even between husbands and wives'.

ℰ *20 October*

One of the handicaps which afflict colonialist peoples is blindness about their own behaviour. Even more than the generality of human beings, they are unable to see themselves as others see them. Not until they cease to be colonialists, so it seems, does the dark cloud of ignorance lift from before their gaze. That, at least, was the opinion of a recent British consul general in East Jerusalem who had spent many years previously in the British Colonial Service. He told me once that it was not until he saw the Israelis strutting around the West Bank so arrogantly, and lording it over the Arabs, that he realised how he must have appeared in the eyes of the native peoples over whom he had at one time exercised power. I was reminded of the consul general's remarks today at lunch. The guests at our table included our friend, Judith Simon, as well as Naomi and Ann, two American friends of hers who are very active in societies for the support of Israel. Usually in our dining hall we all collect our meals from a common table, but today, out of consideration for our guests, I asked Muhammad, our strong, handsome cook, to serve those whom I had invited to our table.

To my astonishment and embarrassment, all our three guests at one point during the course of the meal launched into a loud denunciation of the intransigence of Arabs – and that at the very moment when Muhammad was leaning over them to remove their empty plates and offer them more food! 'You just read the Koran', Ann said, 'and you will understand why we find it impossible to make peace with the Arabs. They are told in the Koran to carry out *jihad*, holy warfare, against us Jews; and all they are waiting for is the opportunity to do so.'

Leaving aside the strange assumption that they are better acquainted with the Koran than the rest of us who were sitting beside them, I could scarcely believe the evidence of my own eyes and ears. Here were three well educated, intelligent and quite amiable middle-class women denouncing a man's people at the very moment he was serving them so pleasantly and courteously. Yet I could not be angry with them when I remembered how many British men and women I had observed in our colonies similarly discussing the 'natives' who were serving them: in each case the British and the Israelis respectively failed to take in that the servant was a human being. They would not have behaved one whit differently had the 'servant' been a robot – such objects do not have feelings!

On the other hand, I did become angry with all three of them when we were drinking coffee together afterwards in our apartment. Though I did not want to tax them directly with their thoughtless behaviour towards Muhammad, I did try indirectly to awaken them to the fact that the man who had been serving them was a human being. I gave them an account of what had happened to him several weeks ago.

It was a Sunday, and Muhammad was driving a friend along a lonely stretch of road between Hebron and Beersheba. The friend was wanting to visit his sick mother in Beersheba, and Muhammad has a battered old car which he uses for such journeys, at the same time charging a small fee to help support his large family. They were travelling along a hill road with no other traffic in sight when suddenly a group of 'Jewish' (i.e. Israeli soldiers) ordered them to stop. The 'Jewish' then ordered them out of the car and told them to lie face down on the road in the dust. Once Muhammad and his friend had done as they were ordered, the 'Jewish' nudged them with their boots and asked them why they were sleeping on this dirty road. Then Muhammad and his friend were made to sweep up the road in the area where they had been lying. After which they were allowed to carry on their way to Beersheba.

Part of my intention in recounting this incident on

Muhammad's Sunday journey was to add that he had only told me about it after I had questioned him; and even then had not done so in blazing anger but resignedly and, as it were, sadly, as if puzzled that human beings should treat other human beings so brutally for no reason whatsoever. However, I hardly managed to add my gloss upon the story before all three guests were each bursting to be first to convince me that Muhammad was lying – 'it is part of the Arab mentality' – and then to quote instance upon instance of Arab brutality.

As regards any incidents of Arab brutality which they had witnessed personally, I replied, I believed them – because I trusted their personal truthfulness in exactly the same measure as I trusted Muhammad's truthfulness.

☙ 23 October

Letter to the Tablet

I said last week that the Jews in Israel are still in a state of traumatic shock because of the Holocaust, and as a result sometimes seem unable to listen to anyone else. Fortunately, however, the pessimistic judgement of my friend which I quoted – 'there is no communication here, not even between husbands and wives' – is not entirely accurate. Apart from anything else, he himself has a wonderful capacity both for listening to others and for communicating with them. He is one of those whom I had in mind when I remarked some months ago that 'these Jewish intellectuals are the salt of the earth'.

The occasion of my remark was the awarding of peace prizes in honour of Sylvia Shine, which took place in Jerusalem in the presence of the mayor, Teddy Kollek, and other notables of the city. A whole series of speakers addressed themselves to the subject of peace with the Arabs; and they did so in a fashion which assured me that the Holocaust, though still an agony, was no longer a trauma for them. But there was one particularly striking speech that came from Rabbi Arthur Herzberg, the well-known American historian of the Jewish people. After rehearsing the injustices which were being perpetrated upon the Arabs of the West Bank by the Begin government, he declared very emphatically: 'This government is poisoning the wells in this part of the world not just for one generation, not just for two generations, but for generation upon generation'. Herzberg's speech was doubly courageous because not only did many many people in Jerusalem disagree with him, but also, since he chooses to live in America, and not in Israel, he lays himself open to the taunt that he is not in the front line and consequently has no right to criticise the policies of the state of Israel.

In fact, of course, the existence of a free-speaking American Jewry may well prove a great blessing to Israel in the long run, since American Jews have a certain breathing space within which they can achieve a sense of proportion and perspective upon Israeli affairs. On the far side of the Atlantic they are not necessarily caught in that obsessional world which encompasses all who live in the Holy Land – even those of us who are temporary sojourners, even indeed remote reviewers of books about the Land, to judge from a *Tablet* review which began: 'Pro-Jew or pro-Arab? The first question one asks of a book on modern Israel must always be this.' So far can the obsession with 'our problem' stretch.

Herzberg's speech, quoted above, was delivered some time before the invasion of Lebanon, though we were all aware even then that the invasion was imminent. But the time of his speech is worth recalling, because the tide of protest against the policies of the Begin government had already begun to swell before that invasion; and the invasion itself has tended to blot out of our minds, and particularly out of foreigners' minds, the volume of protest that was being directed against Israeli policy in the West Bank during the first six months of this year. Some of the critical letters to the Israeli press, for instance, were of unforgettable nobility. I remember especially the one from Professor Abraham Wasserstein of Hebrew University. Precisely in the name of his sister and his parents who had been murdered by the Nazis, Professor Wasserstein denounced the repression being carried out against the Arabs; and his whole letter carried the repeated, compelling refrain, 'I am ashamed.'

Nevertheless, the Israeli invasion of Lebanon has genuinely changed not simply the mood but the very condition of the nation, at a profound level. Indeed, one of my Israeli Jewish friends does not hesitate to say that the nation, during these past months, has been 'undergoing a sea-change'. The kind of self-questioning that one had thought to be confined to small groups of intellectuals has now spread to virtually every branch of the people on account of Lebanon. Which is not to say, of course, that all are agreed as to the answers. For an Israeli, agreeing with anyone else is like surrendering his independence – Israelis are the most argumentative people on earth.

But the debate within the nation during these last few months has demonstrated, first, how profoundly moral is the substance of the Jewish people and, secondly, how strong is the democratic instinct within the country.

When I speak of the Jewish people as profoundly moral, I am not saying that I think their judgements are always right. How could I say that when they are forever contradicting one another? But I mean that the debate about Israeli policies within Israel has been raised to a moral level which is almost unique in the modern world. The contrast, for example, between the quality of Israel's self-questioning and both the American débâcle in Vietnam and the attitude of the British in Northern Ireland is striking beyond words. No one in the USA managed to lift the level of public self-examination about US policy in Vietnam to the moral level; while the British in Ireland have failed miserably over the centuries to do so, and are now bogged down forever, it would seem, in the morass of pragmatism. Only the debate engendered in France by such towering personalities as Mauriac, Marrou and Massignon at the time of the Algerian war of independence seems to me comparable in depth with the present struggle for righteousness in Israel.

No secret was made of the fact that quite a number of the Israeli soldiers doing their duty in Lebanon were against the war from the beginning, while even more of them protested against extending the campaign as far as Beirut. Indeed, some of them on leave from the front held public meetings to protest against what was happening; while all the world knows that a distinguished young soldier, Colonel Eli Geva, asked to be relieved of his command, rather than take part in an attack upon Beirut. Moreover, though relieved of his command, he was not punished for his stand. Neither, apparently, was the son of interior and religious affairs minister, Josef Burg, when he took an open stand against the policies of the government. That such events should take place while the country's soldiers are in action is surely quite extraordinary, and it is scarcely surprising that many people within Israel felt that such events should not be allowed to happen. But in fact they are a sign of a society that is longing to be healthy.

How strong that longing is may be gauged by one of the most moving aspects of the Lebanese campaign: a number of parents of soldiers who died in Lebanon have openly declared that their sons died in an unnecessary war. That is an incredibly courageous statement on the part of parents. What could be more agonising than to acknowledge to oneself and one's community that one's beloved son has died unnecessarily – not for a good cause, but for nothing? I find it hard to imagine how a parent could find the courage to make such a declaration. During the period of the Vietnam war, was it not the seeming impossibility of such a declaration which was one of the psychological obstacles to making peace? If the US were to make peace with the Viet Cong, it was said, it would be tantamount to telling the bereaved parents of thousands of soldiers that their sons had died in vain. How could you do that?

So in order to prove that the dead had not died in vain, you had to send more young men to die after them.

The issue of whether the US action in Vietnam was wrong, or the Israeli action in Lebanon, or the British action in the Falklands, is not one to which I am at the moment addressing myself. I am simply recognising that in virtually any military action, as any soldier knows, there are occasions when you wonder whether what you are doing could not have been avoided, and whether you may not be risking your life in vain. And I suggest that it is a sign of national maturity when such doubts can be openly raised.

But even those of us who live in Israel were amazed, I think, at the demonstration in Tel Aviv when it was calculated that one Israeli in ten gathered in Municipal Square to register their concern about the Lebanon campaign. Naturally we anticipated that certain of our friends would be there – those, for instance, who belong to the *Oz ve Shalom* group, religious Zionists who 'are gravely concerned about the drift in Israeli politics, especially within the religious parties, which threatens to undermine Jewish values and Torah principles for the sake of a parochial ideology'. Nor could we doubt that the *New Outlook* team, whose inspirer, Simha Flapan, has for more than 30 years struggled without ceasing to promote Arab-Jewish friendship, would be in the square. But the crowds in Tel Aviv included many who had never previously participated, or even thought to participate, in such a demonstration. Among them were yeshiva students usually regarded as ultra-nationalist. 'One discerns a certain fall from innocence among these religious soldiers, who suffered a large casualty rate in the war', is how one observer put it. But the shock waves that went throughout the country must not be attributed simply to a large casualty rate among the religious, since sub-sequent weeks have revealed more and more rabbis also declaring themselves – Rabbi Yehuda Amital, for instance, head of the well-known Har Etzion yeshiva, and many others. Also we have lately heard the observant education minister, Zevulun Hammer, recording a change of heart when he said: 'Our minds must remain open to many ways in which our living in Judaea and Samaria can be assured, and we must make every effort to achieve a solution that would not be just military'.

❧ 12 November

Letter to the Tablet
Last week I described the moving attempt within Israel to ensure Jewish values. But in one respect especially this should not be misinterpreted. It should not be seen as providing *carte blanche* for every critic of Israel to indulge his prejudices or his desire to hit back at Jews for any unfair criticism which they may have heaped upon him at some time. In particular it seems to me inexcusable to characterise Israeli policy in language and idiom which gained currency through the dreadful events of the period from 1933 to 1945 in central Europe, using terms such as 'holo-caust' and 'genocide' and 'Gestapo'. If Israeli critics themselves choose to use such exaggerated language, that is their privilege; but it is not a privilege of which others should avail themselves. Admittedly, a section of the Jews in Israel are intent upon driving the Palestinians out of the West Bank on the specious plea, put into currency by Arik Sharon, that 'the Palestinians already have a state – it is east of the Jordan River'. And that same section of the public does not trouble to conceal its delight that 160,000 Palestinians have emigrated in the last 15 years, or its intention of forcing the rest to follow them. But that is not 'genocide'. It is immoral, of course, and cruel, and it is unjust towards the Palestin-ian people who so love their land. But it is not 'genocide'.

Again, it is true that the Arabs on the West Bank are continually being harassed, regularly in minor ways and often in grievous ways; and sometimes Arabs have been killed without due cause. Nor is it any consolation for a bereaved Arab family to be told that virtually every army of occupation one can think of has behaved more ruthlessly than the Israeli army on the West Bank. But no one who knows anything whatsoever of the period from 1933 to 1945, especially of what happened to the Jews, could ever describe the Israeli army as a 'Gestapo'. At no period, for instance, would the Gestapo have anywhere permitted the publication of the English language weekly *Al Fajr*, a radical Arab newspaper which is essential reading for anyone who wishes to keep up with day-to-day events on the West Bank and Gaza.

Again, it is inconceivable that a 'Gestapo' would have allowed any of its officers to behave as certain Israeli officers have been allowed to: they held a press conference denouncing some of the practices of their own army on the West Bank; and their accusations have led to the arrest and sentencing of Israeli soldiers.

Moreover, there are certain groups of people, especially, who should have the basic decency to refrain from such totally inappropriate idiom – the Germans, obviously, but also Western Christians.

British people always seem surprised when I tell them that I know of no single Israeli who does not think that the BBC is adamantly prejudiced against the state of Israel, and that the BBC is in that respect representative of British public opinion. The British would be less surprised if only they could bring themselves to imagine the image of Britain that is the background which Israelis see when they are hearing the pronouncements of the BBC. That image, for most Israelis, is of British colonialists who executed Jewish freedom fighters in the Mandate period, and then, in the person of Ernest Bevin, closed the doors of the Promised Land in the faces of hapless refugees who had survived the Nazi concentration camps. Therefore, when any British person, and particularly a British minister, makes a statement critical of Israel's policies, the Israeli citizen automatically sees the statement as a function of an anti-Israeli, not to say anti-Semitic, stance, which is all that he can expect from the British, granted the image he has of them.

Of course, the Israeli reaction is not balanced. But who should dare to demand balance of a people just emerging from an era of such oppression? Not at any rate the British, and even less the world Christian community, since so much of the persecution of Jews throughout the centuries has been carried out in the name of Christ – not simply by ignorant Christian peasants, but even more by high-ranking Christian prelates. That unpalatable but undeniable fact surely demands of Western Christians, and especially of Christian prelates, that they afford Jews space in which to vent the anger that has been piling up inside them over the centuries. Christians have a calling to stand inside that space and absorb Jewish anger precisely in the name of Christ, who said: 'If anyone presses you to go one mile, go two miles with him'. Western Christians are failing the call when they instantly react by rejecting Jewish anger and hitting back with self-exculpatory apologies.

That sentence might well strike the proper note on which to end this account of the mood in Israel, were it not for the fact that my account leaves out something which I have come to value as the most helpful feature of foreign correspondents' reports. That something is the smell, the feel of everyday life in the country being reported upon. Although, to give a different example, I had read a great deal about the Soviet Union before 1970, it was only in that year, when I went to Russia, that I acquired any feel, sense or smell of everyday life in the country. And the volume of letters I received after broadcasting my impressions of Russia on Radio Four showed me that many other people have the same need as I have, and that it is the retailing of ordinary incidents which satisfied that need. Hence I offer the two following incidents from my own recent experience.

The first took place beside the swimming pool of a kibbutz where Gentiles are welcomed to come and swim, and where I have even encountered a group of Arab boys disporting themselves (which says something).

A Jewish woman fell into conversation with one of the swimmers and discovered, to her surprise, that he was a Catholic priest. At the front of her mind was the knowledge that the genial mayor of Jerusalem, Teddy Kollek, had just turned down an invitation from the Apostolic Delegate to attend a reception in honour of the fourth anniversary of Pope John Paul II's coronation – because the pope had publicly received Yasser Arafat.

So the Jewish woman said: 'What do you think of the pope receiving Yasser Arafat?'

Priest: 'Well, Arafat is not my favourite person. But I expect the pope was trying to act as a sort of bridge builder.'
Woman: 'But how can a spiritual leader condone a terrorist?'
Priest: 'Well he received Yitzhak Shamir, didn't he? And Shamir was one of the leaders of the Stern gang whose founder, Avraham Stern, tried to do a deal with the Nazis. Most people believe that the Stern gang assassinated Count Bernadotte. And who assassinated Lord Moyne? And we know that Begin blew up the King David Hotel and was responsible for the massacre at Deir Yassin. And we know that Arik Sharon was the leader of the 101 squad. It's a funny business trying to sort out when a terrorist ceases to be a terrorist – if ever.'
Woman: 'Do you know, I never thought that way before.'

Anyone conditioned by endless reports of Israel–Arab conflict could be excused for surmising that after the above conversation, priest and woman parted as cool enemies. On the contrary, when the woman discovered that the priest did not have a car, she kindly drove him home.

The second incident occurred in a taxi travelling from Tel Aviv to Haifa carrying six Israelis, five of them Jewish and one of them an Arab, a Christian. The Christian was quietly reading the New Testament as the taxi radio was broadcasting a speech by Menachem Begin. (That also says something: we listen to the radio continuously, as though we are expecting any minute to hear that the Messiah has come in judgement.) When Begin said something particularly harsh, the Arab passenger in the taxi groaned and exclaimed in disgust, 'Begin!' Instantly the taxi driver told him to keep quiet because he did not belong in Israel. At which the Arab equally vehemently retorted that he and his family had lived in the land for hundreds of years before the taxi driver and his family; moreover he himself was an Israeli citizen who always tried to live at peace with everyone. But the taxi driver was not to be appeased, and told his Arab passenger that soon he and all other Arabs would have to get out of Israel.

One could, of course, leave the story at that point. And one would then have simply added one more anecdote to that endless list of stories illustrating Arab–Jewish hostility which many people delight in. But the rest of the incident is far more significant: the five Jewish passengers in the taxi, each and every one of them, sprang to the defence of their Arab fellow citizen and rebuked the taxi driver in no uncertain terms. Some of them (if percentages are anything to go by) must have been supporters of Mr Begin; nevertheless they recognised when a principle was at stake. They exhibited a real sense of what democracy means, and I am not at all confident that a parallel situation, with a taxi full of comparable people, would have produced the same scenario in Birmingham, England, or Birmingham, Alabama.

These are, perhaps, minor incidents but they reflect the hopes of ordinary people. May they not be betrayed by those for whom the destiny of the Holy Land is an 'international issue' or an interesting television documentary, and not, as for the inhabitants of the Land, a matter of life and death.

☙ 1 December

Christmas letter to the Tablet

'It must be simply wonderful to be in Bethlehem at Christmas-time – so long as the Arabs don't play up.' That was the message inscribed last year by a Californian friend of ours on the Christmas card which she sent us. If only she could have foreseen the ever-deepening waves of irony that her message aroused in us she would have been astonished.

After all it *is* a cause for wonder as soon as one wakens each day to draw back the curtains and see from one's windows the town of Bethlehem on a hillside just opposite, its university buildings and the Church of the Nativity so clear in the light of early morning that one feels as though one could easily reach out and touch them. Similarly, were I to walk out on to our terrace and pick up a stone, then – if my cricketing arm has not entirely lost its vigour – I could throw that stone as far as the rocky path running below our west wall which Joseph trod, or so our Arab neighbours tell us, on the eve of the first Christmas as he led his donkey along, bearing Mary and the child within her womb.

How is it, then, that I gave much less immediate assent to our Californian friend's message than I did to the words of *The Times* correspondent, who last year headed his Christmas report with the words, 'O tragic town of Bethlehem'? And not much more immediate assent than I gave to a bitter article by another foreign journalist, entitled, 'O little town of guns and soldiers'?

The answer is simple. Our Californian friend sees Bethlehem and its Arab inhabitants in the light of misapplied fairy tale and mischievous propaganda – whereas the two journalists, in spite of their variously inadequate visions, have at least caught a glimpse of the reality of Christmas in Bethlehem.

Suppose, therefore, that I try to gaze upon this Bethlehem and the Holy Land at Christmas with the eye of faith – even my little faith: do I see anything further than a misplaced fairy tale, mischievous propaganda and unredeemed bitterness?

What I see first of all, with the eye of faith, is Arabs – not 'playing up', as my Californian friend feared, but trying to find some way of putting bread into their mouths. That has been difficult for them this year because much of Bethlehem's prosperity in the past – minimal though it may have been – has been derived from the tourist trade, which is now in decline. And visitors who despise the tourist trade, and speak of the souvenir shops and hawkers as spoiling the pristine atmosphere of the 'little town of Bethlehem', might well pause to remind themselves that it is the profits from those tawdry little shops that have often to feed as many as 20 or 30 mouths in the extended families to which they belong.

For in Bethlehem ('the house of bread', as the Hebrew name signifies), daily bread is not easy to come by, especially for those 15,000 or so Arabs, almost entirely Muslims, who make up the population of the three refugee camps situated on the outskirts of Bethlehem. Many of those in the camps who are able to find work go each day to help construct housing projects for the Israelis. And as one sees them trudging to their work in the morning, one cannot help reflecting on the irony of their position – building fortresses for their new rulers in order to be able to put bread into their own mouths and the mouths of their children. And yet these same Muslim workers never inspire pity. They are too proud, too much their own men, to permit such a response. You feel the truth of that, especially in the afternoons, if you happen to be passing a group as they are waiting by the roadside for a bus to take them out of Israel and back into the West Bank. On such occasions you may observe a handful of them, weary-looking, cement all over their clothes, stone-dust clinging to their eyebrows and their hair; and then the next thing you see is that each of them takes up a stand, shoulder to shoulder with his neighbours, turns towards Mecca and in unison with them begins the rhythmical sequence of ritual gestures prescribed in the prayer of Islam. I myself am still moved by that clean, uncompromising confession of faith, just as much now as when I first encountered it 40 years ago in the desert of Sind.

In that uncompromising position, our Muslim friends are more fortunate, perhaps, than our Christian friends in Bethlehem, because the Christians have to tread a path that is fraught with ambiguity.

To begin with, they are Arabs. Arabic is their language; and the Arabic language is more than a computer-like means of information; it represents a whole world in which people feel themselves at home at their ease, confirmed in their identity. Yet the image which is imposed on them as Arabs by the world outside their home, as by our Californian friend, is an image that alienates. 'Who are these people?' said an American visitor, speaking in the name of her whole tour party, after she had been received by some of our Arab staff. 'They are Arabs', I said. 'Arabs!' cried the tourists in alarm, as if to say: 'Then they are terrorists! And we are in danger of being murdered in our beds!'

There is something almost comic in such a reaction when one knows the real nature of the Arab Christians of Bethlehem and neighbouring Beit Sahur and Beit Jala. Among them one finds gentleness and kindness of a quality that I have experienced nowhere else except in certain parts of Connemara. In fact, the gentlest eyes and voice I have ever known belong to my devout friend Issa. There was even no note of anger in his voice last winter when he explained, at my request, what had happened to him one day the previous week. He said quite simply that, after he had come out of church on that particular day, some Israeli soldiers had surrounded him and several other Arabs walking down the street and made them all stand facing a wall with their hands held high, palms against the wall. They had not been cudgelled, he said; and after they had stood in that position for three hours, the soldiers had just let them go without any explanation. He had suffered no harm, he assured me; the only thing was that his shoulders still ached.

Issa has a most beautiful voice and sings in the choir of St Catherine's, the Catholic church within the Church of the Nativity. But he will not be singing there on Christmas Eve, because Midnight Mass in the Church of the Nativity is really for the tourists. If you want to join in the Mass you have to obtain a ticket beforehand, and then to run a gauntlet of road blocks thrown around the township. Eventually you come to the edge of

Manger Square and meet several walls of soldiers who will quickly let you through into the church once you show your ticket. The efficiency of that operation will spare you the sight of Manger Square itself, where raucous and often drunken young men and women from outside Bethlehem roam around within the walls of soldiery.

So it would not be at all surprising if Issa were to be angry. He has many grounds for being so. He could justifiably be angry against the foreigners who take over his parish church on Christmas Eve. He might very well rage against the Israelis who are occupying his native town, producing conditions which drive his children to emigrate from their own township. It would be understandable if he were to spit in the faces of those evangelical Christians who come from abroad to hail Menachem Begin on the Feast of Tabernacles, and who proclaim that resistance to his policies is 'anti-God'. Nor would it surprise me if Issa were to criticise his own church leaders who maintain such a close clerical control over the people of God that the people are almost asphyxiated.

But Issa does none of these things. When I met him in the bright sunlight of Manger Square on Christmas Day after Mass, and asked him whether he was sad not to have been able to celebrate Midnight Mass in his own church, he smiled and said, 'No. Is better. Last night was good for the tourists. This morning is better for the Arabs – the children come.'

So I hope that this Christmas my Californian friend will worry less about the Arabs 'playing up'. And with the eye of faith, I would like her to see through the 'tragic town of Bethlehem' and the bitterness of 'guns and soldiers' to the lovely, gentle smile of my friend Issa – because peace begins with a smile.

And just in case she did not realise it: Issa is the Arabic name of an earlier native of Bethlehem – Jesus.

❧ 1983

❧ *20 January*

The thought of giving a lecture tomorrow at Nes Amim is making me uncomfortable. (Nes Amim, a Hebrew name, means 'Banner of the Nations'. It is a *moshav*, or land community, established near Haifa mainly through the inspiration of Dutch Reformed Christians, as a witness to Christian solidarity with the Jewish people and an act of repentance for Christian persecution of Jews.) I don't see why I should feel like this, since what I intend to say was, so to speak, cleared by the members of the Ecumenical Fraternity last June when I spoke to them on the same topic: that is, 'The Christian Response to the Holocaust'. All the members of the Fraternity are known throughout Jerusalem to be devoted to the Jewish people, and one of them, a distinguished Hebraist, said to me after my talk last June that it was the only one he had heard on the subject given by a Christian with which he had no quarrel whatsoever. Moreover, the Nes Amim pastor, Arend Boersma, was present on that occasion; and since it is he who prompted the invitation for me to go and speak there, I presume he wants the people at Nes Amim to hear what I have to say.

Yet no matter what consoling considerations I may urge to myself inside my head, the thought of Nes Amim makes my heart heavy – partly, no doubt, because that community has touched off weird vibrations within me ever since I went there six years ago. Before that first visit, I was favourably inclined to them because I agree with their foundational belief that Christians have a duty to make some effort, no matter how inadequate, at reparation towards our Jewish friends for the evils that Christians have inflicted upon Jews. But on arriving at Nes Amim I quickly sensed that, in their effort, many of the members there had fallen into a familiar trap. It is the same trap into which we are all likely to fall when we decide – usually on a generous impulse – to identify

110

ourselves with some group other than our own. Before we know where we are, we start using that repulsive word 'solidarity', and keep repeating that we must show our solidarity with the group with which we have chosen to identify. Since my own primal group is the working class of northern England, I can see the process at work most clearly in the case of those members of the middle class who seem to imagine that the working class needs them to prevaricate on many issues in the name of solidarity – even lying, if need be. Whereas what members of the working class need, above all, is the same as other classes need: that is, truth.

There are so many other examples of this corrupting process at work: in Ireland, for instance, whose history has been bedevilled by Englishmen and Americans taking up the Irish cause. In India and in Africa, among Arabs and among Russians, the same story is repeated.

For very understandable reasons, a number of Dutch people, French people, Germans and others have recently chosen to declare their solidarity with the Jewish people. Many of them, however, it seems to me, have fallen into the trap I spoke about, and now attach more importance to solidarity with the Jewish people than they do to truth. I felt this most strongly the last time I was there, when every one of the Nes Amim members at my table unconditionally defended the Israeli invasion of Lebanon, as well as all the subsequent actions of the Israeli army in that land. One of them even praised the murderous Arik Sharon for being just the tough kind of person that you need for such a situation. So perhaps I should not have been surprised to discover that you cannot be accepted as a full member of the Nes Amim community unless you are prepared to bear arms in defence of Israel, a condition which obviously cuts out pacifists. Yet the state of Israel itself provides more scope for the individual's conscience than that. I can well understand how the people of Nes Amim have come to their position; but should they not ask themselves whether they have taken a wrong turning somewhere along the way?

Amidst this confusion of my mind and my heart, the main source of solace for me is that my host, Pastor Boersma, is a good and truthful man, and presumably there are others at Nes Amim who do not demand that everyone toes the party line. Also,

I take their invitation to go there as a sign of friendship on their part.

❧ *22 January*

Nes Amim

'My worst fears were realised at Nes Amim', is the sentence with which I intended to begin today's entry in this journal – but the sentence itself caused me to pause and ask myself whether it may not be true at a deeper level than I would like to acknowledge. May it not be true that, if one approaches an occasion in a fearful spirit, then that very approach causes whatever one most feared to happen?

Be that as it may, the result of our visit was not happy!

Actually, things seemed to be going very well for a time. My friend, Colin, a medieval historian, and myself were met by young Victor, an ex-student of mine who is working for a year at Nes Amim. We spent a couple of happy hours chatting with him, and then with others over dinner. And there were about 50 or more members who later came to the lecture and followed it most attentively, so that I was feeling rather relaxed by the time I finished speaking. What happened at question time, therefore, caught me off my guard.

A woman asked in strident tones why I had not dealt with the historical responsibility of the Christian Church for creating a mentality which made the Holocaust inevitable. Since such a crucial question (not to say begging of the question!) demands the utmost competence in historical research as well as deep integrity, I turned to Colin and asked him if he would care to make a comment, because his concern for the Jewish people has led him in recent years to study the matter in some depth. Colin kindly agreed, and provided a most careful, nuanced statement, characteristic of the gifted historian that he is.

But evidently such a careful statement was the last thing the woman wanted. What she was demanding of us was a denunciation, particularly of Martin Luther; and in pursuit of her demand, she bombarded Colin with a series of quotations from Luther's coarse writings about Jews, quotations which she reeled off by heart in the manner of someone reciting a catechism. Being a conscientious historian, Colin tried to put Luther's statements into their context without in the least minimising their shamefulness. He then went on to say, quite firmly, that you cannot draw a straight line of causation from Luther's excesses to the annihilation programme of the Jews. 'Hitler's use of Luther', he said, 'was not derived from Luther but from his own psychological condition.'

At that point the woman exploded, and an atmosphere was generated which made it quite impossible for anything sensible to be said. So the meeting was brought to an end.

This morning Colin was clearly still distressed that his well-intentioned comments had not only provoked such a violent reaction but had even raised the suspicion that he, and possibly I, were trying to 'absolve the Christian Church' from any responsibility for the Holocaust, and that maybe we are surreptitiously anti-Semitic.

However, we both felt cheered when young Victor told us that our visit had acted as an occasion of liberation for him. After the meeting he had walked round on his own under the night sky, laughing and laughing out of relief that the *moshav's* suffocating party line had unwittingly been exposed: 'It was just the breath of fresh air that I needed'.

ॐ *24 January*

It is inevitable, I suppose, that I should be continually using up much energy and time worrying about whether this community, of which I am head, is in good heart. On the days when I am exhausted and depressed, the word that comes into my mind to describe some of the scholars is 'merciless'. They want what *they* want; they intend to get it and have no mercy on anyone who gets in their way. Always, on reflection, however, I recognise that the number of them who behave in that fashion is really quite small. On the other hand, in this community as in many others, they are the sort who often make the running, set the tone or fix the agenda – whatever metaphor you wish to use. It is also disturbing that frequently the merciless ones are precisely those who arrive announcing to one and all that their overriding concern is 'community-building' or 'peace-making' – or both!

To some extent I was forewarned about people who go around telling everyone that we must concentrate on 'building community'. I had already come across Bonhoeffer's remark that,

113

if someone arrives on the scene talking perpetually about community, then you can be more or less certain that they will turn out to be a pain in the neck of the existing community on to which they have descended. What such characters usually mean is that they have devised a scenario for a community in which the rest of us play supporting roles to themselves, who are to star as the central characters in the drama. A community can carry one or two people like that, but if you get more than a certain percentage of such prima donnas, the tension of the drama becomes intolerable for the other members.

Lately, in the course of a seminar, I told a story bearing on these matters which I hoped might be heard and taken to heart by our small set of 'community-builders'. It was about my friend Father Aidan when he was asked to help in a mission to an English university. The task given to him was neither to preach nor to lead study groups nor even to celebrate the liturgy, but simply to be around, wandering into coffee bars and common rooms or chatting with students and staff in corridors or at sporting fixtures – in a word, to pick up a sense of what the members of the university were thinking concerning the mission.

In the course of performing his task, however, as he told me later, he stumbled across a puzzle of his own. Never having been a university student himself, he was puzzled to work out 'what made this institution tick'. So he paid particular attention to the members of the university as they circulated, taking notice of how they related to one another. 'And eventually', Aidan said, 'one day the penny dropped. What did those people exchange with one another when they met? You'd be surprised – they exchanged grievances. So the currency of that university is grievance.'

Never previously had I come across that particular insight into the way human societies work: any body of human beings, like any physical body, depends upon its circulation; it depends upon what the members put into the bloodstream of the whole body, because what you will get back when the blood circulates will be what you put in. If you put in grievance, you will get back grievance. If you put in kindness, you will eventually get back kindness. So all of us should examine ourselves honestly and ask ourselves, 'What do I put into circulation within this community?'

Father Aidan's observation about the kind of currency that circulates throughout any body of human beings helped me to understand something that had puzzled me about many monasteries and convents that I have known. It is that, in spite of their high ideals and the striving after goodness of the individual monks or nuns, some fail to form a good community, whereas others seem to manage it naturally. Take, for example, that religious house in Batley. On the face of it, you would not expect it to be outstandingly successful as a community because almost all the individual members go out every day to pursue their own specialities, and they appear to do very little in common – and yet you always feel warm and at home there. After racking my brain for long enough, I finally hit upon the explanation. It is Brother Albert. What could be more surprising! For Albert is now very broken down; he shuffles around the house in his slippers, devotes ages to reading the morning paper, smokes a good deal and spends much of the evening sipping his whiskey and watching television – hardly what they call 'a model religious'. And yet I am convinced that it is mainly Albert who sets the currency of goodness and kindness circulating through that community.

When you ring the monastery door bell, for instance, it is Albert who comes shuffling along and opens the door, always with a kind smile on his face. 'Hello, Donald', he will say, 'How are you? Do come in. When did you eat last? Well, in any case, come and have a cup of tea'. If it happens to be a tramp who calls, Albert will afford the same welcome, but to the tramp he probably says instead, 'Would you like a cigarette?' And so it goes on all the day, with Brother Albert circulating kindness and consideration throughout the whole building, so that when the 'model religious' return in the evening, they find themselves in a current of kindness and consideration.

It was the thought of Brother Albert which, two weeks ago, left me putting one question mark after the brilliant lectures given to us by Father Jerry Murphy O'Connor. Taking as his point of departure the Christian church at Corinth in the first century, Father Jerry drew out of St Paul's letters to the Corinthians certain principles that have to be fulfilled in order to have an authentic community. The principles he stated were so demanding as to scare the living daylights out of us.

So it was partly out of fright and partly out of exasperation that one of our number defiantly asked Father Jerry whether he had ever come across a community that was authentic by his criteria. 'No!' he replied, 'at least, not in the Western world.' 'Well, where then?' came the retort. 'In the base communities of Latin America', said Father Jerry. 'Well, why there?' was the next exasperated rejoinder. 'Because they have no choice', said Father Jerry. 'For them, community is a matter of life and death. And their commitment to one another is, therefore, for life – for good, until death. I know of no communities in the Western world of which you could say the same.'

In those staccato sentences Father Jerry seemed to me to be presenting us with tremendous insights into the meaning of community, but his use of them was flawed through their being given such an all-or-nothing application: either perfect, authentic community or no community worth speaking about. Against that application, however, the figure of Brother Albert shuffling around the Batley house rose in protest. Albert is not perfect; nor are we at Tantur, yet we do achieve some measure of genuine community, if I am to believe what one of our scholars said the other day. Since he is someone whom I have had to rebuke severely in the past for kicking over the traces, it was all the more impressive to hear him saying, 'It is a real miracle that community is achieved here at Tantur, considering that the scholars come for such a short period, and each with their own agenda'.

There was a further implication of what Father Jerry had said which only became clear to me as I thought of one scholar's indignant explosion, 'Well, you can't expect us in the USA to devise an artificial situation of life and death just so that we can have what you call "authentic community"'. The more I thought about that remark, the more I wanted to answer the man, 'You don't need to devise a situation of life and death in the USA – or anywhere else on earth, for that matter. I don't simply mean that every human being is always in a life-and-death situation if only he realises his situation; I mean, even more, that the entire human family, as a family, is now facing death from nuclear weapons and pollution. You don't need to devise any artificial situation; all you need do is to see what is in front of your very eyes.' So perhaps the greatest contribution any of us can make to community-building is to awaken one another to our life-and-death situation, but to do so in such a manner that we don't scare people to death.

∽ *27 January*

Having been asked to speak this afternoon in the Cenacle on Mount Zion, during the service which is part of the Week of Prayer for Christian Unity, I spoke as follows:

We are soon to eat *matza*, i.e. unleavened bread, the bread of affliction, as it is termed in the Scripture, *lehem oni*, as opposed to what the Talmud calls *matza ashirah*, the bread of opulence.

Now very few of us here, I imagine, eat the bread of affliction in the original sense of the term – most of us do not belong to the oppressed people, nor are we hungry, or homeless, or ill-clothed or in prison – all those characteristics which qualify people to eat the bread of affliction.

How then do we here dare to carry on with this ceremony of eating *matzot*? What can we do to avoid making this ceremony into just a piece of play-acting which is simply a part of the annual Jerusalem January round?

May I suggest to you that we should think of what we are about to do as a token of our determination, each in our own calling, truly to eat the bread of affliction by sharing our energies, our very lives, with those who alone give meaning to our ceremony? Those who in the literal sense of the word eat *matza*, the bread of affliction. Those in prison, whether in Teheran or Vladimir or Ramallah; the homeless, whether in Lebanon or Afghanistan or El Salvador; the hungry, the sick and the lonely who are all about us, whether in Kfar Salem, the Musrara or in Gaza.

Whenever we eat bread that is provided for us, we consume part of the life of those persons who have put their energies, which are their life, into that bread. Their lives have been transformed into bread for us. Let us in our turn transform that bread into life for them. Or, as Mother Teresa never tires of saying to her sisters: 'Let the people eat you up.' [At this point in the service each member of the congregation ate a piece of *matza*.]

By eating the bread of affliction together we have signified in God's presence our determination to work for the day when no one whosoever will be hungry or in prison or homeless or lonely or sick. Perhaps that is precisely the manner in which we are called to work in the present age so that under God's providence even Christian unity will be achieved. First the bread of affliction; and only then the bread of the Eucharist.

Until that day dawns let us take courage from the words of the Korean poet, Kim Chi Ha, who has suffered many years of imprisonment, hunger, loneliness and sickness at the hands of a tyrannical government, and who knows what it means to eat the bread of affliction.

The poet says:

> Bread is heaven
> You can't make it on your own
> Bread should be shared
> Bread is heaven
>
> We all see
> The same stars in heaven
> How natural that we
> All share the same bread
>
> Bread is heaven
> As we eat
> God enters us
> Bread is heaven
>
> Oh, bread
> Should be shared and eaten by all
>
> In Jesus' name. Amen.

Not everyone was pleased with my attempt to relate the theme of affliction to the affliction going on under our noses, in this Holy Land.

◌ 5 March

Kifr Harris

Around sunrise this morning, John and I were taken by Khalil, our friend from Bethlehem University, to visit his native village of Kifr Harris, which is situated in the hills to the west of Nablus.

Our day began typically; that is, inauspiciously. The *sheerut* which we were sharing with five Arabs had only travelled a few miles along the road from Jerusalem to Nablus when we were halted at a roadblock. The Israeli soldiers, flourishing their machine guns, ordered us all out of the *sheerut* so as to examine our identity documents. Fortunately the Arabs' documents were beyond suspicion, and the soldiers allowed us all back into the *sheerut*, though not without giving John and myself some hard stares, as if to say what were we up to with these potential terrorists.

Once past the roadblock, however, the whole atmosphere inside the *sheerut* quickly began to change. Our companions visibly relaxed; their bodies became less tense the further we drove from Jerusalem, and they started speaking and breathing more easily.

The change was particularly noticeable in Khalil. As soon as we stopped in Nablus, his face took on a smiling appearance such as I had never seen on him previously. The sounds of children calling to one another, and the greetings of stallholders as we walked along the streets – every aspect of the city seemed to assure him that here he was safe among his own people. Almost like a wealthy landowner displaying the riches of his estate to distinguished visitors, he led us into a café which is owned by one of his relatives, but which, in all conscience, is extremely seedy. The relative was trained as a lawyer in Beirut but does not work as an advocate in the civil courts here because, in common with a score of other lawyers in Nablus, he is 'on strike against the Israeli occupation courts'. For this strike action each of them is paid 100 Jordanian pounds a month by the government in Amman. Those among the Nablus lawyers who do work in the Israeli courts are not ostracised by the people, as one might have expected, because everyone recognises that the Arab community needs to have *some* representatives speaking for them in the Israeli courts.

I asked this striking lawyer what would happen to anyone who tried to protest against the recent imprisonment of the four youths from nearby Jenin. They had been arrested for not informing the police when an alleged terrorist was supposed to have attempted to persuade them to join his organisation. The man laughed incredulously, as if to say, how could anyone ask such a naïve question? He said, if you did so, then you also would be put inside. One of his brothers has been two years in prison already for making such a protest. And since another brother is in Kuwait studying, he himself has to keep the family going by running this decidedly ungrand café.

At mid-morning we left Nablus and drove westwards through hill country dotted with Arab villages. Where the land has been cleared of rocks, the soil is very rich, which is one reason why the Gush Emunim are determined to establish settlements in this area and gradually force out the Arabs. Khalil's own village of Kifr Harris is under particular threat from the Gush Emunim because it is the site of the tomb of Caleb, an Old Testament hero; and the Jewish fanatics regard it as their sacred duty to take over and occupy every such holy place and its vicinity.

However, none of those threats seemed this morning to becloud the mind of Khalil, whose inner joy mounted at every turn of the road that brought us nearer to his beloved village. And his joy was complete when eventually he led us up the rocky path to the door of his home, where his old father came to greet him. Father and son embraced each other long and lovingly.

There was an element of relief in the father's greeting to his son, as we soon learnt from Khalil, because during the previous night a company of Israeli soldiers had descended upon the village, arrested four of the menfolk and taken them away to who knows where. General opinion throughout the village seemed to be that there is an informer among the 3000 inhabitants who must have reported to the authorities some scathing conversations about the Israeli occupation made by the four men arrested.

These sudden swoops in the night upon Arab villages, resulting in arrests, particularly of young men, are a source of constant terror to the people, and Khalil's father had feared that maybe what happened in Kifr Harris had simply been part of a general sweep throughout the whole West Bank. He was frightened that Khalil also, in Bethlehem, had been thrown into jail. However, he soon recovered himself; and his wife began a ritual fussing over John and myself, apologising for the fact that we certainly came from more lavish homes than theirs, and that they could not receive us at the level of honour to which we are accustomed. Still, that ritual was not over-prolonged, and in no time she had an enormous mat spread on the floor with pillows and coverings for each one of us. Sitting between Khalil and ourselves, the old father, now 74 but still very strong and fit, made

120

sure that our cups of coffee were constantly replenished from the handsome pot which was kept hot upon a brazier.

They burn wood from their extensive olive plantations in order to keep themselves warm, but at the same time they leave their doors open to prevent the rooms becoming filled with smoke, an arrangement which probably explains why they are such hardy people – their bodies have to develop a great capacity for the inner regulation of heat and cold. Since I am not endowed with that capacity, I was very glad to be wearing my duffle-coat.

Also, these village Arabs, as I have noticed before, have an equally astonishing capacity for eating, which they assume is shared by all people. This they showed by bringing us great handfuls of nuts, and spoonfuls of the most heavenly honey I have ever tasted – so heavenly, in fact, as to leave me feeling that all the honey I had hitherto tasted cannot have been real honey. Only this honey was real which Khalil's father takes from his 150 hives and whose absolute purity he attributes to the fact that he never gives his bees sugar; hence they feed only on the wild flowers in these unpolluted hills. The old man glowed with delight when we told him that after tasting his honey we would always remember his home as *Beit-al-nahil* (House of the bee).

In the meantime the room had been unceremoniously filling up with children and adults. One of the adults introduced himself as Khalil's uncle, a construction worker, whose workplace is near Tel Aviv. This means that he has to leave the village at 4 a.m. and does not arrive back home until 6 p.m. As a reward for doing that six days a week, he receives only a pittance on which to support his family. He and his wife have nine children, a boy and eight girls, one of whom is now married. Interestingly, he also acts at certain times as muezzin, the one who calls the faithful to prayer. When I learnt this, I began to reflect on the truly popular nature of Islam. You could never have imagined such a character serving as a Christian priest, roughly dressed as he was and with calloused hands. My mind also went back to the day in Cairo when we had visited the ancient Islamic University, the al-Azhar, where we were struck by the very simple, not to say primitive conditions in which the Muslim students from all over the world live and pursue their studies. No wonder, we reflected, that Islam is spreading so rapidly throughout the world when its ministers are prepared to live so simply. We had in mind, by contrast, the numerous young men of Christian families who are taken from

121

peasant homes in Palestine or Africa or India and transported to luxurious seminaries in Rome, London or Chicago, and there transformed into ecclesiastical careerists who are intent on never again returning to the rough life of their tribal ancestors.

After a couple of hours of warm conversation, talking about life in Palestine, England and California, both now and in earlier generations, a great meal was brought in by Khalil's mother and sister, who, along with other unnamed women, served us. We five men all ate from the same enormous platter which was entirely covered with recently made bread, two chickens and beans. This was followed by bowls of the tastiest roasted or cracked wheat gruel accompanied by salads and olives. The meal was made heart-warming, to the point of sacramentality, by the way in which Khalil's father and uncle would regularly pick up some choice piece of meat and place it with evident pleasure on our round of flat bread. This atmosphere of holy hospitality was further heightened by their habit, frequent among Arab hosts, of looking at you now and again during the meal and murmuring '*Ahlehn*' (meaning 'You are truly welcome').

During the course of our meal, one or two children and men quietly sidled into the room and either stood around or sat on the floor watching us eat. Mostly they remained silent but occasionally they whispered to one another, smiling a lot with their eyes. But once we had finished off our meal with delicious goat's cheese and Arab coffee, these spectators began to talk more freely and the whole room became lively as more visitors crowded in.

This enlarged group included someone who was obviously being presented to us as the pride of the village, the teacher of English. She was quite extraordinarily beautiful – and shy at first. She was nervous, I suspected, that the presence of these English speakers might reveal her legendary knowledge of English to be faulty. She need not have feared, for she was very intelligent and she corrected almost instantly any slight mispronunciation or syntactical error which she had made when I pointed it out to her.

For over an hour she read aloud some of the very compli-cated poems which these village children have to study for their examinations, and we discussed the levels of meaning of different phrases, all the time watched intently by the crowd which had now gathered in the room. Eventually I saw that she was beginning to tire and so I spared her by singing for them some of the lovely songs that one meets in Shakespeare's plays. Then, for some reason which I cannot remember, I was persuaded to sing folk songs in Gaelic, which seemed to intrigue them.

But what brought the whole company to the pitch of excitement was theology. Khalil's uncle, the muezzin, having waited for the moment when his question to us would have its most dramatic effect, suddenly said to John and myself without any preliminaries, 'Why did Jesus never marry?' This question led to many others, such as the relationship of the Koran to the gospels; and, inevitably, since we were in an Islamic community, our hosts latched on to the issue of the crucifixion. Afterwards, John and I both said to one another how unlikely it would have been to have had any similar theological discussion in a comparable American or English community.

Fortunately, perhaps, our taxi was by this time waiting to drive us the 20 miles or so down to the Jerusalem road, and so we declined the pressing invitations to stay overnight in the village. We set off eastwards along a road that was now soggy with the late afternoon rain.

We had only been travelling four or five miles when a sight met us which immediately erased from our minds that image of Arabs impressed upon us during the last few hours. The image of Arabs as hospitable and friendly was replaced by the one which Israeli propaganda induces in nervous tourists: Arabs as the supreme terrorists. For about 100 yards in front of us, strung across the road, barring our way, there stood a score of evil-looking Arab men, their keffiyehs drawn tight around their mouths and their shoulders hunched against the pouring rain. They put their hands out, palms towards us, indicating that we were to stop. As they did so I heard John, sitting next to me, catch his breath, and I likewise felt my own heart begin to beat more quickly.

Our driver did stop and wound down the car-window. Two heavily moustached men leaned into the car and began to address him in staccato Arabic sentences. The sky seemed to grow suddenly even darker as they spoke.

Then, as firmly and calmly as I could manage, I said to our driver, 'What do they want?', wondering whether they wanted money or hostages or Lord knows what. 'They say, sir', replied the driver, 'that there has just been a wedding in the village hall and it is the custom for the woman to walk in her fine dress back to her husband's home. But the weather is so bad and the road so muddy that she needs to go in a car. But nobody has a car so, please, could they borrow the taxi for half an hour to take the woman to the husband's home?'

When we instantly agreed to this request, the 'evil-looking terrorists' were transformed in a twinkling into the same warm-hearted Arabs as we had come to know in Kifr Harris. They led us into the village hall as though we were some sort of heroes, and there showered hospitality upon us – endless sweetmeats, unending cups of coffee and, to our dismay, one cigarette after another. And although neither John nor I smoke cigarettes, we both felt it would be churlish to refuse them on this occasion; and so each of us struggled through the task of half-smoking one or two.

For three quarters of an hour we thoroughly enjoyed ourselves, sharing in the celebration of the wedding, so that when our taxi returned and we waved goodbye to our 'captors', I kept thinking to myself that perhaps peace would be achieved if only enemies could be invited to weddings.

Our driver had also received a generous welcome in the village hall, and he told us how much he had enjoyed the day when he finally set us down at a bus stop on the Jerusalem road.

It was a desolate spot. The grey, rain-filled sky was closing in with darkness falling, and we were actually beginning to feel nervous again – after all, this was 'Injun country' – when someone called to us from a barn-like structure behind us. We were being invited to shelter against the rain, and we were informed that the last bus had gone so we would have to hope for a *sheerut*.

In the half-darkness of the barn we discerned three men, all engaged in making brooms. The dominant character among them was a strong-jawed, clear-eyed young fellow, enormously skilful with his hands; he could twist and tighten wire around the broom handle as easily as though it were cotton. A merry, self-confident fellow, he turned out to be the brother of a well-known Arabic author. He himself is a writer and a great reader, mainly of books translated into Arabic. His favourite work is Tolstoy's *War and Peace*, but he also admires Hemingway and Sartre. For Marx and Lenin he has no time at all – too arid and intellectual. His brother is in an Israeli prison, and when I asked him whether he himself had ever been in prison he grinned, threw back his head and exclaimed, 'Not yet!' When I questioned him further as to whether the Palestinian people had created any poems or songs of resistance to Israeli occupation, he answered very affirmatively. To prove his point he sang us one, a haunting one, with the refrain, 'Will you come and visit me in prison, my beloved?' When John then asked him if he knew the name of the poet and composer, he again let out a loud laugh of amusement, put his finger to his breast and said, 'I am the one'.

This fascinating encounter with a genuinely popular culture only came to an end when a *sheerut* drew up, but not before we had discovered that there was a fourth man sitting on straw bales at the far end of the barn. Dressed in a worn *ghalabiyeh* and wearing heavy, broken-down boots, this mild-looking man came outside at the same time as ourselves. He was on his way to the mosque in order to call the faithful to prayer, because he is the local muezzin, another witness to popular Islam.

On the way back to Jerusalem in the darkness, our Arab companions in the *sheerut* grew more and more silent and withdrawn the nearer we drew to the Holy City. They were tensely anticipating the inevitable roadblock, which duly confronted us just outside Jerusalem. This time the Israeli soldiers did not make us get out of the *sheerut*; but they flourished their machine guns all the more vigorously. By the time they waved us on, the atmosphere inside the *sheerut* was electric, and the thought suddenly struck me that any young Arab who puts up with this sort of treatment day after day without engaging in some form of resistance must eventually come to feel that he has no balls, that he has been castrated.

๛ *3 April*

Ein Karem

This has been such a beautiful, relaxing day. To begin with, I was able at dawn to take a long time over my yoga asanas and my breathing exercises. As a result, I have found myself breathing really deeply all day, inhaling peace from the incredibly rich scents which fill this enclosed garden of the Sisters of Sion, who, with the aid of a warming sun, have nurtured such a dense growth of bushes and flowers of every variety. And the variety of bushes and flowers further ensures the presence of a rich variety of birds and insects and bees. I love these sun-blessed places on the earth's surface, where the warmth bathes you in waves coming not only from the sky above but also from the ground below and from every side. How could you not grow relaxed in this peace-filled, scent-laden spot?

For most of the day I walked at my leisure around this womb-like valley of Ein Karem in the middle of which, and on its slopes, the houses of the village nestle, much as Jesus was folded in the womb of Mary when she came from Nazareth to this hill-country of Judaea to visit her cousin Elizabeth, in whose own womb was nestling John, later known as the Baptiser. The route I followed today took me along the hill-tops from the Hadassah Hospital to Kiryat Ha Yovel, where so many Moroccan and Yemeni Jews have settled, and then to the Holocaust memorial at Yad Vashem, and on to Mount Hertzl from where there is so fine a view over the city of Jerusalem.

As you walk around the heights above Ein Karem there is no way you can prevent yourself reflecting that Ein Karem declares itself to be an Arab village which is now occupied by strangers. Even though the ancient terraces are now overgrown on which the Arab villagers once husbanded their olives, nevertheless they speak silently of those who had owned them for centuries. Similarly, the shape of the houses, the straggle of the streets, the steeples of churches overtopping the trees and the tall minaret set above the Spring of the Virgin – all harmonise with the hallowed Arabic name, *ein karem*, 'the spring of the vineyard'.

By contrast, one sees ugly buildings here and there, often bearing signs in Hebrew, whose very shape and location appear to have been stamped upon the landscape by an alien mind. They squat uneasily by the roadsides as if conscious that they do not belong. They are the work of Israelis.

I almost began to hate myself for noticing the contrast between Arab buildings and villages and fields on the one hand, which always seem to have an organic relationship with the landscape, as though they have emerged in harmony with it, and on the other hand Jewish buildings, roads and settlements. Almost all the latter, with the notable exception of those inspired by Teddy Kollek, look as though they have been imported wholesale from some place far across the Atlantic such as New York or Pittsburg. I do not see how any honest person can fail to be struck by the contrast. Even some of my most patriotic Israeli friends agree with one of their number, Naomi, who lately sighed to me,

'Why are our buildings and settlements so ugly compared with the Arab villages?'

So I took comfort later in the day, as I was strolling through Kiryat Ha Yovel, at being able to watch Jewish families relaxing in the evening sun for the start of sabbath while their younger members were playing soccer and basketball with great enthusiasm, and while the fathers of young families were earnestly cleaning their cars or carrying out improvements to their houses. The atmosphere in Kiryat Ha Yovel was pleasant indeed, and I was pleased for these people who must be happier here than ever they were in Morocco or Yemen. Here they obviously feel to be at home.

ও *5 May*

How extraordinarily difficult it is for us, Jews and Christians, really to meet and discuss our beliefs without getting carried away by currents of underground feeling within us that arose thousands of years ago, before any of us were born. The effect is that such currents are continually creating eruptions of anger, resentment and hatred between us that surprise us by their suddenness and violence. Such eruptions can spring up even between Jews and Christians who are personally good friends.

One such incident happened last year when I was just beginning to familiarise myself once more with the many groups around Jerusalem devoted to Christian–Jewish dialogue. In the course of doing so, I kept noticing how often people characterised Christian–Jewish dialogue as 'asymmetrical'. Puzzled as to how this term applied to the dialogue and what were its implications, I turned to Professor Shamir, a very open-minded friend of some years standing. I asked him what the term meant and he replied, 'It means you need us, but we don't need you'. Coming from him, the words themselves startled me; but what took me aback still more was the arrogant tone of this usually genial Jewish friend.

Though even Shamir's attitude was as nothing compared with that of a rabbi who was lecturing not long ago to a large audience composed of both Christians and Jews. He was quite properly praising the heroism of Rabbi Akiba in the year 135, reminding us that under torture from the Romans, Akiba's last words were the defiant, 'Hear, O Israel, the Lord your God is

One'. And then our lecturer added, in a quite venomous voice, 'Unlike the cry of despair from a crucified Jew a few years earlier'.

Nor was it only the Christians in the audience who were stunned by this sudden eruption in the middle of an academic discourse.

Yet I realised last night that Christians should try not to take offence at such fierce remarks, because similar underground currents often produce conflict amongst Jews themselves.

What happened last night was that Professor Horowitz delivered to our group a very well thought-out lecture on the subject of changes since the second Vatican council in the attitude of Catholics towards questions of human rights. As his lecture proceeded, I imperceptibly began, as one does around these parts, to sense a wave of resistance to what he was saying running through the group. The reason for this escaped me at first, but then became crystal clear, as I explained to my guest, Father Michael, during the break for refreshments that always precedes discussion of the lecture.

Father Michael said to me, 'What happens now?' 'I'll tell you what I think is going to happen', was my reply. 'I am pretty sure that some of our Jewish friends here realise, within the penumbra of their minds, that if they accept as true what Horowitz has been saying, then they will also have to accept that present Israeli policies on the West Bank are morally indefensible. But that is what they certainly have no intention of recognising. Their anger over the dilemma in which Horowitz has placed them goes so deep that they cannot face it. And so they will displace their anger on to Horowitz and attack him personally.'

In what followed it was as though the participants were faithfully acting out the script that I had given them, except that the attacks upon Horowitz were even more vicious than I had envisaged.

None of the Christians present said a single word; they seemed paralysed at the animus that was being displayed. And I certainly had no intention of heightening the swirling passions by injecting my diagnosis of what was going on.

ᏋᏋ *6 June*

'Well done, Yorkshire!' I say that because of the lightning response of the TV producer, who was phoning from Leeds this afternoon.

He had telephoned me several days ago asking if I could put him into contact with any Arab Christians who might be willing to give their views of the accord for Lebanon recently drawn up by the Israelis, the Gemayels and the Americans. At first I hesitated to do so, knowing that whenever an Arab raises his head he is liable to get it kicked in. But eventually I gave him the names and phone numbers of three Arab Christians who are strong-minded enough to say 'No' if they don't want to have anything to do with the proposal.

When the man called me up today, he did so in order to thank me for the help I had given – but also to convey his disappointment that none of my Arab friends had proved willing to accede to his request. 'They seemed very reluctant', he said, 'to go into the Israeli television studio in Jerusalem.' 'Does that surprise you?' I commented with astonishment. 'Yes, it does', came the reply. After a short pause, during which I reflected on how little sense even educated people have for the realities of life in this land, I said slowly and deliberately, 'Do you realise that there is almost certainly someone listening to our present conversation?' 'No, I didn't', said the startled voice at the other end of the phone in distant Leeds. But then, quick as a flash, the Yorkshire voice said, 'Well, to whoever is listening . . . *shalom*!'

I hope the listener appreciated the quick wit as much as I did.

ᏋᏋ *21 August*

Never again, I vow, shall I call another human being 'a nut' – not after today. At the same time, I can scarcely be blamed for calling her 'a nut' in the first place, when she phoned one evening two weeks ago.

Our dinner party was in full swing when the phone rang, and our confused receptionist up at the desk announced that a woman wished to speak to me; but he couldn't make out what her name was. So I said, 'Put her through'. Then, when I announced myself over the phone, I was greeted by a staccato voice saying, 'This is . . .', followed by a strange name that I could not catch. But I caught only too well the next sentence: 'I am Jewish and have been in Assisi and there St Francis told me to talk with you'.

Inwardly I emitted a long drawn out groan. 'Here we go again!' I said to myself. Because at least once every week, sometimes twice, and even occasionally more often, some character or other either phones or writes or just appears at our reception desk with a plan for saving the world or announcing the end of the world. And for some unaccountable reason, they have cast me for some role in this impending scenario. Every time it happens I am reminded of the statement by Danby, the great Anglican scholar, that whenever he was lecturing in Jerusalem he could always be confident that at least six members of the audience facing him considered themselves to be the Messiah. Nor do our beloved Arab receptionists seem capable of screening me from these and other unexpected visitors – probably in virtue of the Arabs' admirable inability to understand why anyone would not be glad to welcome any visitor at any time. (That inability had left me one afternoon entertaining in our apartment at one and the same time an Arab shepherd, a German professor and a French cardinal archbishop. The last of these had called because of his concern for Christian–Jewish relations; the German professor wanted to discuss the New Testament, and the Arab shepherd wanted me to expel other shepherds who were grazing their flocks in our grounds over which he claimed a monopoly for his sheep and goats.)

But to return to our messenger from Assisi. I said to her, 'Where are you?', dreading that she would say she was at our reception desk, in which case I would be trapped. To my great relief, however, she said she was phoning from Haifa. That at least gave me a breathing space, and we arranged that she should come to lunch with her husband (who, I gathered, was a famous author) at 12.30 two weeks later, that is, today.

But in view of our initial conversation, I knew it would not prove so simple as that! Nor did it. In subsequent phone calls I was asked to arrange for someone to take her husband and herself along the stations of the cross in the Old City of Jerusalem, because her husband knows nothing whatsoever about Christianity. That experience was tentatively arranged for them, but then it somehow slipped off her programme without a word – and so off mine! Moreover she several times changed the time at which the two of them would arrive for lunch.

Finally it was agreed that lunch would be at 12.30. So, not for the first time, I asked the community if they would be so good as to switch the time for lunch again, from the usual hour of 1 p.m., to which they generously acceded.

But at 12.30 there was no visitor in sight, nor at 12.45, by which time I was wondering if it was my duty to remonstrate rather sternly with our visitor when and if she were to arrive.

Then, at 1 p.m., just as I was about to tap a glass to signal the grace and begin the meal notwithstanding, we heard a noisy clatter along the corridor outside the dining room. The door was flung open and there strode in a big, fat, smiling woman followed by a small, pensive-looking man. And instantly I liked her. Why I should have liked her immediately, I cannot explain. Of course, I can think up reasons, such as that she behaved so warmly towards our Arab cooks, to whom she spoke in voluble Arabic – both accomplishments unusual in our Jewish visitors. But perhaps the real reason, despite my ingrained scepticism, has something to do with St Francis.

I say that because of what happened after lunch. She asked me to provide her with brochures about the work of the Institute and for that purpose we had to go across our garden to my office. There I opened the door and walked straight across to my desk in order to find the required brochures; but scarcely had I begun searching for them than I heard my visitor's powerful voice behind me proclaiming, 'There! I told you I would come to see him'. Astonished, and wondering whom she might be addressing, since there was no one else in our end of the building, I suddenly realised that she was standing reverently in front of a slender board hanging upon the wall upon which I had fixed the full-length portrait by Cimabue of St Francis displaying the stigmata.

Preoccupied as I had been over lunch, I had completely forgotten that I had placed that powerful depiction of St Francis upon the wall of my office. St Francis' eyes are so piercing and unrelenting; and they were saying to me, 'Unbeliever! Never again call anyone "a nut", not even in your mind. If you had been a citizen of Assisi during my lifetime you would probably have called me "a nut".'

[For the sequel to the events of this day, see p. 168.]

♋ 22 August

Letter to the **Tablet**

I don't know why I should have been surprised – after all, every precedent going back thousands of years assures you that trying to act justly in the Holy Land constitutes an invitation for someone to stone you. Still, I was taken aback when I opened the letter. It was from Los Angeles, and had been prompted by an article of mine entitled 'Peace in the Holy Land?' As I read the letter, I had the feeling that the words were jumping out of the pages to bite me: the man was accusing me of having been duped by the Jews into believing their version of recent history, which was all lies. They deserved what had happened to them, he said – and there was more to come.

I felt sorry for the man who had written it – evidently an American Catholic – when I imagined the misery of living within such a skin. At the same time, I was truly grateful to have been the recipient of such a letter, to have myself been the object of an anti-Semitic outpouring. For although I have read much anti-Semitic writing over the years, never before had I experienced the sensation of the filth being heaped on my own head. What it must be like to receive such venom constantly is beyond imagining.

And then there came a second letter, this time from the east coast of the United States, on account of the same article (on peace: God help us!). I was now charged with supporting 'the murderous Arafat'.

By good fortune, however, I had lately been reading a book by Ronald Storrs, *Orientations*, in which Storrs, who was at the time military governor of Jerusalem, describes being summoned to Downing Street by Lloyd George. Storrs feared the worst when the prime minister pointed to a pile of letters of complaint against Storrs and said they were from Arabs. Then he pointed to another pile of accusing letters from Jews. After which Lloyd George assured Storrs that he would be sacked if there were ever to be only one pile.

Storrs comments later: 'Two hours of Arab grievances

drive me into the synagogue, while after an intensive course of
Zionist propaganda, I am prepared to embrace Islam'; he complains also that 'criticism of any Zionist method or proposal'
is considered to be 'equivalent to anti-Zionism, even to anti-
Semitism'.

I sometimes think that nobody whatsoever actually listens to the
Palestinians of the West Bank – neither those who speak in support
of them, or even in their name, nor those who speak against them.
Some people at least listen to our Jewish friends, many of whom
speak the same language as ourselves and, in many cases, went to
the same universities as we did.

So I am all the more eager, when opportunity offers, to
hear the comments of thoughtful Palestinians such as Ahmed
whom I met again two days ago. And, as often happens, he made
me really think.

I was attempting, as always, to 'put the other side', in the
hope of increasing mutual understanding. Frequently there is a
touch of arrogance about such an undertaking, because it assumes
that one has reached a deeper understanding than that of either
side. In the event, the conversation revealed my own impercep-
tiveness.

In response to Ahmed's complaints about the Israeli
occupation of the West Bank, I was trying to argue that it is less
harsh than most occupations one knows about. He looked at me
sadly, as though called upon to enlighten a moron, and then said:
'We have been occupied by the Turks, by the British, by Jordan.
None of them were good. There was much cruelty from all of
them. *But none of them stole our land*. What is happening at the
moment is not occupation; it is conquest and stealing. And you
watch it as though it was a play on television.'

Failing so frequently to serve as a bridge can be discouraging, so
for encouragement I looked again at my journal for one day in
March of this year.

This morning I walked southwards out of Tiberias alongside
the Jewish cemetery on my right, with the Sea of Galilee to the
east, on my left. The cemetery is beautifully kept. Whenever
I pass it, there are usually groups of religious Jews present,
tending the graves of their beloved dead. There is always

something very moving about seeing one's fellow human beings making their fragile protest against the seeming finality of death.

But when I came to the end of the Jewish cemetery, I walked immediately into a different world, a wilderness through which there ran an overgrown path leading up the hill. For about a quarter of a mile I walked along the unused path, past ancient rubbish dumps and rusty abandoned bodies of cars. Gradually, I became invisible to the rest of the world, buried from sight by the tall, luxuriant yellow bushes on both sides. By now, however, through the bushes to one side, I could just make out some more graves – Muslim graves this time. They were totally abandoned except by the brilliant anemones and marigolds in which they nestled. And then, the path having turned, I again observed the high graves of the Jewish cemetery some ten yards away to my right.

Standing there in the warm sunlight, all I could see eastwards over the yellow bushes were the Golan Heights, while westwards the land rose towards Mount Tabor. Scores of martins were skimming over and around me, and myriads of insects were humming as they passed from flower to flower; so that all of nature seemed to be crying, 'Life! Life!' And in a strangely compelling way the Muslims and the Jews, on either side of me, though dead, were also present in their such different cemeteries, the one so bereft of human care and the other so graced with it.

In the presence of the living dead, I was sure that neither Muslims nor Jews would now mind if a lone Christian, standing between them, offered a prayer for all the commonalty of the dead, a prayer that all of us, Christians, Muslims and Jews, might even one day become human enough to tend one another's graves.

Walking slowly back, afterwards, the Lord put a happy thought into my mind. When the winter rains sweep across that hillside, they inevitably carry certain particles of the Muslim dead down into the Jewish cemetery: at the resurrection we shall rise as one body.

৵ *10 September*

Sometimes you really do feel that there is an Evil One, a Satan, at work in the world, and especially here in the Holy Land. Late on Thursday afternoon, I even seemed to smell the traces of his passage among us, much as one can sometimes scent the recent presence of a leopard in the wadis above Ein Gedi.

I was pacing around the Institute, which is almost empty at the moment, in a certain anxiety about how things were going to work out the next day, Friday, because that was when we were to host the first Christian–Muslim Dialogue Conference ever to be held in this land. My anxiety was due not only to the fact that we were just about to step into unknown territory which might well prove to be a minefield, but also because it has taken Geries and myself about 18 months to prepare the ground for the conference. At times it has seemed as though the mistrust and suspicion between Muslims and Christians hereabouts is so ingrained that we would never manage to bring them together. And I don't think, in fact, that we would have managed to do so had it not been for the goodwill of Sheikh Muhammad al Imam al Husseini. He it was who, so to speak, came to stand as guarantor of the good faith of Geries and myself in face of the local Muslim community – he is our protector, as it were. And his readiness to be so sprang entirely, I am sure, from a source which is so little recognised in modern society; that is, the heart. The moment that the sheikh and I met about a year ago, our hearts told us that we were brothers, and we each of us trusted our hearts. There have been difficulties since that moment, inevitably, but our mutual trust has each time smoothed them out.

All the same, the Evil One nearly outwitted us on Thursday afternoon! I was walking along the corridor leading towards our reception desk when I happened to glance up at the notice-board. To my horror, I saw pinned upon it a leaflet announcing a series of meetings to be held this very weekend in Bethlehem, at which Abdul al Haqq, a convert from Islam to Christianity, would be speaking! For an instant a shiver ran down my spine as I envisaged what would happen the next day if our Muslim brothers and sisters were to arrive and see such leaflets fixed upon our notice-boards. They would all have left instantly.

I had the leaflet off the board before anyone could utter

the proverbial 'Jack Robinson', and went straightaway to Issa, the receptionist on duty, to find out if he had seen who had pinned the leaflet there. But he had not himself noticed it, nor seen any stranger come in who might have done the deed. Nor did my subsequent enquiries of others shed any light upon the identity of the mischief-maker. However, I was less concerned about that than I was to go round the whole Institute with my eyes skinned, looking to see whether there were any more of the offending leaflets about the place. I discovered two more before supper time. However, although I sent Geries and the others to scour the place, thankfully no more were found. All the same, I did not sleep as well as usual on Thursday evening – troubled, I expect, by a deep fear that I might have failed to detect one of the leaflets. And I was even more troubled, perhaps, by an awareness of how near we had come to seeing all our work of the past 18 months brought to nought. Also I was disturbed by the depressing realisation that there are forces at work in the world so malicious as to want to destroy brotherhood.

However, in the event, the forces of good and not the forces of evil prevailed, thank God. Indeed, on Friday afternoon I was even able to have a good relaxed laugh at something which happened, even though it was at my own expense.

As rector of the Institute I clearly had to welcome our guests on Friday afternoon, all 200 of them, virtually all Arabs. Equally clearly, I had to ask for an interpreter to translate my words into Arabic. As far as I could make out, the man appointed to do so made quite a reasonable job of the translation. But no sooner had the first session ended than a number of the delegates crowded around me to complain about the terrible mess the interpreter had made of translating my speech. From the haughty manner in which they criticised the wretched fellow, I realised that in part, at least, their indignation was a way of indicating to me how much better they themselves understood both English and Arabic than he does. However, Brother Bartomeu, who was standing nearby and listening to all this, provided me with a more charitable explanation: 'The interpreter was so hesistant', said Bartomeu, 'because he was waiting for you to say something. You simply stood there with your hands folded and spoke in your normal quiet, soft voice. On such an occasion as this, Arabs expect a speaker to shout and gesture and generally behave dramatically. So your interpreter was waiting for you to do that; only then would he have known that you were saying something worth translating.'

Subsequently the truth of Bartomeu's reading of Arab modes dawned upon me. I recalled how startled I had been at the speech following my own when the dear sheikh, the gentlest of men, kept punching the air and shaking his head, bellowing away, his eyes gleaming with excitement at what he was himself saying. In fact, I became alarmed at the level of passion he was both displaying and evoking in his audience. 'Goodness', I thought, 'he sounds as though he is calling for *jihad*!' So I turned to the man sitting next to me and whispered, 'What is the sheikh saying?' The man gave a gleaming, happy smile and whispered back, 'He is thanking you for your loving generosity in inviting us all to this historic conference'.

❧ *13 September*

My apprehension about the repercussions of our Muslim–Christian conference have proved to be well grounded. From one section after another of the Israeli establishment I have already been receiving signals – in the unattributable fashion customary around here – that the Jews are displeased about our initiative and suspicious of what we are cooking up. How can there ever be peace in the Middle East as long as gestures of friendship between any two groups are automatically regarded as gestures of hostility against a third group?

Also, the sending of these signals makes me very cross with the media workers stationed in Jerusalem. Having recognised beforehand that our conference was likely to be misunderstood and misrepresented, I had invited 17 journalists, TV and radio reporters to come to dinner at the Institute when I would have explained to them what we were about so that there could be no misunderstanding. There is one question in particular that was bound to be raised yet again, and to which I have replied until I am blue in the face. But I must continue to answer it. The question is, 'Why do you hold a Muslim–Christian conference and not a Christian–Jewish conference?' The answer, which I seem to have to keep repeating over and over again, is that, in the first place, there are numerous Christian institutions and centres in Jerusalem devoted to dialogue between Jews and Christians but not a single one devoted to Muslim–Christian dialogue. Moreover, here at Tantur Jewish scholars come in and out the whole time, whereas we can hardly ever draw a Muslim into our circle. Again, a number of Jewish scholars have given Tantur lectures but not a single Muslim has done so . . .

If the media people had transmitted my answer to the public, the suspicions to which we are now subject might have been dampened. Whereas not a single one of those invited turned up to dinner; and only two of them had the grace to reply – Jennie Goldman, the warm-hearted producer from *Kol Israel*, who was already engaged, and David Richardson of the *Jerusalem Post*, who had been called to military duty in Lebanon.

The behaviour of journalists frequently makes me seriously doubt whether journalism as it is practised can be regarded as what the Buddhists call 'right means of livelihood'.

৶ *8 October*

When those Jerusalem divines two years ago declared themselves so shocked at my proposal to place the question of nuclear weapons on the agenda for the Jewish, Christian and Muslim divines who had assembled in the holy city of Jerusalem, I was at first astonished. Had they dug themselves so deeply into their various pits precisely in order not to be able to see anything outside their own particular pit?

Now, with the benefit of two years' living in the Jerusalem community, I find their behaviour not so much astonishing as weird – eerie!

During these two years I have heard the following statements. I have heard a highly respected rabbi say that if Israel is ever in danger, then he would be prepared for Israel to use nuclear weapons. When someone pointed out to him that such action might result in the destruction of all life on earth, he replied, 'Then so be it'. I have heard a Christian Palestinian priest say that if the only way for the Palestinians to secure justice is by way of a third world war with nuclear weapons and all their consequences, then 'OK'. And I have heard a Muslim sheikh declare that if Islam is threatened, then Muslims would be justified in using nuclear weapons.

When I look upon Jerusalem, aware of all these necrophilous passions swirling over and within the city with such intensity, and then call to mind these priests of various faiths all mumbling away at the bottom of their separate pits, convinced that their particular mumblings are the only way the world can be saved; and when I further remind myself that they are all highly educated, and even in a sense intelligent within the limits of their own worlds, then an eerie feeling comes over me of the unreality of it all.

❧ *18 October*

Letter to the **Tablet**

I never get used to the drive to Lod, no matter how many times I travel down that twisting road from the Judaean heights to the plain where Ben-Gurion airport fronts the Mediterranean. It is as though that thin line through the hills brings out the very worst characteristics of Israeli motorists – boiling aggression and scowling faces which go far to explaining why Israel has such an appalling record of death and injury on its highways.

And yet, though the journey generally scares me to death, I am always delighted eventually, when I get there, to be able to watch arriving passengers coming through the airport barriers. Waiting and watching becomes a kind of sacrament. From the very way in which the individual men and women walk, you can almost read off in what manner each walks with God. And from their faces, especially from the glance of their eyes, you are drawn into one aspect after another of the human drama – the farce, the comedy and the tragedy.

But in every body and every face and every eye, there is one invariable, one constant: that is, the desire for recognition. It is true, of course, that certain of the arrivals try to hide their desire. Many of the English do so, as do priests and religious in general; but the effort is no good – it only underlines the desire.

However, there are some people who never seem to hide their desire for recognition, and that is the Israelis. As soon as those who are waiting and those arriving catch one another's eyes, there is a veritable explosion of joy. Their faces light up; they laugh uninhibitedly; they wave fit to shake their arms off and then rush to the end of the barriers to embrace one another time and time again. In a sense all this has nothing to do with me, as I stand there patiently waiting for the plane that will bring my sober English friends; but none the less it always happens that I once more find myself pulled into the drama – smiling slightly to myself at first, until finally I am laughing along with the chief characters, and tingling with delight as I observe their happiness.

The only shadow that clouds my delight arises when I remember that I have still to drive up that dreadful road under threat from all those ill-tempered Israelis. At which point I have to ask myself whether the faces on the road and those in the airport can possibly belong to the same people. The answer is undoubtedly, yes, they do. But how can that be?

The explanation, I believe, lies in that matter of recognition. Watching those habitually closed, fearful faces, and then seeing them suddenly open up into joy and happiness in the moment of recognition, I cannot help feeling that what this people needs is to be truly recognised. Then they would change – beyond recognition.

It was eerie watching the parade of Arab Scouts in East Jerusalem as they marched to commemorate the massacre in the Palestinian refugee camps of Sabra and Chatila. They marched in a wonderfully disciplined and dignified fashion to the solemn beat of their drums. They commanded the warmest admiration from all those watching the march – from all, that is to say, except the Jewish soldiers in their bottle-green battledress with their sub-machine-guns grimly at the ready. The eyes of the soldiers were here, there and everywhere, scanning the crowds for the least sign of trouble. They seemed isolated and cold, alien beings from another world.

Yet it was not their isolation nor the menacing beat of the drums in the hot sunshine which provided an explanation for my sense of eeriness. It was rather the calm, untroubled, totally controlled manner in which the Arabs – both in the crowds and more especially in the parade – completely ignored the presence, the existence of the Jewish soldiers.

I had noticed on previous occasions the skilful way in which Arabs manage to conduct themselves in the presence of Jews, as though those Jews simply did not exist. The first time was a year or two ago, in the staunchly Arab town of Hebron. I was standing only a few yards away from a Jewish soldier when an Arab whom I knew slightly saw me from a distance and came towards me to greet me. He set off to do so on a line that threatened to take him straight through the body of the Jewish soldier standing near me; so much so that I involuntarily lifted my hand to alert him to the danger, as if he had somehow failed to notice the soldier. In the event, however, my Arab friend passed within a hair's breadth of the Jewish soldier without even the slightest glance. Somehow or other he managed to reduce the soldier to a status even below that of a ghost. And that was what made me feel eerie, both in Hebron and in East Jerusalem.

After the parade, as I walked homewards along the Bethlehem road, which was quiet and almost deserted because of the holy day, I was pondering upon a story concerning the triumph of Nazism – a story that has haunted me for many years. It is told by Karl Stern in his marvellously illuminating autobiography, *Pillar of Fire*. There Stern describes how he travelled by train back to his cosy little home-town in Bavaria just as the Nazi infection was beginning to take hold of the minds of Germans. His father met him at the station. And while the two of them were walking back home together as night was falling, they kept encountering fellow citizens of their acquaintance on the way. Some of these would no longer greet Karl and his father because of the Sterns being Jewish. It is precisely with such little acts of cowardice and hostility that all the terrible events of our terrible world begin – the lying, the tortures and the killings. Likewise the work of reconciliation begins with the act of greeting. Simply to greet another person, to recognise that person, is to partake in the sacrament of peace. 'Lost in wonder' is doubtless a cliché, but I have to say that no other phrase so well expresses the admiration I hold for Da'oud, my Arab Christian friend. He has lost his family lands to Jews and has had to endure almost daily harassment from them, yet I have never heard him speak even one word of hatred for them. When I call to mind the simmering hatred for Germans and Japanese which so many of us Britishers still harbour, the contrast helps me to understand how he manages to say: 'If we do not love our enemies, then we cannot call ourselves Christians'.

Nevertheless, he was very downcast indeed the other day. A close friend of his had suddenly been arrested, and Da'oud had lain awake all night recalling all the fearful stories he had heard about the treatment of Arabs in prison and imagining what might be happening to his friend. But above all, he was shattered by the killing of Palestinian refugees by their fellow Arabs in Baddawi camp north of Tripoli. For him, the forces closing in on the Palestinians seemed to signify the extinction of the Palestinian people – his people – and their centuries-old culture. And the nations of the world were standing by, watching this final act, not concerned for the men, women and children being destroyed but hovering over them like vultures, waiting to see what pickings of power and wealth they might secure for themselves.

Within an hour of listening to my Arab friend, in despair at his abandonment by all the world, I found myself in a totally different atmosphere – the atmosphere of what St John precisely calls 'the world', where ambitious men and *soignée* women together generate that peculiar smell of mingled power, wealth and sexuality.

Since my friend Menachem truly does not belong to that world, in spite of his high office, he quickly drew me aside and began to speak of the events in Tripoli. After a time, he said to me: 'Of course, I am deeply sorry for what has happened – especially to the women and children. But surely everyone in the world must now understand the fears of us Israelis, and why we need to be strong: if the Palestinians do such terrible things to one another, it cannot be imagined what they would do to us Jews if they were given half a chance.'

As we were driving home afterwards I began to day-dream about the peace that might come about if only Da'oud and Menachem were to get to know one another. Unfortunately, there is a seemingly endless abyss between them over which no greetings can be heard.

ॐ *27 October*

Last night could have proved to be disastrous to this community for the rest of the year. It may yet do so, of course, but I am not as fearful of that happening as I was last night. Still, if it does cause harm, most of the blame will be mine for issuing at the community meeting a rebuke which came from the wrong place inside me. As soon as I had spoken, I knew it had come from the wrong place. So I immediately apologised. But that was already too late; the damage had been done. Other members of a community may be able to get away with such transgressions, but when the head of a community commits the same transgression the consequences both for the whole community and for himself are inevitably more serious.

I, of all people, should have known better in view of all the times during the past 40 years that I have given thanks for what I always think of, in traditional Celtic fashion, as 'The Three Great Rebukes That Stopped Donald In His Tracks.' The first occurred in 1943 after I had entertained a barrack room of my fellow soldiers by running dialectical rings around a raw-boned Scot and his conservative political opinions. In the end, confused and totally exasperated, the good man bawled along the length of the barrack room, 'The trouble with you is that you're too bloody clever to live long!' With those words of an unquestionably good man, all my cleverness was reduced to dust and blown out of the room.

My second rebuke took place in the French Carmelite monastery of Avon. There I made a sly remark one afternoon about the number of devout old ladies who used to come swarming around the friars – at which one of the friars, Father Philippe, looked at me with steely eyes and asked, 'And who else do they have, except us?' My third Great Rebuke was administered by that most endearing of men, professor of Old Irish at Dublin University, Gerard Murphy. In the excitement of a high-spirited conversation among a group of us, I made a snide observation about Arnold Toynbee, tracing his ideological changes to his marital changes, only to be met with the deep-voiced admonition, 'Let us be very careful before we start taking away a man's good name'.

I have received other rebukes in the years between, of course, but those just cited are the ones that stand out in my memory as issuing from a clean heart. And because they were directed from a clean heart, each of the rebukes found its mark in a rotten point in my own heart, thereby touching off a process of healing within me. The healing process, I have always realised, is still far from complete; but that in no way diminishes my gratitude towards my three rebukers. And it was in the light of my very gratitude towards them that I was now able not only to see how the rebuke I had issued had boomeranged back into my own heart, but, even further, to find the determination not to sleep until I had uncovered that area of decay within me that had flared up into my angry words.

So it was that I went up on to the spacious flat roof of the Institute after the meeting, and began to pace the length of it, forwards and backwards, time and again, for hour upon hour, trying to examine honestly not just the events of the evening but all the events throughout the whole of yesterday which had led to my flare-up. Nor was it long before I realised that my search had to go further back still, over months and years, in order to uncover the sources of my feeling of resentment against Alan and his circle. Because the more resolutely I tried to examine all aspects of the incident, the clearer it became that, by yesterday evening, I was on the point of exploding with suppressed resentment, some of which had been boiling up within me for much of my life.

I felt that I had been working harder for half a century than most other people around me, partly through the need to earn my keep in this world and partly through a twisted sense of duty. And now I had run into a group of scholars who do not work half so hard yet are wealthier, who have been given the privilege of studying but who choose instead to sit for hours around the coffee room, gossiping and idly scheming. I also resented the way I had been isolated during the course of the meeting. Such were only a few of the reflections that kept running through my head as I paced up and down in the darkness. And they could easily have been turned into a long bill of accusation against the community in general, had I not seen my own resentment so clearly in the light of my Three Great Rebukes.

Was there something in myself, for instance, which, despite all of my pretentions to duty, would have preferred to live a leisurely life with plenty of money? With time to sit around, drinking coffee and gossiping? If not, then why do I object to others who live like that? Out of unacknowledged envy?

Objectively, of course, it is right that people who are not working hard enough to justify their wealth, and who are forever mouthing high-flown sentiments over their coffee cups, should be shown the error of their ways. But who has the right to show them? The only answer I could give to that question was that, even though I was not the one to have administered the rebuke, nevertheless I was glad it had been administered, because it was needed.

And how fortunate I was in having the opportunity to

deal with all my turmoil on the high roof of the Institute, against the background of the silence of the Judaean hills, and to be walking in the darkness of a moonless night, comforted by the glistening joy of myriads of stars. Under the influence of the night sky, the silence, the soft breeze from off the Judaean desert and the sweet smell of the pine trees that reach up over the roof's edge, I found myself beginning to breathe more deeply and slowly. My whole body became more and more relaxed, until eventually my heart melted and a deep peace came welling up within me, permeating my whole being.

I went down to our apartment a different person from the one who had climbed the stairs some hours previously. And I was doubly thankful that I had so firmly turned down Dorothy's suggestion that I should discuss with her the events of the evening. I refused because I needed all my resources to handle my own inner conflicts, without taking on board the conflicts that anyone else might have brought to the situation. It is such a profound illusion to imagine that 'talking it over' is always a help – doing so often has precisely the effect of 'talking over' the real issues and sealing them under a wax of words.

But something very remarkable then happened. Although I felt at peace when I lay down to sleep, for some reason I did not sleep. Instead, I continued to work away all night through those areas of myself that had been revealed as rotten. But I did so peacefully, no longer in turmoil. Certainly I cannot have slept for more than an hour, because I clearly heard the muezzins calling the pre-dawn prayer from several of our neighbouring mosques, and the distant stirring of the traffic while it was still dark as the Arab day-labourers began their journey from the West Bank into Jerusalem. But what amazed me was that, far from feeling worn out from all my mental struggle, my heart was light, my mind clear, and I was ready to greet the new day with a smile and to regard my fellow human beings in the most benevolent light.

The whole episode has been a great lesson to me: if only you work away at the rotten areas of yourself on which the light of Christ has been shed, then the burden of Christ will prove so light as to be no burden at all.

൙ *31 October*

Visit to Ma'hadda

I still don't know whether we made the right decision when we agreed that a small group of us should spend the day in the Arab village of Ma'hadda, which sits in a fold of the mountains eastwards of the city of Hebron. Two weeks ago we had witnessed for ourselves the damage done to a different Arab village by Jewish settlers, in order to punish the Arabs for receiving foreigners and for revealing to them the injustices committed by the settlers and the Israeli army. As a result, we resolved to be more careful than ever not to put Arabs into danger by contacting them unnecessarily. On the other hand, the message we had received from Ma'hadda was that they were prepared to take the risk of reprisals at the hands of the Israelis if, as a result of our visit, their miserable situation were to become better known in the West.

This unheralded exchange of messages with the villagers also placed me in a rather delicate situation. In order not to attract attention, our party had to number not more than nine plus our driver; and I knew that more than that number of scholars wished to go. I also knew which ones I wanted to see visiting Ma'hadda – responsible people who would behave discreetly and afterwards quietly do whatever they could to help the villagers. But there are two or three scholars, decent enough in their own milieu, who nevertheless are always wanting to get in on every act and who will always blather about it afterwards. They are precisely the ones, moreover, who kick up a fuss if they do not get what they want. I have already heard rumblings from them about what criteria I adopted for the make-up of the party – and I can hardly explain my criteria to them!

In the event, the day went smoothly enough. We were taken to the middle of Ma'hadda where there stands a rather pathetic shrine, still not finished, in memory of the two young schoolboys of Ma'hadda who were shot dead by Israeli soldiers. We drank coffee with the boys' fathers in the village centre and learned how the Fascist rabbi Kahane had sent messages to them, after the boys' death, telling the villagers how many shekels Arab blood was worth – not many. The elders of the village also showed us where the Jews were steadily encroaching upon their ancestral lands in an attempt to drive them out – an attempt, the elders said, which would never succeed because now they would rather die than leave: the deaths of the two boys had in a way sanctified their *sumud*, their steadfastness to the land.

But the most striking and chilling incident occurred as I was walking alone with the most imposing of the elders. When the subject came up in our conversation of the massacre of Palestinians in Sabra and Chatilla, this strong-boned, broad-shouldered representative of the villagers turned towards me and said very deliberately, 'We can get more children in one night than the Jews can kill in all their Sabra and Chatillas'. In speaking the words, a note of defiance came into his voice, arising out of the very depths of his being, and I was chilled by the realisation that the war between Jews and Arabs is now taking place no longer at the level of diplomacy, economics and politics. That level is comparatively superficial. The fight is now being fought deep down in the loins of these peoples.

৫৪ *21 November*

I received a message today from Ma'hadda to say that since our visit, 14 men of the village have been arrested and are now being held in Hebron. Whether the arrests are in consequence of our visit we cannot be sure, but the elders who received us three weeks ago did say that there were two paid informers in the community who were keeping an eye on us, and would undoubtedly give a full account of our doings to the Israeli HQ in Hebron.

৫৪ *16 December*

'Once you raise the issue of peace with people, you automatically raise the demons inside them', is a saying of my Jesuit friend, Gerry Hughes, of which I yesterday witnessed the truth.

The first demon popped up in the shape of a Christian bishop, no more than a minute after Landrum Bolling had concluded his lecture for the opening of our Peace Academy. It was my manner of opening the afternoon's proceedings that triggered the demon's appearance.

What I had done was to share with the invited guests –

Jews, Christian, Muslims and agnostics to the number of several hundred – the dilemma of inaugurating anything in a society as dividing as ours is nowadays. By contrast, I said, it would have been comparatively easy for our Roman predecessors on this very same hill-top to have carried out an inauguration that would have been almost universally acceptable in the ancient world. In those days, we need have done no more than hire an augur who would have interpreted for us the omens provided by the flight, the singing, the feeding and the entrails of the multitude of birds that live around Tantur, and on the basis of his interpretation the augur would have advised us what path we were to follow. But having invited not only Christians but also Jews, Muslims and agnostics to share in the inauguration, it would have been offensive to one lot or another to have begun, *In nomine patris et filii et spiritus sancti*, or *Bismillah-aRahman a Rahim*, or *Baruch ata adonai eleynu.* After quoting these three blessings to illustrate our dilemma, I had asked everyone present to join for a minute in the universal sacrament, the sacrament of silence. I had also secretly hoped that those in the gathering whose hearts were in pure silence might thereby receive all the three blessings I had very deliberately and liturgically pronounced – the Latin one, the Arabic one and the Hebrew one.

My eirenical efforts proved in vain. For no sooner were the guests streaming out of the lecture hall towards our reception room than this excitable bishop appeared before me and subjected me to a voluble attack for having sold the pass – 'a Christian institution should always use a Christian ritual, no matter who is present', he almost shouted.

I was rescued from his further excoriation, however, by the press around me of a crowd of well-wishers, one of whom, my friend, Bill Clark, an Israeli conservationist, presented me with a most beautiful box. Because of the crush of people I had no opportunity to examine it more closely, apart from admiring its fine finish. I was still carrying it in my hands a quarter of an hour later, as I was passing our coffee room on my way to the reception, when I noticed our Muslim friends all sitting there apart from all the rest. Straightaway I realised that they had declined to go on to the reception because wine, the forbidden drink, was laid out for guests in our dining hall and they did not wish to be associated with it. So I decided that I must join them, if only for a short time, in the coffee room.

As I went in to welcome them, I noticed that the beautiful box in my hand was a musical one; and so, after the customary greetings, I showed it to the sheikhs for their admiration, instinctively opening it as I did so, not knowing or considering what tune it might play. After only a few notes, however, I realised to my consternation that it was playing the popular Israeli song, *Shalom, shalom, shalom aleikhem*. The Hebrew words are, of course, all about peace but, unfortunately, due to the twists of history, the song in Arab ears sounds like a Jewish war-cry. As quick as a flash, and before my Muslim friends had time to pick out the tune, I snapped the box shut, smiled at my guests and asked them to excuse me as I now had to go to receive other guests.

Happily most of our other guests were by now well into the swing of the reception, everyone chatting away in best Jerusalem style, greeting one another like long-lost friends, even though they had met one another half a dozen times at similar receptions during the past month. But even here the occasional demon put in an appearance – in the form, this time, of one Jewish professor who buttonholed me and asked me what on earth we teach our scholars at Tantur. I tried to explain to him that we don't programmatically teach them anything, since they are senior theologians who learn on their own. But that was no excuse for my remissness. 'One of your scholars', he trumpeted indignantly, 'has been speaking to me of what he calls "the West Bank". Doesn't he realise that there is no such place? It is Judaea and Samaria, and has been since the beginning. You should teach them better.'

For myself, after all these years, such encounters are no longer very disturbing; they are par for the course. But just as everyone was beginning to drift away around 9 p.m., young Bob, one of the Peace Pilgrims, came up to me looking shocked and hurt. He told me in considerable distress that he had been talking to one of our guests and had referred to 'Palestine'. To his astonishment, not even his youth had saved him from a fierce onslaught for having used such a pernicious name. He looked quite dazed, still trying to figure out why peace seemed so much more difficult in Jerusalem than it ever had been on the 12,000 kilometres from Seattle to ... Palestine? the West Bank? Judaea and Samaria? Whatever the name, 'there be demons'.

৶ *26 December*

What impressive people there are among the Bethlehem Peace Pilgrims! From the very old to the very young.

I have been astonished at the maturity of the youngsters. As, for instance, when one of them, a slim, bespectacled girl, was asked at a moment's notice to summarise what the pilgrimage had come to mean for her. Modestly, yet in quite a composed manner, she formulated her answer in a few beautifully balanced sentences. In brief, she said that a pilgrim is 'one who asks':

> We asked for food; and it was given to us. We asked for shelter; and it was given to us. We asked for encouragement; and it was given to us in abundance. And now we are asking God for peace for all the earth... and we have faith that peace also will surely be given to us.

But in outward appearance, at least, the most striking member of the pilgrim group, with his mahogany-coloured face and luxuriant, silken white beard, is Father George Zabelka. He it was who in 1945 had served on Tinian Island in the Pacific, as chaplain to the Allied airmen who went on to drop bombs on Hiroshima and Nagasaki. His observations on the pilgrimage I found specially intriguing.

According to Father George, the country in which they encountered the most stubborn polarisation in the debate about nuclear weapons was England. By contrast, in Northern Ireland, in spite of the warlike atmosphere, they found the people to be wonderfully warm, and open to discussion of the issue. The country where the populace seemed to have been best educated by their government on nuclear matters was Greece.

But it was after they had landed at Haifa and had begun to thread their way through Israel and the West Bank that they walked into a seemingly impenetrable wall, resistant to the witness for peace they had been trying to offer over the course of their 12,000-kilometre pilgrimage. That resistance, constituted by mutual suspicion, hatred, lying and the burning resentment of the Arabs against their oppressors – all these obstacles, Father George said, meant that 'it is this last stage of our journey, through the Holy Land, that has revealed to us the point of it all. For me, these last days of our approach to Jerusalem have crystallised what it is all about. It is here, where we have met the greatest resistance to our message of peace, that peace on earth will be born again.'

Unbeknown to himself, Father George was affirming what I had said recently at the inauguration of our Academy of Peace: 'Already, thousands of years ago, the skein of human destiny began to coil itself around the city of Jerusalem, one end being twisted around the city and the other end threatening to entangle the whole earth'. The same sentiment was expressed to me some months ago by Herr Brandt, the German TV producer, who had been making documentaries about Jerusalem and Tantur. I met him near our reception desk one Sunday morning when the place was deserted and rather forlorn-looking, though not so forlorn as Herr Brandt looked. He seemed so depressed, in fact, that I thought to cheer him up by inviting him to come to our apartment for a cup of coffee.

He followed me down to our apartment in silence and remained silent for a while as he took his first mouthfuls of coffee. And then, raising his head as if it were leaden with weariness, he said despairingly, *'Hier ist alles vergiftet'* ('Here' – that is, in Jerusalem – 'everything is poisoned'). What had caused him such despair was an incident from the previous day, when he had been trying to get a picture of the status within the Christian community of the Orthodox Church in Jerusalem. In order to do so he had interviewed a Catholic priest, a German, who is well known to be close in spirit to the Orthodox, namely Father Düssing – as gentle a man as you will meet and amazingly well informed on all questions concerning the Orthodox Church. Typical of his benevolent and clean-hearted approach to life and to his fellow human beings, Father Düssing had come to revere and love Orthodoxy not through study of Byzantine art or through the mystical teachings of Mount Athos, but by way of long, harsh years as a prisoner of war in Russia, years of which he speaks with no trace of bitterness but rather with an abiding gratitude for their having brought him into contact with Russians.

It was no more than 20 minutes after conducting the interview with Father Düssing, sighed Herr Brandt, that a messenger arrived, despatched by a Roman Catholic prelate, to protest against Brandt for his taking the views of Father Düssing as an accurate indicator of the position of the Orthodox Church in Jerusalem. Everyone in Jerusalem knows, the message went on, that Father Düssing sees every deed of the Orthodox through rose-tinted spectacles. 'Presumably', Herr Brandt said, 'the Roman Catholic authorities would have been happier if I had managed to present a person prepared to divulge some scandal about the Orthodox. *Hier ist alles vergiftet.*'

'A golden bowl filled with scorpions' is the Arab description to correspond to Herr Brandt's experience, and I am sure that young Dean McFalls would not quarrel with that description after his own treatment since arriving in this 'City of Peace'. Throughout much of the Peace Pilgrimage, Dean has been acting as their spokesperson and seems to have done the job very well – until he found himself in this 'golden bowl', where he is completely out of his depth! When questioned by the local press as to the kind of reception the pilgrims had received between Haifa and Jerusalem from Jews and Arabs, he answered very honestly and, as he thought, in a balanced and peaceable fashion. From the way in which he was immediately castigated by both Jews and Arabs and their respective supporters, he is beginning to learn that what the rest of the world means by balance and peace bears no relationship to what the words mean in Jerusalem. When I spoke with him today, his eyes were the eyes of a man who had just been shell-shocked.

Many of these issues came up this evening when I invited the senior members of the pilgrimage to come to our apartment for a drink. But what intrigued me most was the answer they gave to a question I put to them. I said, 'You have all walked 12,000 kilometres, and you have been received by every kind of person, from the lowest to the highest, including many religious leaders. Could you say which, if any, of those people has most impressed you?'

They all sat silently for a while before beginning to exchange comments. Then all of a sudden they came to an agreement. 'Yes, we were most impressed by the mayor of Marzobotto. He is a Communist, and Marzobotto is a Communist town south of Bologna.' I have to confess that their answer tickled me: Christian pilgrim reports that it was not a Christian dignatory but a Communist mayor who had most impressed them!

๏ *27 December*

Letter to the Tablet

How mysterious is the process by which certain truths dawn upon one! In the past, I never took seriously some statements made by my friend Hassan Askari, who teaches at Selly Oak, Birmingham, even though I have the deepest regard for him and his perceptions. It was more than ten years ago that he wrote:

> The Palestinian question is neither a Russian question nor an American question. It is neither a socialist nor a capitalist issue ... The Palestinian question is a question concerning the People of the Book ... The whole world will either be saved or will perish on account of it ... The life and death of the human spirit depends upon the way in which the Palestinian question is resolved.

Since I am extremely sceptical of all such eschatological declarations, especially when they are so firmly linked with specific issues, I had thought Professor Askari's pronouncement to be a great exaggeration. But, standing before several hundred Jews, Muslims and Christians and addressing them, at the opening of our Peace Academy, as I looked down upon the audience I suddenly became convinced that Hassan is right: the life and death of the human spirit depends upon the way in which the Palestinian question is resolved.

Having been formed in the critical Oxford tradition, however, my mind immediately started to explain my conviction away, on the ground that I was simply on a personal 'high' because so many of my aspirations seemed at that moment to be converging and confirming one another.

Among the audience, for instance, were the Bethlehem Peace Pilgrims who had set off on foot on Good Friday, 1982, from the Trident nuclear submarine base at Bangor (near Seattle), the home of the deadliest weapon system on earth. Well before they had set out, in 1981, I had seen a notice of their intended pilgrimage in a newspaper and had written to their initiator, Father Jack Morris SJ, to offer the pilgrims hospitality at Tantur on the last stage of their journey to Bethlehem. And here they were now, some 18 months and 7,000 miles later, about 20 of them, weather-beaten and looking deeply drained of energy; yet steadfast, and confirmed in their resolve to make peace.

Also, we had managed, against all the odds, to have available for sale in our auditorium a little booklet entitled *The Possession and Use of Nuclear Weapons in the Light of Torah, Gospel and Sharia*. As I explain in my preface to the booklet, the task of finding a rabbi on the one hand and a sheikh on the other prepared to deliver the lectures on which the booklet is based was no easy one – nobody in these parts is eager to take up the nuclear issue because of a general awareness, all the more agonising through being suppressed, that one might thereby touch off the final explosion.

Yet eventually Rabbi Pinhas Peli, of Ben-Gurion University in Beersheba, and Sheikh Muhammad al Husseini, judge of the Islamic Court in Jerusalem, generously took the risk. And there the two of them were, sitting in front of me, my Jewish friend and my Muslim friend, come to help inaugurate our Academy of Peace.

So I was seeing realised before my own eyes another of my aspirations – an aspiration that I always associate with my dead friend, the Russian thinker Nikolai Fyodorov. Fyodorov used to say that the restoration of kinship among humankind requires that those who do not generally speak to one another should begin to speak with one another. And this was what happened during the reception that went on for several hours after the inaugural lecture: Jews and Arabs, both Muslim and Christian, who would otherwise never have anything to do with one another, were together in the same company. I do not say that they all came to love, or even to like, one another, but they did at least begin to recognise one another as human beings and not demons.

And all this was happening by virtue of the Peace Academy which we were inaugurating at Tantur. I had recognised the desirability of it already two years before. I had felt in those days that none of us had quite woken up to the potentiality of our Institute, unique in the Middle East, as a location for peacemaking. For, according to international law, we were situated in occupied territory; whereas, according to Israeli law, we belonged in the municipality of Jerusalem. The scholars who have come to us belong to different Christian traditions, while the staff has always included Christians, Muslims and Jews. And here now was our international president, Landrum Bolling, explaining to

our guests just what had prompted the founding of the Academy
of Peace as part of our work.

For him, also, the day represented a climax, since
throughout his life as scholar, journalist and fund-raiser, his two
main concerns have been peacemaking and the convergence of
world faiths. He said:

> The nuclear issue is essentially a moral issue. No nation has
> the right to use nuclear arms, no matter how just its cause, and
> set off the kind of global conflagration that would threaten the
> continuation of life on this planet. That is a declaration on
> which the adherents of all religious faiths can unite ... [More-
> over,] we must begin the quest for peace with the cultivation
> of the individual's search for inner calm, strength, serenity –
> the peace within.

The Inter-Faith Academy of Peace will provide a location where
scholars of all faiths are to be invited to learn together how to
live in peace and to make peace. Some scholars will come for two
or three months, and others for nine months. As a team, they will
be responsible for issuing a quarterly bulletin so as to make the
results of their studies and experiences available in the market-
place. From the beginning it is being made clear to scholars that
they are not being invited into an ivory tower. Tantur is in the
eye of most of the whirlwinds that swirl around the Middle East –
'a high-risk venture', as Bolling put it.

ᏒᎤ *28 December*

As I was sitting at my desk in the rector's office early
this afternoon, I experienced a profound sense of peace. It was
one of those ecstatically beautiful days such as Palestine in winter
sometimes bestows upon us. The brilliant light of the afternoon
sun was flooding over the white stones of the enclosure in which
my office is situated. A fresh wind was rippling the surface of the
pool which stretches the length of the courtyard and draws one's
gaze beyond the high walls of the Institute eastwards towards the
tiny Arab village of Umm Tuba, the minaret of its mosque just
visible beyond a bend of the hill. Often, sitting at my desk, I hear
the call of the muezzin echoing from that minaret across the stony
hills around Ramat Rachel and Bethlehem, and ruminate in awe

upon the mystery of human existence, thinking how strange it is that within two miles of our modern, American-style way of life there should stand village communities, such as Umm Tuba, the pattern of whose culture is worlds apart from ours and goes back to far more ancient roots.

The enclosed courtyard and the ancient landscape always give me the sense of being protected and at peace. That was particularly true this afternoon, since there was no one in the library. All the scholars were out for the day, our Arab domestic staff had all gone home, and quiet prevailed throughout the building. I was looking forward to several hours without interruption, during which I could work steadily through the backlog of Institute business that had accumulated on my desk.

Just then the phone rang. It was Geries, our receptionist, to say that someone had arrived at the reception desk, unannounced and without an appointment, and wishing to speak with me. At which moment I could have sworn that the backlog on my desk grinned up at me as if to say, 'You're not going to get rid of us today!' Heavy of heart, I muttered, 'Who is he?' 'He says he is a theologian from Strasburg', came the reply from Geries, who plies a quiet line of mockery at human absurdity. 'A theologian from Strasburg'; the phrase sounded like the title of a play on the life of a present-day Martin Bucer who had wandered into the Holy Land, possibly to torture my brain on his forerunner's subject of the Eucharist.

'Bring him across', I said to Geries, at the same time making a mental resolution to welcome this wandering theologian in the manner that St Benedict orders us to receive guests: 'All guests to the monastery should be welcomed as Christ, because he will say, "I was a stranger and you took me in" '.

As so often happens when one fears the worst, the reality, in this case a Strasburg theologian, proved on the contrary to be quite pleasant. Long-winded he certainly was, but pleasant; and so it was not too difficult to give him my full attention for an hour and a half, in spite of the pile of papers staring up at me from my desk. And he himself seemed very contented with his visit, after he had taken a cup of tea, when I accompanied him across our garden to bid him farewell.

But the farewell did not last long – no more, in fact, than two or three minutes. Because I was just on the point of stepping into my office once more when the same man burst through the doors of our administration wing almost convulsed with excitement, and in broken, agitated English gasped something about a young man being hurt. I quickly realised there was no way that the cause of his excitement was going to become clear to me through his incoherent words, and so I told him to show me what was wrong.

It had to be something very urgent because our unathletic-looking theologian from Strasburg broke out into a clod-hopping run as he led me along rocky paths towards a rather remote quarter of our grounds. There no words were needed to tell me what was amiss: our Arab worker, Fawzi, had somehow managed to pinion himself between the branch of an olive tree and the seat of the tractor which he had been driving. It was certainly a dramatic sight – Fawzi suspended in silhouette against the pale evening sky and the distant hills of Moab – like some sacrificial victim, with his left arm trapped firmly by a branch of the olive tree and the seat of the tractor neatly slotted against his arched backbone, as if holding him in place for the *coup de grâce*. To make matters worse, two of our Arab employees now rushed up and, in their anguish at Fawzi's cries, began frantically to try to move the tractor, not realising that if they lost control of it on the slope then the tractor would slip and the seat would thrust violently upwards and might break Fawzi's spine.

In that moment I bitterly regretted my inadequate Arabic which left me unable to explain the danger. But fortunately Geries now arrived and translated my warning. Better still, I was able to direct him to send for the paramedics to come immediately from the Husseini Hospital in Beit Jala.

In the mean time Fawzi was getting more and more desperate, having been suspended in this manner for at least half an hour; fearing moreover that he was never again to see his wife and children. And though I tried to reassure him, I was myself worried on account of his left arm, which was now deathly cold due to the lack of circulation. I was frightened that gangrene might soon set in.

We all began to breathe easier again, therefore, when we heard the roar of the paramedics' ambulance along the bottom road some 80 yards below us, followed by the tremendous clanging of a fire brigade bell. At which point something extraordinary happened.

Standing at a bus stop on the bottom road, as the ambulance and the fire brigade roared towards the distant entrance to the Institute, was a little group of Arab construction workers. They are to be seen at the same stop every evening waiting to catch the Hebron bus, weary from the long day which sucks them into Israel in the early hours and then disgorges them back on to the West Bank in the evening. Today there were about eight of them standing together at the stop, their eyes turned towards Jerusalem, awaiting their bus. As soon as they heard the alarm bell of the fire brigade and saw the ambulance speeding past, they looked round and caught a glimpse of us among the olive trees. Within seconds they had all scrambled over our seven-foot outer wall, and despite their heavy boots they were positively flying up the slope to where Fawzi was trapped, their eyes blazing with determination to aid whoever was in distress.

Never have I seen a group of men respond so spontaneously and instantly to a cry for help. Even now I do not understand how they managed to get over the wall so quickly – as though, in spite of the weariness in their limbs from the day's labour, some invisible spring-heels enabled them to leap over the wall at one bound. And, of course, they proved invaluable at helping the paramedics to bend the olive branch slowly, to hold the tractor from slipping, and then, very gently, to draw Fawzi out of his trap, almost as though they were delivering a new-born baby.

Back now from the Husseini Hospital, relieved that Fawzi's back is not broken nor his arm in danger of gangrene, I wonder again at the fine and incredibly complex web of human relations. Suppose that our theologian from Strasburg had not called this afternoon, I might have spent a peaceful few hours clearing my desk; but then he would not have heard Fawzi's cries, and with darkness and the chill of night setting in, perhaps Fawzi would now be dead, his wife a widow and his children orphans.

◈ *31 December*

'So and so has flipped.' That is a sentence which Dorothy and I often find ourselves saying to one another rather wearily and with slight exasperation. We do so when one or other of us discovers that a member of our community has 'flipped' from a condition of seeing everything through Jewish eyes to seeing everything through Arab eyes, or vice versa (which happens less frequently).

The usual pattern is that a scholar comes to Tantur with a highly idealised picture of Israel and of Jewish achievement in the land, and with an equally distorted image of Arabs as terrorists. Then they personally experience some harassment by Israelis, or else they see the day-to-day oppression endured by Arabs, and they flip – now Arabs can do no wrong, and Israelis can do nothing right!

Americans, with their simplistic view of the world and their anti-Arab media, are particularly prone to flip. But it can happen to almost anyone – even, in a strange way, to a Jew! I am thinking of the evening when Sarah Rosenblum picked us up in her car to drive us to Bethlehem, where all three of us were to have dinner with some American friends. A Jewish immigrant from South Africa, Sarah had pooh-poohed the suggestion that Bethlehem in the dark was no place for a Jewish person to be visiting. During the course of that evening she made one or two derogatory remarks about 'the Arab mentality', especially their habit of forever bewailing their 'oppression'. Not wanting an argument, the rest of us kept quiet. But Sarah received a marvellously apt riposte that same night as we were returning home around 11 p.m.

By this late hour, the Israeli army had established a roadblock on the Jerusalem road, and as we approached it Dorothy and I naturally anticipated that Sarah would slow down and stop. Instead she kept going at the same speed, until two soldiers brandished their machine guns at us. They made her stop and ordered her to wind down the car window. 'What the hell do you think you are doing?' they shouted at her, and made her reverse back to the line of the roadblock. She was so shocked that she said very little; I could only conclude she had thought that Jews do not have to take notice of roadblocks! Moreover, she had almost certainly not taken it in that the two soldiers were not in fact Jews but were Druse. Some Druse may well be ready to serve in the Israeli army, but that does not mean they love Jews, whom they even enjoy taking down a peg.

Once the short altercation was over, Sarah drove on silently for about half a mile and then burst out indignantly, 'This place is getting like South Africa!' God forgive me, but I nearly cracked out laughing to see how she had so quickly changed her tune: the very slightest touch of harassment on one's own skin, and one flips.

A more serious case, however, faced me this afternoon when I returned to find awaiting me two American journalists, a writer and a photographer from the *Middletown Gazette*. They were beside themselves with anger.

Their story was that they had come with a group of fellow citizens from Middletown, a Jewish group who had collected $75,000 to establish a project in Galilee for which they expect to be able to raise altogether $3 million within the next two years. The Jewish group had offered to pay all the journalists' expenses for the ten-day tour, but the two of them had wisely declined on the ground that they wished to retain their professional independence, a decision for which they were now heartily grateful.

For the first week of their stay in Israel they had been kept very busy going from one Jewish project to another, with all of which they had been most impressed, as they also had been with the Jewish officials, rabbis and media workers to whom they had been introduced. But as the days went by, they became increasingly conscious of a niggle at the back of their minds: why was it that the group leader always headed them off when they tried to broach the subject of the Arabs? And especially when they suggested exploring the West Bank? They began to feel that they were being brainwashed when this latter suggestion was always greeted with the words, 'There's no point – so little there to see'. The photographer, Fred, was particularly sensitive on account of an incident on the plane coming over. Sitting next to an Israeli woman, he had asked, in the course of their conversation, what was to happen to the Arabs. She replied, 'We should annihilate them'.

So Fred and his colleague, Doug, had cut loose from the party and headed for Jerusalem. This morning they had spent several hours at the memorial to the Holocaust victims at Yad Vashem, and then driven from there straight to the refugee camp at Deheishe, where some 8000 Arabs live in desperate conditions. As I looked at their faces, it was clear that both of them were in a state of shock as a result of both these experiences.

Then they started telling me how the experience of Yad Vashem and of Deheishe seemed to them all of a piece; and they had been reinforced in this impression by the interview they had just concluded with the Arab mayor of Bethlehem, Elias Freij.

He, on learning that they had come straight from Yad Vashem, had commented that, 'The Jews, in their turn, are trying to put a holocaust on us', and had gone on to speak of the 'genocide' of the Palestinian people.

Fred and Doug nearly jumped out of their chairs when they saw my reaction to these statements. 'What on earth does Freij mean?' I exclaimed. 'None of his family have been taken to death camps and executed! In fact, as far as I know, none of them has even been arrested by the Israelis. There is no Treblinka on the West Bank. Arabs are allowed to leave the country if they wish. You are free to go into Deheishe and take photographs and publish them in the world press. There is much oppression on the West Bank, and I see it every day of my life, but the degree of oppression here is light-years distant from what happened to the Jews in Europe. It is simply immoral, and no service to anyone, to use terms like "holocaust" and "genocide" in that irresponsible fashion.'

Poor dears! They looked as though my reaction had just given a final turn to the violent tumble-dryer in which they had been tossed about these last ten days, buffeted by Jews, Arabs, Muslims, Christians – and now by this exasperated Englishman. And perhaps there was more yet to come. Fred, the photographer, explained rather plaintively that he had just telephoned his official Israeli contact in Tel Aviv to discover whether, on leaving Israel, he would have to clear his photographs with a censor. 'Don't worry', his contact said calmly. 'The authorities already know that you have been in Deheishe.'

The speed of the Israeli intelligence network had left Fred and Doug open-mouthed and eager to get back to Middletown.

ᥦ 1984

ᥦ *2 February*

Arnold phoned this morning to say that he would like to talk with me. He asked if I would go into Jerusalem to meet him in some quiet spot where we could talk undisturbed; so I suggested the garden of Christ Church, near the Jaffa Gate, and that is where we met about 11 a.m.

He is worn out – and I am not surprised – through his endless showing of *The Work*, a slide show which he asked permission to present to our scholars in October. It is really the story of his life: how, as a boy of 12 he was taken to Auschwitz: how at the selection he was sent one way – eventually to survive – and his father was sent the other way – into the gas chamber.

Arnold survived through the goodness of older prisoners and his own power of fantasy – he convinced himself that he was really a bird and could have flown out of Auschwitz whenever he chose. After being rescued by the Americans and taken to the US, he managed to suppress completely the experience of Auschwitz from his consciousness. He married and had children. Some ten years ago he thought that if he were to have his concentration camp tattoo-number erased from his arm, that would prove that he had never been in Auschwitz.

At which point, the suppressed Auschwitz experience exploded inside him and fragmented his life. He went to pieces: his marriage broke up and his children were estranged from him. He was lost; and realised that he would have to return to Auschwitz to examine the camp registers showing that he indeed had been there. He would then have to pick up the thread and follow it into the present.

When he did that, something amazing happened. As if it were a revelation from God, he was brought to see that the Holocaust of which the Jews were the victims is also a foreshadowing of a nuclear holocaust which is to be the fate of the whole human family, unless human beings are awakened to the peril. Arnold has a call from God to ensure that the human family does not go blindly into death as so many Jews did. Hence his slide show, *The Work*, is the story of his own life, and a warning to the whole human family.

When I agreed to his showing *The Work* one evening last October, I had no idea of the powerful effect it was going to have on the Tantur community. Normally they are a loquacious group, ready to discuss anything whatsoever at a moment's notice. But after Arnold had finished his presentation that evening in October, all of them sat quite still, and silent. After a time, I quietly suggested that we should disperse in silence; and we did so, much as worshippers reverently move away from the altar after receiving communion.

These events were going through my mind as Arnold told me of his weariness, and asked whether he might come and live with us until he feels better. I also remembered hearing of objections being raised some years ago against a rabbi being lodged for a week at Tantur on the grounds that it is a Christian institution. In the case of Arnold, I was not prepared to take any notice of such objections. He is coming here tomorrow.

✑ *27 February*

I know that one should never look for rewards but, at the same time, there would be something wrong with you if you did not feel deeply thankful when they come along. Certainly this evening brought perhaps the most rewarding moment of my whole time at Tantur, when our Jewish friend, Arnold, came into our apartment to take his leave. Having been with us for four weeks by now, he says that he feels at peace with himself and ready to carry on with his work.

As we sat together drinking tea, I realised that Arnold was struggling to get something out which was very important to him, something for which he could not find adequate words. Since he could not manage it, he began instead to ask me how much he should pay for his stay with us. The dear man – I knew how little money he has. And his hesitancy moved me to the verge of tears, as I am often moved when I see poor people made aware of their lack of money. That is probably because their lack of money reveals their powerlessness and consequent vulnerability. And for the same reason, so many of those sermons I hear on 'the cross', and on Christianity as 'the way of powerlessness', sound hollow to me because I know that the preacher has money, as well as education and social esteem, and he himself, therefore, is far from powerless.

For one brief moment, there was a flicker in Arnold's eyes and a movement of his hands in which I thought I perceived the shadow of his helplessness, years gone by, in the concentration camp. But he relaxed when I laughed and said I could hardly ask a guest to pay us for hospitality! But then I realised that to leave the matter there might only render Arnold's feeling of impotence more acute; and so I said, truthfully enough, that many of our guests made small contributions to our staff fund, and he might like to do the same.

But all of this, in any case, was just a form of clearing the way for what he had really come to tell me.

'During the course of my life, Don', Arnold said very deliberately, 'many, many Christians have spoken to me about how much they loved me, and what they intended to do for me. But in every case it eventually became clear that ultimately, somewhere at the back of their minds, they were wanting me to convert – and my being aware of that eliminated everything they had previously said to me or done for me. It was really a way of saying to me, "We don't accept you until and unless you convert. As a Jew, you don't really exist for us until you convert."

'But here, at Tantur, for the first time, I feel that I have been completely accepted as I am, by everyone in the community. In the five weeks I have been with you, in the dining hall, the seminar room, on field trips, over coffee, at no time have I ever felt any breath of a suggestion that I should convert. And I want just to thank you for that.'

Soon afterwards Arnold stood up to say 'Good night', and leave our apartment. For my own part I sat without moving for a long time, reflecting on what he had said, my whole being suffused with joy, and with gratitude to the entire community here for having maintained a clean heart towards Arnold during his stay with us.

At the same time, I remained puzzled by what seems to be an inner contradiction in my own attitude towards our Jewish friends. I do not work or pray for their conversion. Yet whenever one of my Jewish friends becomes a Christian, I have to acknowledge that joy springs up in my heart, just as it does when I hear of anyone of whatever tradition finding Christ. I know that some Christians of my acquaintance who specialise in Jewish–Christian dialogue would frown upon my joy because they are so fiercely opposed to Jews converting in any circumstances.

But do even those Christians seriously suggest that it would in some way have been better, for instance, if Edith Stein, the brilliant Jewish agnostic philosopher who became a Carmelite nun and died in Auschwitz, had never been converted? Anyone who studies her life must surely recognise that it was through her conversion that she became one of the unquestionably holy people of the twentieth century. Such was the impression she made upon all who met her, as for example the Dutchman who encountered her in the transit camp on the way to Auschwitz:

> The one nun who caught my attention immediately and whom I have never forgotten in spite of the many horrible episodes which I have seen, was the woman with a smile that was not a mask but a warm radiance . . . I knew this was truly a great woman. In the hell of Westerbork she lived only a few days, walked among the prisoners, talking and praying like a saint. Yes, that's what she was . . . She spoke in such a humble and clear way that anybody who listened to her was seized. A talk with her was like a voyage into another world.

Following a strict interpretation of Jewish law one would have to believe, nevertheless, that Edith Stein, as an apostate from Judaism, has 'lost her part in the world to come'. There has to be something wrong about a law which so condemns a saint.

☙ *29 February*

One of the saddest and most depressing features of living in the Middle East is the fact that you can so often predict how people are going to react to some event. What makes this experience so sad and depressing is that it seems almost to prove beyond a doubt that no one is prepared for any new initiative or imaginative liberation from inculcated patterns of behaviour.

Some weeks ago, for instance, Dorothy and I were discussing the film *Gandhi*, which we had seen in England, and wondering how it would be received when it was shown in Israel. 'I'll guess', I said to Dorothy. 'The Israelis will really dislike it because they will want not to receive the message of the film. But, at the same time, because of their liberal, democratic heritage they will not want to admit how much they dislike it. So they will criticise it fiercely for any small errors or technical failings that they can point to in order to distract attention from the message.'

Reading the review of *Gandhi* in the *Jerusalem Post*, you might have imagined that I had managed to substitute myself for the paper's film critic and had written the review specifically in order to prove the accuracy of my prediction. The reviewer writes exactly what I foresaw.

৶ *25 March*

They say that the family is *scola caritatis*, a school of charity, and I have often mused that the cricket ground is, in its own way, a school, not perhaps of charity but of a certain discipline preparing you for *caritas*. This evening, at least, I feel that my long years on the cricket field may have helped to stem internal warfare in this community.

Once again it was the Eucharist around which the animosity centred. Earlier in the week our announced celebrant, Father Ailred, as gentle, kindly and modest a man as you could wish to meet, had issued the customary declaration which is mandatory upon all celebrants to outline the eucharistic faith and practice which is traditional in his or her own Church. And though Ailred's statement was very much the conventional Roman Catholic one that has now been accepted for a couple of years without any sharp reaction, I was not surprised that I soon heard murmurings against him. My antennae had early this session picked up stirrings in Tantur of what Goethe named *der Geist der stets verneint*, the spirit of negation, for which reason I was not taken aback by the murmurings.

All the same, it was not very pleasant to go into chapel this morning and find almost no non-Catholics present. Clearly a group of scholars had organised a boycott of the Mass.

Poor Father Ailred! You could see from the expression on his face as he processed towards the altar that his heart went into his boots when he saw the chapel half-empty. He had worked so faithfully at his declaration in an effort to avoid offending anyone. And when it came to the homily, I truly regretted that the others were not present, because Ailred spoke such humble, careful words as should, I am sure, have melted the hearts of the boycotters if they had been present. Then agony was piled upon agony when the moment for communion arrived and one or two of the non-Catholics who were present walked out.

Our Sunday Eucharist is invariably followed by a joyful time of real celebration, the common meal to which everyone comes, including wives, husbands and children as well as visitors. But for many of the Catholics, the prospect of joining in that meal today, a barbecue in the garden, now seemed unbearable. A number of them went off to their rooms without speaking – torn, as I later learnt, between their wounded feelings and their Christian desire to live at peace with their fellows. They sat silently in their rooms, wondering whether to boycott the meal.

Though I myself scarcely had any other choice but to join the barbecue straightaway, I must also acknowledge that doing so took no great effort on my part. Which does not mean that I was not distressed when I crossed into the garden and faced a crowd of people already well into their meat and their wine, not even having had the decency to wait for Mass to end. There was something gross about the scene; so it was at least fitting that no one, it seems, had asked a blessing on the meal.

Still, I soon found myself chatting to all and sundry as though nothing untoward had occurred, as though they had all been present at our Sunday Eucharist as usual. And soon the Catholics who had gone to their rooms came and put a brave face on the matter.

What intrigues me now as I examine my motives for behaving as I did, is that the image which served most powerfully as a springboard for my behaviour was not, I believe, a specifically Christian one. It may not even have been a very commendable one. What was in my mind as I strolled over this morning to the barbecue crowd, some of whom avoided my gaze, was the image of an opening batsman in a cricket team.

The opening batsman in a cricket team usually has to face the fiercest fast bowling, and is often struck painful blows on his thighs, his arms, his head and other tender places. The natural reaction, on being struck, is obviously to wince and start rubbing the bruised spot. But already 50 years ago, in Yorkshire, where I started as an opening batsman, it was drummed into me that you do not wince when struck; and, above all, you do not give the fast bowler the satisfaction of seeing you rub the bruised spot. So I did not say a single word to any of the boycotters about their behaviour. At a certain level, I even enjoyed not giving them the satisfaction of seeing that I had so much as noticed their absence.

Which leaves me with a puzzle. I am pretty sure that the misery of those Catholics who went to their rooms arose out of a more Christian source than my feigned insouciance. On the other hand, I am equally sure that if I had behaved as they did we should have soon become locked in internal warfare.

Is cricket, therefore, a necessary *praeparatio evangelica* for Christianity?

ᴇᴆ *16 April*

So now I know what St Francis was up to with my friend from Haifa! During the course of her visit to us, I was greatly taken by her husband – a quiet, gentle man. He had about him an air which is quite unmistakable, the same air that I have virtually always sensed about men who survived the Japanese prison camps of the second world war. Obviously you can't put your finger on it, otherwise you would not have to describe it as 'an air'; but it is, indeed, unmistakable. The air about such men has something to do with their having gone further into suffering and the depths both of human cruelty and of fidelity than one ever imagined possible, and yet having emerged still compassionate, gentle human beings. Such people are indelibly marked, as by a sacrament.

And he was one of those people. We learnt that he had spent years in Auschwitz and, on being liberated, was overwhelmed by the need to tell the story of Auschwitz and its victims. So, after making his way to Tel Aviv, he had straightaway established himself in an abandoned concrete bunker and, like some hermit vowed to a secret cult, he had devoted himself night and day to describing the world of Auschwitz. When the books that he wrote appeared in print, the Jewish reading public quickly recognised that here was someone truly inspired to give voice to their sufferings. But the identity of that someone was something they could never find out, because he so determinedly and skilfully projected his anonymity.

No one could penetrate his secret – not until my 'nutty' friend from Haifa came along and tracked him down in his bunker. Not only that: after 18 months of relentlessly wooing him, she married him.

But it was in her moment of seeming triumph that her troubles began. Over the course of the next ten years, the man from Auschwitz slowly recovered in mind and body, step by step, from the trauma of the concentration camp; but his young wife, on the other hand, descended by a parallel series of steps into a condition of terror comparable to the terror he had known in Auschwitz. That double terror is heartbreakingly described by her in a book which she later wrote, entitled *The Prisoner*. There we learn of the pathetic means by which she attempted to keep her terror at bay: that is, by reaching for food as her saviour. What happened to her in consequence was grotesque.

As a result of eating so much and so frequently, she grew incredibly fat – so fat indeed that taxi drivers used to refuse to allow her to ride in their taxis. But each such public humiliation could not shame her into controlling her voracious appetite. She would, for instance, bake a huge chocolate cake in the morning for the birthday of one of her children, and then eat the whole of it herself by lunch-time. This left her time to bake another cake before her two children arrived home from school in the afternoon; hence no one would know the extent of her eating.

The story could well, of course, have had a tragic ending. But, as we learn from her own account of her struggle in *The Prisoner*, that was happily not the case. For by virtue of separating herself from her family and making a year-long pilgrimage, she finally recovered. The fever left her, and she emerged as the smiling figure who burst through our dining-room doors – half an hour late for lunch, it is true, but immediately likeable in spite of everything.

Yet that was by no means the end of the matter, for there remains a further story within that story, which in its turn stood within an earlier story.

For some obscure reason, after reading *The Prisoner*, I felt that it might be meant for Arnold, my Jewish friend who had himself been in Auschwitz as a boy. So without making a big deal of the matter, I handed him a copy of the book, commenting that it might interest him.

My comment, to put it at its very mildest, was an understatement, as I was to learn some weeks later when Arnold telephoned me. He could scarcely contain himself with astonishment at what had happened as a result of my lending him *The Prisoner.*

After he had begun to read the book, so he told me, he started to do something he had never done before. He began to read passages of the book out loud for the benefit of Teresa, the woman he had lived with for a year or two, a most attractive and radiant person who yet had lately been suffering from one unspecifiable ailment after another. Eventually both Teresa and Arnold became so absorbed in the book that they read the whole of it out loud to one another, each taking turns to do so. Slowly they came to realise that the story in the book was their story also: just as Arnold had been recovering from 'Auschwitz fever', so Teresa had by the same token been picking up the infection ever more desperately. But, thanks be to God, their very reading of *The Prisoner* out loud to one another had proved to be a healing process. And though still feeling fragile, as one does after a fever has left one, Teresa was once more the radiant person we had first met. Interestingly enough, the process had also left them both very clear in their minds that they should soon separate for at least a year – no longer under a cloud threatening bitterness but with light hearts and ever deeper love for one another.

The more I reflect upon these intertwined stories, the surer I become that there is such an infection as 'Auschwitz fever' from which certain victims of the concentration camps manage to recover, but which other people close to them may at the same time pick up. How these latter people themselves recover is not easy to understand, but I am convinced that we do need to understand it, because at the collective level the whole Jewish people has been a victim of the concentration camps and has caught 'Auschwitz fever'. Anyone who chooses to come close to the Jewish people, therefore, exposes himself to the risk of becoming infected, which is why so many high-minded people choose to distance themselves from Israel, pretending that the event of Auschwitz was nothing to do with them. I suspect, however, that their behaviour has less to do with high-mindedness than with a selfish fear of infection.

170

১ *17 April*

Our time at Tantur is the first period of my life that I have spent continuously among professional religious, and it has awakened in me a deeper sympathy for them in certain respects. At the moment I am being made particularly aware of the spiritual peril that they run into through their having to use tremendous, mystery-laden words so constantly that they are almost bound to trivialise and banalise the awesome realities to which the words are pointing. If they do not succumb to that temptation, then they must become saints – and in order not to succumb they have to become saints.

I say this on account of the number of occasions during these past few weeks when I have heard so many people mouthing 'forgiving' and 'forgiveness' as though it were the easiest thing in the world, talking so glibly as to make my hair stand on end in disbelief.

Dorothy and I were the only lay-folk, for instance, at a house Mass celebrated – and very beautifully celebrated – by Father Francis. All the scriptural passages appointed to be read at the Mass turned upon forgiveness, about which Father Francis spoke a few modest but penetrating words, before inviting the rest of us to contribute our thoughts on the matter. And almost immediately I grew exasperated at the ease with which all the other religious present slipped instantly into pious ecclesiastical clichés, as though through years of practice it had become second nature to them to side-step every difficulty in forgiving. They seemed to assume that we all know what it means to forgive, whereas in reality we only begin to get a glimpse of what it means after we have been trying our very sincerest to forgive someone. And every time, it seems to me, we fall short of complete forgiveness. Perhaps that is why Jesus tells us that we have to forgive those who offend us seventy times seven. This last phrase is usually explained by the learned as a way of saying 'for ever'; and in one sense they are right – but it is better to stick to Jesus' idiom because 'seventy times seven' makes us begin mentally counting and envisioning the number of occasions, one after another, in long succession, when we shall have to pick ourselves up again after yet another failure to forgive completely. The phrase should also signify to us how much practice we all need at trying to forgive.

Of course, that phrase, like every powerful phrase, is particularly susceptible to misunderstanding, and I suspect that some of my own abortive struggles to forgive have been flawed by my having imbibed such a misconception of forgiveness as a youngster. In accordance with my misconception, forgiving for me was a discrete act – so separate that one could distinguish every such act from every other and actually count the number of them, even adding them up, for instance, to seventy times seven.

The other flaw in my notion of forgiving was my belief that the very generosity of the act would of itself and instantly achieve reconciliation between the alienated parties – and that would be an end of the matter. The matter in dispute had now been dissolved away!

In real life, however, it is not like that, as I have been discovering all over again during the past months. Time after time, I have forgiven a person both by word and in my heart, only to find that same person within an hour committing that very same offence once more. Similarly, there have been occasions when I have been forgiven, yet have found myself soon afterwards on the point of committing the same offence once again. The matter of the dispute has still been lodged somewhere inside me and is going to take a long time – perhaps seventy times a lifetime – before it is dissolved.

The conclusion I am bound to come to, therefore, is that when we speak of forgiveness we should have in mind not so much a series of discrete acts (though it is that) as a continuous lifelong condition. There is no moment when one is not in need of forgiveness, nor any moment when one does not need to be forgiving.

Everything I have written down so far is all well and good, and I believe that the practice of reflection in this fashion actually does help one to behave better in future. But, of course, these abstract formulations cannot conceal from me the awareness that they are all circling around the quite concrete matter of my relationship with Walter.

I feel it would be a comfort, and would make life easier, if I could tell myself that he and I had obviously been incompatible from the beginning. Because then I could do what the great Buddhist scholar, Edward Conze, did when he and my friend, Father

Colman, had a fierce dispute at their first encounter. Conze asked Father Colman what his astrological sign was. And when Conze realised that both of them were Scorpios, he said, 'That explains why we shall never get along together'. Except, of course, that once they had realised their 'incompatibility' they got on quite well! But that is not true of Walter and myself. We cannot say that our individual chemistries are incompatible. Admittedly, questions were raised in my mind on account of certain traits in his original application to come here as a scholar. Still, that is the case with virtually every application form one ever reads.

No. Something went wrong somewhere along the line that has led to the present unease between us. 'Unease', however, is too anodyne a word to describe how I feel on Sundays in chapel, when the moment comes for everyone to exchange a sign of peace with every other member of our Christian community gathered around the altar. When Walter and I then greet one another, I am sure that both he and I are genuinely sincere in wishing peace to one another. Yet even in that moment I remain aware at one level that, in no time whatsoever after the Eucharist is finished, he will do something or say something behind my back calculated to undermine me and to make life very difficult for me. His habit of doing so seems to be almost a conditioned reflex, as automatic as the drug addict's reaching for his fix.

However, it is a total waste of energy – as well as being spiritually destructive – for me to draw up inside my head a bill of accusation against Walter, listing all the occasions when he has given me grounds for charging him with betraying me. Is this not a case for applying the ancient Catholic maxim of *lectio benevolentior* ('the more benevolent reading, or interpretation'), according to which, when the behaviour of someone is difficult to comprehend, one adopts the more favourable interpretation of their actions? So when Walter goes behind my back and does or says something that causes me endless trouble, may it not be that what he wants to achieve is actually in his eyes for the common good of the community? But he is unable to take me into his confidence. Is this because he does not have the courage to confront me, or because he is afraid for my sake, on the ground that, until his scheme comes to successful fruition, I shall feel threatened by it?

Have there not, in the past, been occasions when I have myself 'gone behind someone's back' in the hope of sparing them some experience or some decision that I believed would prove terribly painful for them? And whenever my subterfuge has been revealed, has my conduct not seemed like an act of betrayal? In any case, I am supposed to have learnt years ago to be very slow to speak of 'betrayal', ever since I fell into a trench during the second world war.

What happened was one of those incidents that our Zen Buddhist friends often cite as occasions of enlightenment.

At the time, we were young infantrymen doing our basic training, and on this particular day Sergeant Major Reid had made us run here, there and everywhere, so that we finished up breathless on a grassy verge where he formed us up in a single rank and allowed us to get our breath back. Once we were composed, he called us to attention and then gave the order, 'Two paces backwards... March!' Like good soldiers we obeyed his order, took two steps backwards and fell down into a deep trench behind us which we had not noticed – much to the delight of Sergeant Major Reid, who almost doubled up with laughter.

Though I doubt whether he was aware of having done so, the sergeant major had, in fact, subjected at least one member of our section, namely myself, to one of those shocks which Zen masters often cause in their disciples so as to provoke enlightenment or realisation. Because, ever since falling into that trench, I have realised with complete awareness that we human beings do not have eyes in the back of our heads. That may seem a platitudinous thing to say, but it has consequences that are far from platitudinous: it means that when we are trying to move into a correct and just position with regard to someone in front of us, we almost inevitably move into an incorrect or unjust position with regard to someone behind us whom we had not seen – stepping on their toes, for instance.

And when someone steps on our toes, we do not generally say to ourselves, 'He did that because he was trying to behave justly towards A or B; and, since he is a finite creature with finite limited vision, he did not see, or foresee, the pain his movements were going to cause me'. Instead, we invariably interpret the pain caused as having been willed by the person who caused the pain, and therefore we regard him as an enemy, or, in many cases, as a traitor to us.

I am reminded of the psychiatrist in San Francisco who

was speaking with a Dominican friend of mine and regretting how little he could really help his clients. He said:

> You know, the people who come to me for help are in the end all of them asking the same basic, fundamental question. They are all saying to me, 'Is there somewhere a friend who will not in the final resort betray one?' I would love to be able to say, 'Yes. There is'. But I cannot do so because I am an agnostic, and only if I believed in God could I say, 'Yes'. But human beings will always in the end betray.

What the psychiatrist said is both penetrating and helpful, but I do query his use of the word 'betrayal'. Would it not be more accurate to say that human beings will always in the end let one down – at least in some measure, because we are finite creatures and cannot see all round us? We can never see all the consequences of our actions towards others, or even towards ourselves. This is not to deny, of course, that there are occasions when someone delivers us into evil out of malice or selfishness. But once we adopt the *lectio benevolentior*, we find that the percentage of occasions when we feel betrayed diminishes – though, correspondingly, the percentage of occasions when we feel let down increases.

But in both cases we feel hurt, and in order to protect our hurt feelings we react with feelings of our own. After all, we are not unfeeling stones but highly sensitive creatures. Nevertheless, if, in reaction, we allow our feelings to dominate us, then a dark cloud blinds our eyes and a hard lump lies upon our hearts to block the spirit of truth, which is the Holy Spirit of forgiveness. The Holy Spirit cannot then enter our hearts and cleanse us.

In this seeming impasse I have asked myself, 'What can I do to make the miracle of forgiveness possible?' And, by the grace of God, I have arrived at a conclusion that I am beginning to find really helpful: if one honestly observes the distinctive character of one's reactive feelings and analyses them relentlessly, then the mere desire for truth sustaining that observation and analysis will of itself begin to disperse the darkness over one's eyes and dissolve the lump lying heavy upon one's heart. The only trouble is that the process of observation and analysis may unearth truths about oneself which one would rather not know. As it has done in my own case.

I was shocked to discover that my way of dealing with hurt feelings is by having recourse to a corresponding feeling of contempt for those whom I judge to have inflicted the hurt upon me. This salutary discovery would not have been possible, I believe, without the unwitting aid of others. I had never, for instance, forgotten the quiet comment of Archbishop Dwyer of Birmingham when he was meeting a small group of us, university teachers, gathered to appoint a university chaplain. In response to one of our number who was speaking harshly of a candidate, the archbishop said, 'We put ourselves into danger whenever we speak with contempt of another human being'. Whether the man rebuked heard the archbishop's rebuke I cannot say, but I certainly did. The archbishop had sensitised a spot within me that, since then, has always been primed to send out a danger signal whenever I have strayed into contempt.

And I also believe that my discovery owes something to one of the scholars here who, despite being described by a visiting luminary as 'an interfering busybody', has nevertheless helped me. Out of good will, I am sure, this man pointed out to me that when the head of an institution, from a height of six feet six inches, corrects a much smaller member of the institution, it can be rather frightening. So I should be aware of the effect I could have upon those so far below me in physical stature. At first, this explanation of the effect I have sometimes had on people seemed to let me off the hook, but then I thought to myself that I know other people of my height who do not appear to produce the same effect. So there must be some other factor present in my own attitude; and I believe that I have pinpointed it. It is an attitude of contempt, a habit of raising my head and going silent, as if to say, 'How can I be expected to have any dealings with such mean-minded people as these? They are not our sort.'

There was something of that in my attitude towards the religious who were blathering away about forgiveness at the house Mass. I was the only person there who kept silence. And I doubt whether that was a holy silence.

ℰ 18 April

There have been times during recent years when I have been nigh to despair about many spiritual teachers, including some with world-wide reputations. The ones in question, for all their high-sounding books and conferences, often do not know how to behave with that consideration for others which could simply be taken for granted even, say, among the rough, scarcely educated brickyard workers in my native Claremount.

The latest of the species, who descended upon us in February, seemed to imagine that the sole *raison d'être* of Tantur was to ensure that his recent book is granted the maximum publicity. Not only that, but he insisted on my taking him to all those important centres of learning in Jerusalem where I have friends, in order to show them the book. And typically, when we were invited to lunch at the Biblical College, he further insisted on sitting next to the dean, whom he clearly tagged both as important and a person of his own intellectual stature. Not once did he turn to the little man sitting on his right, an inconspicuous, rather gnome-like creature named Genia.

Actually, it was in its own way rather comic to watch this spiritual teacher rattling away throughout the lunch, trying to impress the dean, all the while totally unaware that the little man sitting on his right is probably the most learned man in the place – as well as being a saint! The dean himself once said about him, 'Of all the men I have ever met, he is the one least touched by original sin'!

What joy it was, therefore, today – and a cleansing contrast – to glance around our seminar room and to look upon the faces of so many authentic spiritual teachers who are taking part in our seminar on the 'The Peoples of the Book in the Light of Asia'. Sitting very upright at the head of the table, as leader of the seminar, was the noble figure of Dom Bede Griffiths, whose reputation and glamorous appearance had attracted a good number of visitors. At a far corner from him, my Jewish kabbalistic friend, Avraham Weiner, was quietly taking notes, while gazing at me from the opposite side of the table was the radiant face of my Seraphic brother, Father Marco Malagolo. Just to see even one of these blessed men in our company would have been enough for my cup of joy to flow over, but there were present others who are similarly spirit-filled if not so easily detected. In particular, sitting next to me was God's special gift to me for this term, Sadhu Ittyavirah.

If ever my devotion to the Icon of Unexpected Joy has wavered in the past it should not do so henceforth, after the appearance of Sadhu Ittyavirah, or Itty, as he asks us to call him. Because when I read his book, *Echoing the Father's Love*, ten years ago and learnt something about his life, I never imagined that I should meet and become friends with this sadhu, about whom numerous articles have been written in religious journals. Not only that, but we discovered that we are of the same age (born in 1923), and that I was once stationed for six months near his native village in Kerala. Moreover – what seemed to make us brothers even more – we had both been members of the task force named 'Zipper' which was being mounted to land in Malaya at the time when the atom bomb brought the war to an end. It delights both of us to wonder at the strange ways of providence by which that young Indian soldier and that young British soldier, sailing unknown to one another across the Indian Ocean in the same convoy nearly 40 years ago, should now find their lives converging by manifold ways upon the holy city of Jerusalem.

At the end of the war, this son of a poor Kerala family had trained for many years to become a Jesuit priest, and was indeed within three months of ordination when he was forcibly struck by the thought, 'India does not need another Jesuit priest. What it needs is a Christian sadhu who, like any Hindu holy man, will wander throughout the land witnessing to the love of God, only eating what is given by God's children and sleeping in whatever shelter is offered or else under the open sky.'

For almost 30 years Itty did precisely that, and became quite famous in the course of doing so. As a result, people were constantly seeking his opinion on every subject under the sun. One day, for example, a group of journalists in Madras heard that his wanderings were soon to bring him to their city, and so they went to meet him, 'this vagabond and newspaper boy in the name of God'. They said to him, 'Sadhu, you have traversed much of India and seen every aspect of Indian life, what is the great task facing our country?' Every question anticipates a certain answer, and in this case the journalists were expecting this holy man to issue some profound statement about the spiritual crisis facing the Indian people. Instead, he just gave them his radiant smile and said, 'Food'. Then he continued his wanderings.

Now Itty is no longer a vagabond. He is married, has a little son and received worldly acclaim in 1981 when he shared the Albert Schweitzer Peace Prize along with the great guitarist, Segovia. With the money he received, Itty has set up the Schweitzer Institute of Prayer and Research on a modest plot of land near his native village. His motivation for so doing springs from his conviction that modern science has gone astray because scientific research has taken place outside prayer; and he hopes that science will become more fruitful, more of a blessing for humanity, if at least one or two scientists prove ready to spend some time at the tiny Schweitzer Institute. And though most observers dismiss his scheme as wildly quixotic, who is to deny the truth of Itty's intuition in the age of nuclear terror, when pollution produced by humanity's devilish ingenuity is penetrating earth and sea and sky, and is corrupting not only the bodies of all earth's inhabitants but even the very heart of humankind?

What for me put the seal on the authenticity of Itty's life and teaching was the explanation he gave to me of why he had abandoned his status of sadhu in order to become an ordinary householder. He told me that when he reached his mid-fifties, he began to feel his bones aching more and more as a result of his vagabond life. In his approaching old age he felt that he was going to need comfort such as he had not known for 30 years. So he decided to get married. He did so, having first sought the advice and consent of his ecclesiastical superior.

This explanation for his change of status was simply given, with no trace of affectation or defensiveness. It completely captivated me. As he spoke I could almost hear, as a sort of counter-echo, how the voices of certain spiritual teachers would have sounded if they had taken a similar step. They would have elevated their action to the status of a prophetic statement or a further stage in their spiritual journey or a return to the original lifestyle of the sadhu. Instead, Itty just said that his bones were beginning to ache and that he needed some comfort in his old age.

Of course, anyone who can speak with such simplicity is, in his own person, a prophetic statement.

৶ 5 May

Extract from a letter to the Tablet

It is only a few weeks since the bloody climax to the hijacking of the Egged bus on the Tel Aviv to Ashkelon route, and yet the details of it and of the human beings caught in the drama of that Thursday night are already becoming blurred in most of our minds. Too much happens in the modern world for us to take it in.

But for some reason, I continue to be haunted by the thought of Irit Portugez. Irit was the 19-year-old woman soldier killed along with the hijackers. She was on her way home that night to Moshav Cochav Michael, doubtless going on leave in order to celebrate the sabbath with her family. As with families all over the world, they would already have been anticipating with joy the return of their daughter. So I have continued to picture Irit as one of those thousands of girl soldiers one sees in Israel, usually so neat and trim and innocent-looking – you cannot make a woman look like a tough, uncompromising soldier in the way that you can a man. The ones I have encountered have been uniformly pleasant and kind and helpful.

And apparently the hijackers also were young, and scarcely ruthless enough to be successful terrorists – at one point they stopped the bus in order to allow a pregnant woman to get off. The passengers themselves later said that the four Arabs treated them well.

There also remains in my memory another image of that night. Ze'ev Bukshenshpan, an Israeli Defence Force combat medic who was a passenger on the bus, and himself only 26, proved to be the hero of the occasion by the way in which he cared for the wounded. And aiding him were Irit and Jamal, the latter one of the hijackers, a youngster still in his teens, who helped Ze'ev by holding a flashlight while Ze'ev was inserting a plasma needle into one of the wounded. That moment now stands in my mind like a scene from one of Rembrandt's night pictures – the three young people bending over the wounded man, their features etched against the darkness by the light of the torch which Jamal was holding. For a moment the three of them were held together, bent not upon destroying but upon saving life. Yet within hours, Irit and Jamal had been blasted into eternity, whereas Ze'ev, by a different fate, lives on to marry the woman he loves. May he have long life and see his children's children.

The truth about what happened on that fateful evening was suppressed by the Israeli authorities. Photographs were banned by the censors because they showed two of the hijackers being led away from the bus, alive and on their own two feet. The photographs contradicted the first official story that all the hijackers had been killed in the storming of the bus. Then an

Israeli newspaper was suspended for taking up the *New York Times'* revelation that the two hijackers who survived the storming of the bus had been killed by their captors.

Subsequently three members of the Israeli internal security service, Shin Bet, were dismissed for having leaked the truth about the incident.

A saddening feature about the reporting of this tragedy was that the local Arab newspaper never spoke of Irit Portugez or Ze'ev Buskshenshpan, any more than the Jewish newspaper named Subdi, Majdi or Jamal, who for them remained anonymous. The enemy must never be allowed to be a human being.

Nearly all our visitors who come to stay with us for any length of time eventually ask the same question: 'How on earth do people manage to remain sane in the midst of all the tension and craziness of this place?'

To this question there are many answers: such as, for instance, the shining example of all the holy people in our tension-riddled city. One day I hope to write about them. But there is an even simpler answer which, sadly, is beyond the experience of almost everyone outside Israel. I am speaking of the sabbath. Of the sabbath it is eminently true to say, 'Taste and see that it is good', for unless you taste it, you cannot appreciate its goodness.

And you may taste it in the most unlikely places. After all, Netanya is a Mediterranean holiday centre where you would expect to encounter the usual noise of the modern entertainment world – anything but the quiet of the sabbath. Yet when we arrived there at lunch-time on Friday, you could already feel the town settling steadily into the silence of the holy day. The volume of traffic had gradually diminished; the shops were closing their doors; and even the pedestrians were beginning to move more slowly, their voices quieter as they greeted one another, '*Shabbat Shalom*'. By the time the sun was setting over the Mediterranean, the beach was unpeopled and those of us sitting on benches or strolling along the tree-lined seafront were beginning to breath more unhurriedly, scenting the fragrance of the sabbath.

When I looked up towards the hotel where we were staying, there, to my joy, I saw that the common room was now lit up and filled with my Jewish fellow guests dressed in their prayer shawls and wearing their yarmulkas. At that moment it seemed completely right and proper for them to be davening* on behalf also of those of us outside – except that I did not feel outside, because I was being embraced within the light to lighten the Gentiles.

A strange thought then entered my head: how I wish that the spiritually starving youngsters from Liverpool, Newcastle, Stoke and other cities might taste the sweetness of the sabbath! Because then they might again see goodness. But England no longer knows 'the mystery of the sabbath ... the table wreathed with precious mystery. Deep and hidden, beyond the reach of the word'. So her hungry children never taste sabbath and cannot, therefore, see goodness.

◦ঽ *8 May*

Yet another twist to the saga of *koinonia*! After numerous failures over the past three years, I managed to persuade an Orthodox scholar to come and live at Tantur for a term. Since Vladimir, the scholar in question, is Russian Orthodox and belongs to the Moscow patriarchate, his coming here did not cause the complications with the Orthodox patriarch of Jerusalem that, say, an Orthodox from Greece might have caused – Vladimir is a Swiss citizen.

Vladimir's presence has been a great joy to all of us and he has communicated to us some of his own enthusiasm for the riches of the Russian Orthodox tradition. In particular, he gave us such glowing accounts of the Russian celebration of Easter that a number of scholars asked whether they might accompany him to the Easter service this year.

Only now have I been told the sickening story of what happened when they went.

When the moment came for communion, Vladimir went up to receive, but the priest in front of whom he stood questioned him, 'Are you Orthodox?' 'Yes', answered Vladimir. 'To whom did you make your confession?' In response Vladimir named the priest, only to be told, 'I have never heard of him'. At which the celebrant passed on. And Vladimir had to return, heavy-hearted, to take his place beside his dismayed Tantur friends.

* A form of prayer characterised by swaying of the body.

Certain Westerners, inevitably, will in future listen to glowing accounts of the Russian Orthodox Easter with some reserve.

ༀ *20 May*

Tonight I feel as though an enormous load has been lifted from both my head and my heart. What happened this evening at dinner was enough to make you believe in God and goodness.

At no meal in which I have partaken since coming to Tantur have I felt a stronger current of unfeigned good will, fellowship and holy joy in each other's company than I experienced this evening. All five of us at our table joined easily in the conversation, which was at one time concerned with social affairs and another time devoted to theological issues, always serious but also humorous with lots of relaxed laughter. Above all, the current of feeling around the table was one of warmth and trust.

Only towards the very end of the meal did I suddenly realise that the four men sharing this heart-warming occasion with me were precisely the same four whom I had previously characterised in my mind as 'malcontents'. And a few minutes later, as we were bidding each other 'Good night and sleep well', I found myself reflecting, 'Well, if you had told me three months ago that these four could be in such harmony with me and would be showing such respect and affection for me personally, I would never never have believed you'.

In those days, an accidental discovery had left me shaking with anger against them – though perhaps my anger arose less from their conduct than from that of the misguided character who indirectly transmitted to me the caustic remarks about my running of the Institute which he had elicited from them. For although I could tell without any difficulty, on account of both the nature and the tone of each complaint, which of them had said what, nevertheless the whole circumstance surrounding the incident was so messy that if I had confronted each of them individually, our relations would have been strained for the rest of our time together.

So, instead, I decided to take to heart the criticisms levelled at myself as honestly as I could manage but, above all, to regard my knowledge of their criticisms as privileged, as having been given in trust to someone, and therefore I was under an obligation not to take advantage of it. In the last few months that has not been easy. After all, it is now almost 50 years since I discovered an ability within myself to hit people off with a phrase; and it would have been easy enough for me to finish off each of these four with a polite but deadly gesture of characterisation.

I hope that my determination not to indulge my ability owed at least something to the inspiration of the Holy Spirit, but I am bound wrily to recognise that my Yorkshire sense of economy also had a bearing on it. After all, for nigh on 40 years I had been investing precious energy into curbing a fatal capacity for hitting off with a word people who have crossed me. Was I now going to blow that lifetime's investment just for the satisfaction of hurting someone who had hurt me? 'Not likely!' said the thrifty York-shireman inside me.

But that motive of economy alone would not have been enough to maintain my resolution in face of the many subsequent moments of temptation to break it. The factor that gave most weight to my resolve illustrates the benefits of having affirmed one's beliefs and opinions in the public forum so clearly that one cannot stifle them in the private forum situated within oneself. In this case, having so often and so firmly voiced the need to control one's tongue, I kept hearing some of my own words whenever I faced temptation: 'As the Buddhists teach, "Learn, whenever you are on the point of speaking, to swallow your own words. If you can't swallow them, how can you expect others to do so?" ' 'Becoming holy is not at all complicated. All we have to do is what St James tells us: control our tongues, and then everything else in our life will fall into place.' Or, those golden words attributed to St Seraphim of Sarov, 'Keep away from the spilling of speech. Instead of condemning others, strive to reach inner peace. Keep silent, refrain from judgement. This will raise you above the deadly arrows of slander, insult, outrage, and will shield your glowing hearts against the evil that creeps around.'

But perhaps it is something that I have read, rather than anything I have said, which has in a manner stunned me into silence – by the power of its conviction drawn from a thousand-years-old tradition. That is, the book entitled *Guard Your Tongue* (Jerusalem, 1975) a practical guide to avoiding derogatory speech based on the teachings of a Polish rabbi, Chofetz Chayim. Until I had studied Chofetz Chayim's compendium on the myriad ways in which one can sin through *leshon hora* (one's tongue of evil), I had never realised how much of our everyday conversation is corrupted through derogatory speech. Here one learns to appreciate the great strength of the rabbinic tradition, in that it does not allow one to escape into generalities but rather rubs one's nose in the concrete details of human behaviour. As, for example, if a person with whom you are conversing on the telephone insists on relating derogatory information, you should rebuke him even if the derogatory information is true. If this is not possible, you must find an excuse to hang up, saying 'Excuse me, something has just come up' (i.e. the derogatory information), and break off the conversation. No wonder that some rabbis go so far as to say that tale-bearing is even more sinful than the cardinal sins of murder, adultery and idolatry. And no wonder that it is a Jewish saint, James, who compares the evil tongue to the very tiniest spark which sets a huge stack of timber on fire, just as the tongue can send up a whole community in flames.

It is thanks to all these teachers – Chofetz Chayim, St Seraphim, St James and our Buddhist friends – that I have managed to traverse these past few months without offending against the 'malcontents'. Let that be a warning not to fall into the fashionable pose of scorning teaching in the name of experience. True teachers illuminate the path ahead of us so that we become aware of pitfalls and do not strike our feet against a stone, neither scandalised nor scandalising.

I am still breathing with relief, moreover, through becoming aware of what a close shave it was – just one hard word from me during these last few months and that wonderful atmosphere at dinner this evening would have been quite impossible.

❧ *30 May*

Even as it was happening, you could sense that tonight's encounter at Hebrew University between Professor Leibowicz and Professor Emile Fackenheim was to be historic, and that it would be talked about for a long time to come. For the four of us from Tantur who were present it was a particular privilege to be there, since we were the only Christians in the lecture hall. This meant that the 50 or so Jewish professors and students in the hall were hardly conscious of us. Consequently our Jewish brethren argued very openly with one another and expressed themselves in a way that people only feel free to do when no one but family is present – as, for instance, Leibowicz did when referring to Christianity as 'the enemy of Judaism'.

The impetus for this historic confrontation was provided by the publication of Fackenheim's latest book, *To Mend the World*, a work in which he reaffirms how vitally important it is for Jews to remain faithful to their traditions, and especially for the centrality henceforth in Jewish religious thought of the Holocaust and the state of Israel.

In his introduction to the discussion, it was again the Holocaust and the state of Israel which Fackenheim emphasised, along with his well-known assertion that every Jew must be faithful to his traditions so as not to give Hitler a 'posthumous victory'.

When Leibowicz stood up to reply, his approach to the lectern was grave and dramatic, not without a touch of the histrionic. His bald head topped by a skull cap, his face pale with age and study, this prophet of Israel leaned his right elbow on the lectern and placed the long, bony fingers of his right hand against his cheek. Then slowly, as if wearied by the folly of his fellow human beings, he declared, 'If I had read Professor Fackenheim's book before accepting the invitation to come here and discuss it, I would never have agreed to do so. The book is totally alien to my way of thinking and has nothing to do with Judaism, in my understanding of Judaism.'

I had never heard a discussion between two academics to be initiated in such an uncompromising, aggressive fashion. Hence my sympathies went out immediately to the discomforted Fackenheim, in spite of the fact that I have in the past been scandalised by the way in which he seems to me to distort history for polemical purposes.

At the same time, I was utterly fascinated at the manner in which Leibowicz relentlessly pursued the logic of his own position. 'Faith', he said, 'is not a conclusion from empirical data; it has nothing to do with experience. It is a decision. It is *mitzvah* in this miserable world.' He went on to say that there is no religious meaning to be found in the Holocaust, nor does he attach any religious significance to the existence of the state of Israel (even though he himself worked to establish the state) because there is no meaning in history. God is beyond history; he is beyond space and time; therefore to look for a Messiah in history is a form of idolatry. Which is why 'Christianity is the enemy of Judaism'.

To all of which Fackenheim had no reply. How can you reply to any such fundamentalist who, in effect, begins by declaring that there is no ground for discussion and that nothing you say will affect his fundamental position? Once you grant Leibowicz's narrow view of logic, then he was the victor of the evening and Fackenheim was revealed to be confused. Nevertheless, our little group of Christians felt close to Fackenheim – though he might not have been pleased to learn it – because, as one of my friends afterwards summed it up, 'at least his confusions are Christian confusions'.

But for me the reward for attending the debate did not emerge from the intellectual encounter, but from an incident that occurred when we were leaving the hall as some desultory wrangling was still in progress. Just as I was passing the back rows of the audience, my glance fell upon Mrs Pnina Peli, Mrs Fackenheim and Moshe Greenberg. I smiled at them and they smiled back, and I received from them such a warm feeling, a feeling of real friendship, a sense that these Jewish friends have become an important part of my life. That is a reality which no theological differences can obscure, much less destroy.

ᏇᏕ *31 August*

Looking back upon the World Conference of Religious for Peace, which I have just attended in Nairobi, it is borne in upon me once more how vital the spiritual dimension is for all of us who aspire to work for peace, yet how little regard is paid to spiritual discipline at so many of these meetings. It is as though we doff our hats to the Spirit at the beginning and then say, 'Now let us put that aside and get on with the serious business'.

I am thinking particularly of last Friday. We had been asked to fast for part of the day as an expression of our solidarity with the oppressed people of South Africa, and to meet in the main forum for common prayer at 12.30 p.m. Already we had been informed of the presence among us of Graham Stanton, an Anglican priest, who had been imprisoned in South Africa by the

Botha regime and had only been released a day or two previously. He was to speak at the meeting.

As it turned out, there were only half a dozen people present by the time appointed, including Stanton himself, clearly a very sensitive man who had about him that same indefinable air of having touched something ultimate which one invariably finds among the survivors of the Japanese POW camps of the second world war. He waited patiently, along with the rest of us, for more members of the conference to arrive. A few did so. But the attendance was still sparse even three-quarters of an hour later, at which time it was decided to wait no longer but to begin the service of intercession.

Similarly, the organisers of the conference had encouraged members to take part in a meditation session in the evenings at 9.30, the sessions being led by a different person on each occasion, in accordance with the various traditions represented among us. In the event, the number of meditators never rose above one in fifty of the conference members.

And in one area at least of our work you could trace the destructive effect of this neglect of spiritual discipline, in much the same way as you can trace the path of poisoned blood in a limb whose immunisation capacity has been undermined. This area was that of the Middle East workshop where some 25 of us spent two whole days in the same room thrashing out the issue of peacemaking in the Middle East. There were present Jews from Israel, the US and Canada; Christians from the US, Britain, Canada, Israel and the Philippines – as well as Muslims from Egypt, Pakistan, Iran and the Sudan.

There were some elevating moments during those tense two days, above all when three women managed to slice a path through the macho rhetoric that was clogging the room up. One of the women came from the West Bank, a Christian; the second, Jewish, came from Israel, while the third was a Muslim from Lebanon. They stood together for a period in a mutual embrace that cleansed the atmosphere for a time. The image of those three is memorable.

But there were some very bad experiences as well, especially when interventions were made by the Iranians, spokesmen for Ayatollah Khomeini, who had muscled in on the conference. Their terrifying mentality was revealed when they were asked to comment on the accusation that many people in

188

Iran are being persecuted on account of their religion. The Iranians' answer was even more stunning than the questioner had anticipated. The reply came, 'There is no persecution or discrimination against Jews, Christians and Zoroastrians, the Peoples of the Book. They are all allowed to fight in the war and are all buried in martyrs' cemeteries.' Not only those words but also the faces from which the words emerged, hard as if set in stone, made me think of Cromwell and his Ironsides – as did their emotionless voices when a Jewish participant exclaimed, 'So you are planning to capture Jerusalem and destroy the Jews in Israel?' Tonelessly they replied, 'It will not be necessary for us to do so – God will do so in order to punish you.'

But the behaviour of the Khomeini followers was not the most disturbing aspect of the Middle East workshop. After all, they had marched into the meeting unbidden and we scarcely expected better of them. Far more difficult to comprehend and justify is what happened to the six or seven Jewish members of the workshop.

Almost from the first minute that we gathered in that stuffy room, the Jews present were subjected to a stream of accusations from other members of the group on account of the oppression practised upon the Palestinians by the Zionist state of Israel. Coming at the very beginning, this expression of hostility raised the tension within the room to such a height that henceforth, no matter what subject we might ostensibly be discussing, everyone knew in their nerve endings that the iniquities of Israel were likely to break in upon our discussions at any second.

The result was what anyone with even a grain of intelligence could have predicted: the Jews felt themselves cornered, since they were being made to feel personally responsible for every iniquitous policy practised by the state of Israel. Naturally, in reaction they displayed the less amiable features of their own personalities.

To watch all this happening almost reduced me to despair. Nevertheless I tried to deter the most persistent accusers by catching them at a coffee break and retailing to them the story of the French zoo whose directors affixed a notice to the cage of one of the animals. The notice read, *Cet animal est très méchant. Quand on l'attaque, il se défend.* ('This animal is very wicked. When you attack it, it defends itself.') I was hoping that the story might induce them at least to modify their own behaviour; but there was precious little evidence that it had done so.

Their attitude, in fact, brought to mind again the classical teaching that stupidity is not simply the result of some mechanical or technical error, but is rather the consequence of some self-induced moral obtuseness. They appeared unable to see that our Jewish colleagues, by the very fact of joining in such a peace conference, had shown themselves prepared to face criticism from their right-wing fellow citizens in Israel, who were likely to accuse them of 'consorting with the enemy'. Indeed, some of these Jews had already suffered obloquy for standing up in defence of the rights of West Bank Arabs. And now, as a reward for defending West Bank Arabs, they were being attacked by other Arabs! It is hardly surprising that, after two days, they themselves began to sound like members of the Israeli right-wing Likud party.

❧ 1 September

Letter to the Tablet *on conviviality*

The deep resonance of the word only struck me as I was sitting, away from Tantur, in the corner of a grubby foodstall on a back street of Larnaca. Beside me a cheery-looking Cypriot workman was eating his boiled eggs and drinking his beer with unselfconscious gusto. I also was glad of the beer, after the hot morning wandering around this quarter of the town. In particular my mind was filled with images of various mosques which I had seen, now abandoned and decaying but still dignified by the nobility of their minarets. But what haunted me even more was the realisation that, in this quarter of the town, both Greek and Turkish Cypriots must once have lived cheek by jowl; and no matter what tensions and animosities they may have experienced, nevertheless in some measure they had practised conviviality. Whereas now, some ten years after the ideologues had their way, there were no Turkish Cypriots in this part of the island, just as there are no Greek Cypriots in the northern part. So today neither Turks nor Greeks have the least chance any longer to practise conviviality.

'*Con-vivere*', I thought to myself. What a wonderful word! To live-with others. Could there be any greater grace than the grace to live with others?

Of course, they had quarrelled throughout the centuries, these Greek and Turkish neighbours. But at the same time, they had seen one another celebrating the birth of children; they had watched, and even shared in, one another's marriage feasts; and at a death in the community, they had been touched by the others' mourning. They had at least known that the others were human beings and not demons. But now they never see one another. They are as invisible as demons, and therefore they can demonise one another.

I was reminded of an earlier day in Jerusalem, when I had walked into the home of some friends who lived in the Old City. They had greeted me warmly and asked: 'Where have you been, Donald?' 'Over in West Jerusalem', I replied, brightly enough. There was a silence: West Jerusalem is Jewish. Eventually one of my friends said: 'Oh! We never go there now'. 'Why not?' 'Because we find it so uncongenial.'

It so happened that I had spent quite some time in Jerusalem that morning, sitting on a bench in the open space below the Great Synagogue, named Liberty Bell Gardens, watching scores of young children playing on the grass and hiding in the bushes – some of them handicapped children carefully tended by their teachers. They all seemed so happy! And there was joy in my heart as I watched them; until suddenly, like a hammer blow, the thought struck me that a generation ago these same children, utterly delightful, absorbed in their games, would have been herded off in cattle trucks to die in gas chambers, simply because they were Jewish.

Sparked by that vivid memory, I said to my friends: 'In that case, perhaps it would be a good idea for you to make a point of going into West Jerusalem at least once a week. Just sit on a bench or at a café table, and watch the people going about their everyday tasks, and you will soon begin to feel for them as human beings. What you are doing now is to keep away from the people of West Jerusalem so that you are then in a position to demonise them.'

Of course, I realised why my friends adopted their position: they had seen their Arab neighbours ill-treated; they knew only too well the difference between the facilities given to Jewish children and those available for Arab children. But when all that is said, and much more in the same vein, does not my joy in the security of those Jewish children afford some chance, however slim, of conviviality? Whereas practising apartheid, standing at a distance, only exacerbates ideological differences.

Strangely enough, there are some who stand at a distance for seemingly good reasons. A number of my liberal Jewish friends in Israel, for instance, including a leading writer, absolutely refuse to enter the West Bank while the West Bank is under Israeli occupation, because, so they say, even to pass through that area at present would risk placing themselves, as Jews, in the ranks of the oppressors. But should my writer friend not take that risk in order to be able to convey to his readers the feel of everyday life on the West Bank? Because, as it is, Israelis in general – even liberal ones – have almost no sense of what life is like for a people who yet live only a few miles away.

A much greater risk was taken lately by our Arab staff. They joined us on an outing into Israel, to the beach at Netanya. For them it was most daring, because they always fear what might happen to them in Israel – that they might be arrested, for example, and vanish forever into an Israeli prison. One or two of the older among them, moreover, had never in all their years ventured to the coast. But in the company of us Europeans and Americans, they seemed to feel protected.

And they were greatly rewarded not only by the pleasures of the beach, but even more by moments of real conviviality.

At first our Israeli neighbours on the beach looked very surprised to see some 30 Arabs, accompanied by one or two Westerners, settling themselves on the sands with numerous large hampers of food and drink. Indeed, a few of them, when they saw our hampers all set out, assumed that the food and drink was for sale and hesitantly came across to try to buy some of it – to the merriment of Jews and Arabs alike when their mistake was discovered.

But perhaps the *pièce de résistance* occurred when some of the younger Arab women in our party switched on a transistor and spontaneously broke into dancing. There were smiles all round; and from then on, for the rest of the day, the atmosphere was easy and friendly.

But both the worst and the best was yet to come. In the evening, just as we were preparing to board our bus and go up again to Jerusalem, our cook Da'oud was suddenly taken ill, wracked in great pain. Realising that it might be very serious, I ordered our driver to head northwards immediately to a hospital which, as it turned out, is situated in an area wholly populated by Orthodox Jews. This became obvious to me as soon as Yakoub and I started shepherding Da'oud through the emergency waiting room. Because that afternoon it was serving as the antenatal clinic and was full of manifestly pregnant women dressed in Orthodox fashion and being attended to by doctors and attendants, all of whom were wearing kippas. Women, doctors and attendants understandably looked startled at the sight of the writhing Da'oud being propelled along by a hefty, heavily-moustachioed Arab and a tall, bearded Westerner. However, the doctors quickly recovered and rose to the emergency.

Two hours later, we were able to help Da'oud back on to the bus, a much relieved man – just as we ourselves were now much wiser by whatever wisdom accrues to one through sitting patiently and quietly for two hours surrounded by pregnant Orthodox Jewish women – a wisdom which I felt to be considerable.

Yet the best, as I said, was still to come. On arriving back at Tantur, and before alighting from the bus, we prayed a prayer of gratitude to God for the wonderful day we had shared together, and last of all thanked him for the kindness and skill of the Jewish doctors who had restored Da'oud to us. It was a sincere, heartfelt prayer, a perfect ending to our outing.

'And another thing', as Yakoub said the next morning at coffee time, as he dramatically recited the great deeds of yesterday for anyone who would listen. 'And another thing', he repeated in his thunderous voice. 'They only charged us 4000 shekels. On the West Bank that would have cost us 16,000 – no! 20,000 shekels!' For some reason this perpendicular drop from the sublime to the shekel was too much for his audience, with the result that they almost fell off their chairs with laughter. Palestinian Arabs have such a ready sense of humour.

Of course I am aware, more than I dare say, that the Jewish–Arab conflict is not to be camouflaged by stories such as I retail here. But even in conflict, one flash of conviviality is worth more than a whole generation of apartheid, whether physical or ideological.

193

♋ *17 October*

Letter to the **Tablet**

As the time for my departure from Tantur approaches, and with it the end of this series of extracts from my Jerusalem journal, I realise that during the past four years I may well have failed to communicate the impact on our everyday lives of events that take place actually within sight of our Institute. So this month, instead of trying to reflect on the entries in my journal so as to extract a general theme from them, I decided simply to record in all their abruptness certain events of this sort, and show how they have struck us – or, rather, how we have stubbed our toes on them.

As, for instance, happened when I drew the bedroom curtains one morning, not long after my return from my visit to Nairobi. Some 600 yards away, across the valley towards the hilltop settlement of Gilo, there was now an enormous heap of rubble where previously had stood a two-storey family house. And strewn about the hillside below the rubble were uprooted olive trees and almond trees from which the family had drawn their living.

I walked up the hill later that day to discover what had happened, and was able to piece together a confusing story from the broken English of Muhanna, a sturdy middle-aged man who had lived in the house along with his simple brother Mahfouz and his 85-year-old father, Salman Saleb Arab. The old man, all his days a land-worker, had lived in the house for over 50 years until one morning recently. On that morning, a group of men brandishing guns had arrived with a bulldozer; they had thrown everything out of the house – furniture, clothes, appliances and the rest – and within half an hour had reduced the Arab house to rubble. The family were left to sleep out under the open sky beside their ruined home, until the Red Cross provided them with a tent. But even that had been torn down by the time I arrived.

Who were the members of this group that had behaved so barbarously? 'Settlers', said Muhanna. I understood why he said that, because West Bank Arabs always assume that civilians toting guns are Jewish settlers, but I doubted whether that was the case. The settlers may be ruthless, but this was not their style. And my doubts proved to be well-founded: the men in question had been hired by a wealthy Jew who lives in Los Angeles and who claims that he is the owner of the land.

But even in the gloom of such miserable happenings, human beings can be sources of astonishing illumination. Sitting there on his heap, like the patriarch Job, the old man calmly smoked a cigarette, lifted his hands towards the heavens and said, 'It is the will of God'. And the vigorous Muhanna, though more excited, also showed no bitterness. 'God is good', he said. 'There is room for us all, Jews and Muslims and Christians.'

Yet the incident most calculated to dumbfound a Western mind was to occur several days later. While Dorothy, my wife, and I sat with the family on some rickety old boxes, two agents of the contractor drew up in their car. As they were walking across the rubble towards us, they began to look sheepish at the unexpected sight of two Westerners sitting there. But whereas I gazed stonily at them, our Arab friends did not. *'Ahlan, wa sahlan'*, they called out – 'Welcome, welcome'. 'This is overdoing traditional Arab hospitality', I said to myself. But more was to come. The contractors later asked a neighbouring European family if they might leave the notorious bulldozer for safety on their land. Indignantly, the Europeans refused – but the Arabs themselves allowed the bulldozer to stand on their property.

And there were other good moments which showed that, although this part of the world may sometimes seem like the Wild West, nevertheless Israel remains a democracy, in spite of all the strains upon it. My wife, for instance, wrote a letter to the *Jerusalem Post* about our neighbours' plight which prompted a compassionate freelance reporter to publish a full-length article on the incident. And nothing could have been prompter than the response of Teddy Kollek, one of the great city mayors of this century, when I informed him of what had happened. Immediately he sent along Amir Heshin, his adviser on Arab affairs, to investigate. He, on seeing the condition of the Arabs, straightaway bought food for them out of his own pocket. And I have no doubt that justice of some sort will now be achieved.

In the meantime, there had taken place the drama at our gatehouse. It was Sunday morning and our skilful handyman, Yakoub, was sitting on his porch drinking coffee with that air of leisured satisfaction which in itself is already a vote of confidence in God. Suddenly he heard cries of alarm just beyond the gate, and rushed out to see what was happening. There he saw three

Israeli soldiers running away from a smoking truck, while a fourth was gripping the absurdly inadequate fire extinguisher provided in an attempt to prevent the vehicle from going up in flames. Instantly Yakoub dashed back into his house, seized a proper fire extinguisher and within minutes had the smoke quelled and the danger of an explosion averted.

The terrified soldiers hardly knew how to believe their luck. They had been driving to Hebron from the Allenby Bridge on the Jordan when something had gone wrong with the truck's petrol system. Now they realised that they might all have gone up in flames. But what were they to make of this Arab who had saved the day? Especially after he invited them into his home to have some coffee and cakes, and to telephone their commanding officer at the Allenby Bridge to come and make a report on the accident?

When he told me all this next day, Yakoub was bubbling with laughter as he described how the Israeli soldiers had hesitated before accepting his invitation – they clearly thought he might be a 'terrorist'. However, they calmed down after spending a few hours drinking his coffee until the arrival of their commanding officer, who was even more fulsome than they in his thanks to Yakoub.

'That's all very well, you being a hero, Yakoub', I said, 'but who is going to replace our fire extinguisher?' 'They will, professor. I told them it was not mine, but the Institute's. And', he continued with a sly smile, 'perhaps they will also send us a spare one. And', slyer still, 'perhaps they will even give me a note to say that in future Yakoub must not be kept waiting at the Allenby Bridge when I am going to Amman?' I shouldn't bet on it, Yakoub.

During this same period we had been hearing the sound of drums beating and a crowd singing for several nights. The sound came from the courtyard of the hostel in the care of the Salvatorian Fathers from Lebanon, which is situated about 200 yards south of us, on the rocky path towards Bethlehem where the local people say that Joseph, Mary and the donkey travelled. On Wednesday afternoon, as she was walking past the hostel, Dorothy discovered the source of the singing and drum-beating. It came from some 30 or 40 people of all ages from Lebanon who were making merry in the courtyard.

For a few minutes Dorothy stood watching, enjoying the occasion but declining the repeated invitations to join in the dancing. Then, before she knew what was happening, an enormously fat and jolly Lebanese woman seized her by the arm and swept her into the company of the dancers, all of whom began clapping to encourage their new recruit.

She whirled around with them for a quarter of an hour, but then excused herself as she had to go into Bethlehem. Still out of breath but smiling to herself, she was startled 100 yards later to find herself confronted by an Israeli soldier carrying a machine gun slung across his chest. It was the stark contrast, within such a short distance, between the merriment and the machine gun which made her jump. The young soldier, however, was extremely pleasant and kindly; he realised how he had given her a fright and went out of his way to assure her there was nothing to worry about – 'Just some trouble in Deheishe'.

Deheishe is a camp of some 8000 refugees which lies about two kilometres south of us on the Hebron road. Its name is known to many in Israel, because the inhabitants of the camp are often in conflict with the Jewish settlers who have to pass by Deheishe on their way to their settlement overlooking Hebron. For us at Tantur, the camp is more than a name: it is part of our everyday awareness since, apart from anything else, our gardener lives there. He often comes to work on a donkey. Whenever I see this, I remember how the Institute has available a Peugeot, a Volkswagen and a Fiat. And I am reminded of Jesus. Many days our gardener cannot come, because his camp has been placed under curfew.

'The trouble in Deheishe' that day had centred around the racist member of the Israeli parliament, Rabbi Kahane. Kahane, who advocates expelling all Arabs from Israel and the West Bank, had gone into the camp accompanied by military officers, soldiers and journalists. He had conducted afternoon prayers in face of the camp mosque and had declared, 'I will show these dogs that just as *they* can wander about Tel Aviv, so *I* can move about here'.

Reflecting on all the other incidents from *il piccolo mundo di Tantur* recounted here, I can find some sign of redemption. But for Kahane in Deheishe I can find none.

ᙓ *23 October*

I have not been very successful in trying to bring the Christian members of our Arab staff into the worship life of the community. Soon after I took over as rector I was dismayed to discover that, when the community was ferried into Jerusalem each year to take part in Christian unity services, it was customary for the expatriates (scholars and monks) to go into the service but for our drivers, Sami and Yakoub, to remain outside until the service was over. So the foreign Christians went in and the native Christians remained outside! Which provided an ironic comment on a community dedicated, as we are, to the search for Christian unity.

At first I was inclined to rail within my own mind at the colonialist attitude on the part of the expatriates towards the local Christians which this customary behaviour exemplified. And doubtless there was some justification for my railing; but since those days I have come to realise that the Arab Christians have their own way of dealing with such situations – although for expatriates to say that the Arabs themselves prefer the customary way is only an unwitting way of acknowledging the Arabs have been cowed by colonialism. Indeed they have. Nevertheless, that is by no means the whole story: the Arabs have shown that, when they deem a situation sufficiently serious, they are quite capable of taking over the reins and guiding events in the direction that they consider proper, as they proved at Lane's funeral.

And they are infinitely better than us at celebrating funerals; perhaps because, in their lowliness and poverty, they are nearer than we are to nothingness and death, and are therefore more serious about life. I certainly felt the full power of their seriousness one morning two months ago, when I went into Bethlehem to take part in the funeral service for Carlos' mother in the Church of the Nativity (Carlos being one of our two night guards).

In best Arab fashion they had been very vague about the time at which the funeral procession was supposed to come into church, whether at 10 or 10.30. So, in order not to be late, I arrived at 10, only to find almost no one there. But that in the event proved to be a blessing, because among the patient people of Bethlehem waiting is itself a mode of communion. Their capacity for waiting has shown itself over thousands of years as they have watched one after another of their conquerors come and go while they themselves have quietly survived. And all that grinding history is written on the faces of these men and women as they come into church, cross themselves and then sit quietly, looking straight ahead towards the altar. Their faces are weather-beaten from the burning sun of summer and the fierce winds of winter that do indeed beat upon Bethlehem. All the faces are heavily lined, the men with thick moustaches and generally a stubble of beard. And all of them, men and women, are wearing cheap, worn clothes and much-mended shoes. But their apparent drabness is defied and overcome by the proud and skilful way in which their head-dress is set, the traditional keffiyeh, patterned in both red and grey. Their faces are extraordinarily beautiful, reminiscent of the sort of beauty that one also finds among the Irish of Connemara.

After the service, only the men accompany the coffin to the graveyard, the women going apart to prepare the funeral meal. So I was one of about 50 men who made our way through the traffic of Manger Square and up Milk Grotto Street. It was there that I was moved to tears when I gazed over the heads of my companions as they filled the whole width of Milk Grotto Street, between the open shops on one side and the high walls on the other, moving along like some powerful river. Unhurried, they moved in unison, in spite of some of the older men occasionally stumbling; and everywhere you could see the heads bowed in sorrow, the shoulders bent from years of toil, and at every step the keffiyehs rising and falling like the waves of the sea. In that moment the funeral procession symbolised for me almost everything there is to say about our human condition: the agony of a creature doomed to know death, the hope that springs from knowing poverty, and the capacity for compassion which binds us into one.

And how well, how instinctively, these Arabs of Bethlehem know the way that ceremony should be accomplished. Without hesitation and with no need for books or an orchestrating priest or official, they knew when to stop to allow the close relatives to go forward, in what order to present their condolences to the line of chief mourners and in what manner to take their leave so as to bring that part of the ceremony to a close with dignity and due order.

I believe it was the funeral of Carlos' mother that drew him and me close together, just as his fellow night guard, Akel, and I had already been drawn together by my sharing Akel's sorrow over the death of his new-born child.

And now, almost every night, we meet for a short space of time and commune with one another – though I think Akel and Carlos would show a proper hesitation about using the high-sounding word 'commune'. But that is what really happens when they come up to the roof each night in the course of their guard duties, and often find me walking up and down under the vast night sky of Judaea. Even on a moonless night they are able to pick out my figure in the darkness and greet me, '*Kif halak, doctur?*'

Usually we speak for no more than five or ten minutes, but in that time I seem to learn far more than I generally learn from the seminars of the day just gone. And I dearly hope that I shall never forget what they said last night, each speaking in turn, antiphonally supporting one another:

'Why do men lie to one another, *doctur*?'
'Because they forget about death.'
'There is only one moment when men recognise truth.'
'That is when they stand at the grave-side looking down.'
'Then they walk away.'
'And 20 yards later they forget the truth.'
'They begin to lie again.'

As Akel and Carlos intoned these truths, like two sides of a choir responding to one another, I gazed at their strongly-boned faces silhouetted against the faint lights of Bethlehem and remembered how often I had seen such men as these being treated by Western tourists as though they were uneducated and therefore ignorant. Will the educated never learn that truth only comes through hardship?

❧ *6 December*

Last night I kept being wakened by the noise of the fierce wind that was whistling around these bleak hills. And each time I awoke, I found myself thinking of the Arabs in their tent on the hillside opposite. I have told them so often that they can come and live in Tantur if the weather gets too bad, but Muhanna and his father are very reluctant to do so. I know that some of their reluctance is due to their fear that once they leave their tent empty, it will be interpreted as a sign that they have given up the struggle, and a signal to Shawli and his toughs to take over their land. However, there is another factor at work. Ever since I showed Muhanna the room in Tantur where I thought his father might be comfortable, I have been aware that Muhanna is uneasy; he senses that some members of the Tantur community at all levels are opposed to his father coming to stay in our buildings. One or two of those opponents are frightened that the pilfering from the Institute which they practise might be revealed – as if I didn't know about it! But there are others whose reasons are more despicable.

However, I felt that I had to go up the hill this morning to urge the Arabs to think again about coming in, otherwise I am afraid Salman might die. I was even more afraid when I did go up and I crawled into his tent, because at first I couldn't make out whether what lay on the camp bed was simply a pile of clothes or whether Salman lay hidden amidst them. And when eventually I did discover him and gently roused him, the cries he gave were like the mewing of a helpless kitten before its eyes are yet open. Of course, his eyes, already almost sightless, gave him no light in the darkness of the tent, and so he clung on to my hands with his own hands, still so firm and muscular, while clasping his rosary beads between thumb and forefinger. The old man and I sat together like that for some considerable time, he swaying backwards and forwards slightly as he praised and gave thanks to God, and I trying in the Spirit to stay close to the movement of Salman's spirit.

But then I heard a movement outside the tent and Muhanna appeared, the tough skin of his face and hands seemingly unaffected by the harsh winds. When I went out to speak with him he was as explosive as ever, ready to take on all opponents. He recited for me a list of dignitaries and officials from whom he had in vain sought help, Christian, Jewish, Muslim, to fight his case. As though chanting a litany he intoned of one after another: 'Mayor X say he has no money! Hah!', at which he gave a great roar of contempt; 'King Y! He has no money!' – an even more mirthful roar!

Finally he repeated his litany of contempt, naming each

of the misers and saying after each name, 'He think he is big man. No big man.' He ended by saying decisively, 'No man big . . . only God', and then, in a wonderful flash of afterthought, 'and my father'. Thinking of the bundle of clothes inside the tent, I suspected that Muhanna's afterthought came straight from God himself.

ঙ 10 December

From where inside ourselves do certain words or deeds suddenly erupt? They astonish us just as much as they astonish others.

Today the committee was discussing whether it would be prudent of the Institute to take in our unhoused Arab friends up the hill. The general feeling was that it would be unwise of us to do so, and when the other members were waiting for me to agree I suddenly heard the words, '*Kutum hogia*! Finish! If they wish to come they are welcome.'

And then I realised that it was I who had emitted that authoritative Urdu exclamation which puts an end to any further discussion of the issue. It is, perhaps, 40 years ago since I last used the phrase, since I was a soldier in India, in fact. *Kutum hogia* must have exploded out of the gulf between the suffering of the Arabs and the easy speeches flowing from us, who only yesterday had been standing in chapel piously singing, 'Whatsoever you do to the least of my brethren, that you do unto me'.

ঙ 26 December

What a marvellous evening we had last night, in spite of there not being very many people in the house, and in spite of our not having organised any celebrations! In fact, a capacity for such spontaneous celebration may well be the distinctive sign of an authentic community. And spontaneous it certainly was! We were all sitting around the music room chatting amiably, though in a slightly desultory fashion, when Ed began to play some lively tunes on the piano. The mercurial Sara immediately turned to Simha and said, 'Simha, now we are celebrating Christmas in a Christian community, so you must dance with me'. Since Sara has been unsuccessfully inviting her husband Simha to dance with her for almost 50 years, ever since they arrived in Palestine as Jewish immigrants from Poland, she can hardly have believed that Simha was going to change his tune at this late stage, when they are already both in their seventies. But it is a tribute to Sara's unending zest for life that one could still hear in her voice a note of hope, as if from a teenage girl.

'I will dance with you, Sara', said Simha in his slow, patient manner of speaking – and then, after a pause, he gave her the answer he has been giving to her for decades – 'when there is peace between Jews and Arabs.'

On seeing Sara's exasperation, I took hold of her hand and drew her into the middle of the room. And in no time the two of us were whirling around and across the room in a form of dance invented on the spot. And not only Sara and myself; because for the next half-hour, Alexa and Joseph and Mike and Robin and several others swept around, changing partners and improvising steps as Ed at the piano skilfully interwove tune upon tune. Sara's eyes, always unusually brilliant for a 72-year-old, were like Hallowe'en sparklers by the time we eventually sat down.

After the party I kept thanking God that our first Jewish scholar at Tantur has been Simha. I knew nothing about him three years ago when Richard happened to say to me, 'Simha Flapan is the best man I have ever met in my life', and soon afterwards Raphael independently made virtually the same comment. Believing, as I do, with my Sufi friends, that life does not offer us arguments but signs for which we have to be on the watch, I decided then and there that I was meant to see more of this Simha Flapan. I have since learnt that Simha was brought up in a Polish town as one of the town's very few Jews. His family were not observant but secular and socialist, and he has told me that he never experienced any anti-Semitism there. After immigrating to Palestine in 1930, he became very active in MAPAM (the United Workers Party), working especially for understanding between Jews and Arabs. In 1957, at the prompting of Martin Buber, he founded and edited *New Outlook*, a radical monthly journal devoted to Middle East issues, and so he has been working tirelessly for peace in the Middle East for some 40 years. It amazes us all that in spite of almost daily set-backs, Simha never shows the least trace of becoming down-hearted. He has all the traditional socialist virtues.

For months I had no idea how alien Tantur must have seemed at first to Sara when Simha agreed that they should live here for eight months. Apparently, last August, after they had inspected the apartment allotted to them, they were on the bus back to Tel Aviv when Sara turned to Simha and exclaimed, 'Simha! After all these years, now in my old age you take me to live in a monastery! It is too much!' With much raising of her eyebrows and exclamations of disbelief, Sara told us this story three weeks ago when Dorothy and I were taking coffee in their apartment. What had prompted her to do so was the fact that Father Joe O'Connor, the Jesuit, and Father Hank Beninati, the Maryknoller, had called in for half an hour to say goodbye before they returned to the US. And as they were on the point of leaving, Sara had flung her arms round each of them in turn and given each of them a loving embrace, which they had returned equally warmly.

Once the door had closed behind them, Sara stood for a few seconds as if dumbstruck and then, her eyes seeming to open wider with every word, she said in astonishment, 'I would never have believed it! I come to love Roman Catholic priests and put my arms around them! If you had said that to me six months ago I would have laughed at you and said you must be crazy.' She added, 'This is the best community I have lived in during my life'.

Simha smiled at this but said nothing, though I believe I could guess the phrase that was in his head, a favourite phrase of his: 'As always, Sara, you exaggerate'. For Simha is through and through a political animal, and it is the political insights afforded by his time at Tantur for which he is specially grateful. In particular he says that, for all the years he has spent in Tel Aviv trying to persuade his fellow Jews to understand the Arabs of the West Bank, nevertheless he himself had never appreciated what it must be like to be an Arab on the West Bank until he had spent these months among us. Here he has seen with his own eyes the daily harassment to which Arabs are subjected, and he has heard with his own ears the injustices and miseries which the Arab in the street has to endure – and has heard it not from the lips of intellectuals in conferences but from the lips of ordinary men and women who have little interest in politics. Living here has changed his sense of the situation in a way that could never have happened while he was living in Tel Aviv.

In another respect also he has been changed: much to

his own surprise, he has come to understand and sympathise with those Israeli soldiers who are responsible for order on the West Bank. That happened only a few days ago.

The occasion arose out of my having invited several Israeli officers and soldiers, both male and female, to come and have lunch with us. When Simha and Sara heard that a group of Israeli soldiers would be at lunch with us, I think they were rather shocked at first – as though we were adopting the role of collaborators, like the Vichyite French under the Nazis or the Judenrat in Eastern Europe. In fact, they did say at first that they would not come in to lunch that day. However, when I pointed out to them that as they were almost the only fluent Hebrew speakers in Tantur, they would be in the best position to help me act as a good host, they kindly agreed to come.

And what a revelation that was for them! I placed them next to the two most senior officers at one table, while I engaged the junior members of the party at a different table. Naturally I kept glancing in their direction with some anxiety, but soon I relaxed on seeing that all four of them were talking earnestly and good humouredly – and without pause! So much so that the four of them continued their conversation long after the rest of the community had finished lunch and drifted along to the coffee room.

But eventually the two officers glanced at their watches and suddenly realised how long they had stayed talking. No time for coffee! So up they sprang, quickly collected their forces and bade us all a friendly farewell.

When I took Simha and Sara along to the coffee room they were aglow with gratitude for having had the opportunity to talk so freely and at length with some of the military men responsible for maintaining law and order on the West Bank. They were really astonished to discover what enlightened views these soldiers had on many issues. And they were impressed, above all, by the soldiers' intelligent and sympathetic analysis of the position of the West Bank Arabs. 'They have a much better judgement of the situation', said Simha, 'than the politicians in the Knesset whose orders they have to carry out.' And when he said that, I could not help wondering to myself whether this may not have been the very first opportunity for these two Peace Now activists, Simha and Sara, to have had a really human discussion with military men, a type which they perceive as alien. If so, that is certainly a plus to Tantur's account.

And yet I wonder if any of these incidents with Simha and Sara will remain as vivid before my mind's eye in future years as one which occurred three Sundays ago. The incident sprouted a form of comicality that seems to flourish on theological territory.

For several weeks I had been pestered with schoolmarmish notes from Henry, one of our scholars, who objects to our singing the doxology as the blessing for our Sunday lunch. He considers it very reprehensible that we invoke Father, Son and Holy Spirit when there are Jewish guests present. (Why do so many Americans insist on sending 'memoranda' instead of just coming and having a word with me? It is in every sense a noxious habit because once someone has committed themselves to paper, they then feel they have to stick to it with a stubbornness that would be dissolved in a warm face-to-face discussion. Also, I have to confess that I was a bit irritated at being instructed on Jewish–Christian relations by someone who was not even born when I was already wrestling with the matter.)

In any case, three Sundays ago, no sooner had we all – or almost all! – finished singing the doxology than Henry indignantly rushed across to the table where Simha and Sara were standing and apologised profusely to them for the bad manners of the community in singing the doxology, despite their presence.

Even from a distance, and hemmed in by scholars intent upon their meat roast, I was able to observe Simha's reaction. He was completely nonplussed by Henry's excited address to him. What he does not seem to have known is that Simha is just about as secular as a human being can get – not in a fiercely anti-religious fashion, but in the way of someone for whom words such as 'god' or 'gods' or 'saviour' belong in a foreign language which is used mainly by reactionaries and fanatics – although, it is true, a few of his friends do occasionally use it.

So he gently assured Henry that he and Sara were not in the least offended by the doxology, and were all the time enjoying the opportunity to observe the customs of Christians. All of this he told me afterwards with a little wry smile, leaving me with the impression that, like some field anthropologist, he would be most disappointed if the tribe among whom he was living and whose manners he was studying should in any way truncate their customs out of a mistaken regard for him.

Indeed, he assured me that as a result of living in Tantur, his curiosity about religion had been aroused and he was even thinking that if he had time he might at some future date investigate the Jewish religion to which his ancestors belonged but of which he knows nothing.

❧1985

❧ *1 February*

It was a great blessing to have begun keeping a journal all those years ago. The practice now seems to have become fashionable with people who are 'into spirituality'. And good luck to them and their mentors. Nevertheless I am grateful that I found the way into the habit on my own, spontaneously, which is why I have refrained from reading any instructions concerning the practice, out of fear that I might spoil the spontaneity. What I have found most valuable about it over the years is the way in which a journal gradually reveals the distinctive threads out of which one's own life is meant to be woven. For instance, I was amazed, not long ago, to discover from my very first journal that already, by the age of 15, I was gnawing away at the distinction between a mystery and a problem, and at the need for myth in the attempt to express experience.

And the experience during the past month of having Father Enomiya-Lasalle living here beside us has revealed to me a thread of desire that has been running strongly throughout my life, without my ever having seen its continuity until now. For a seemingly unrelated purpose, I picked up one of my ancient journals and began to peruse it. There, to my astonishment, I noticed how strong and persistent in its pages has been the longing for transparency. And then it dawned on me that it was only in the light of Father Enomiya-Lasalle that I was now seeing the truth of it. That lovely old man came into my life at exactly the right moment. I am not at all sure that I could have received what he has to teach me at an earlier period of my life, and later might have been too late.

Nor was I immediately aware, when we first met, what a profound impression he was to leave upon me. Apart from the fact that I am tired of 'spiritual masters' who jet around the world and frequently land on my doorstep, I had many years ago read Father Enomiya's book, *Zen: The Way to Enlightenment*, and had not felt myself specially enlightened at the end of it. On the other hand, you must be able to learn something from a Catholic of Huguenot ancestry, born in Westphalia, who was wounded as a young soldier in the first world war, became a Jesuit, founded a settlement in the Tokyo slums for the care of the destitute and was within one kilometre of the spot where the first atom bomb dropped on to Hiroshima. Since which date he has become a Japanese citizen, received the freedom of Hiroshima and graduated as a Zen master. Moreover he continues to go round the world at the age of 86, teaching Zen meditation in Spain, Germany, Italy and who knows where else – fulfilling a programme that might kill off a man half his age.

Yet although it only took a few days to realise that there was something very remarkable in this small, slight, boyish-looking, humorous, courteous character who had landed among us, I could not focus on what that something was until the occasion of his lecture three weeks ago, entitled 'The Way of Zen. The Way of Christ'. My dim-wittedness was overcome not by what he said but by just one gesture.

Perched upon the elevated platform in our lecture hall, I introduced him to our learned audience drawn from all quarters of Jerusalem, which included Christian prelates and professors and rabbis of various sorts, as well as one or two Zen *aficionados*. Accordingly, Father Enomiya stood up at the lectern to deliver his lecture; and after talking for a few minutes, commented that one should not make the full lotus position into a *sine qua non* for the practice of meditation. 'All the same', he continued, 'it is well for all of you to know how to take up the position.' Forthwith, before the startled gaze of our audience, this old man of 86 nipped up on to the table at which I was sitting and took up the full lotus position. At this point, from my seat of privilege, gazing down the length of the hall, I saw row upon row of eyes nearly popping out of heads attached to the shoulders of Jerusalem dignitaries who are not accustomed to informality at any time, least of all during an academic lecture.

However, after explaining several points about the full lotus position, Father Enomiya slid down from the table, returned to the lecturn and went on with his lecture as calmly as before.

The striking feature for me of that incident was the completely natural way in which he did what he felt he needed to do. For him it was simple: no embarrassment, no hesitation, no trace of playing to the gallery; in a word, the action of a free man. And since that day, there have been so many similar incidents which I have been observing with growing attention and gratitude.

Just to give one other example. At the dinner table one evening, a scholar was holding forth who knows that Father Enomiya has incurred the severe censure of the pope's favourite theologian, Hans Urs von Balthasar. Von Balthasar maintains that Enomiya is undermining Catholic faith by adopting Zen practices, which carry the taint of Buddhism. Our voluble scholar quoted one particularly critical statement about Enomiya, attributed to von Balthasar, and then turned to Father Enomiya and, in a challenging voice, stated, 'He did say that about you, didn't he, Father Enomiya?' Without any trace of anger, indeed with a little smile, Father Enomiya said, 'Yes, I believe so'. He did not say one word more, but simply got on with his eating. The scholar's question was clearly intended to sow mischief both here and abroad, and the rest of us at table were silently waiting to hear what Father Enomiya was about to say in defence of himself or in criticism of von Balthasar. But he did nothing of the sort. He had answered the question; the matter was now at rest, so he applied himself to eating the grilled fish on his plate with proper Zen concentration and gusto.

Yesterday afternoon the seal was put upon my conviction that we had here a truly transparent human being, when it came to discussing the financial reckoning for his time among us. That could have been very tricky and complicated because of calculating how much of his air fare we should cover (since he was also visiting other institutions in Europe), how much we should pay him for his lecture and how much he owed us for the food and lodging of himself and his companions. In the event, I have never known any such transaction pass more quickly and more smoothly, and to the complete satisfaction of both parties. From which I am inclined to conclude that the ultimate test of transparency – indeed, of spirituality in general – is money; that is, whether we are straight about money.

How often does one encounter people prepared to disclose their political or religious beliefs, their family background, sexual relationships and every other aspect of their lives, but as soon as it comes to their money they shut up like a clam! In so doing, they reveal where their treasure is: 'Where your treasure is, there is your heart also' – in money.

The signs of a transparent human being, therefore, are simplicity and freedom. They only appear in someone when that person gets beyond vanity and beyond fear.

❧ *27 February*

Although it was a burial which has made this day so memorable, nevertheless Ruth's burial was an occasion of joy and, above all, it brought a sense of fulfilment.

We could never have guessed, when we met Ruth and Günther in 1982, that the two of them were going to become so dear to us, nor that I should be called upon to play such a part in the events of today. My first sight of Günther in 1982 was shocking, even somewhat unnerving. At the Rest Centre on Mount Carmel, where we were staying, I could hardly believe that there was life in the skeleton-like figure I saw sitting at the dinner table to which Dorothy and I had been assigned. It was his eyes which first riveted my attention, before I had even noticed the corpse-like pallor of his face and the skull bone that was almost surfacing through the skin: Günther's eyes looked as though they were about to leave their sockets in a spasm of terror. Some unimaginably terrifying experience had left their wild traces upon him. And yet when he began to speak, his voice was reverent and gentle and sure, so that you immediately knew him to be a man who had actually overcome terror and despair.

And so it proved when, over the course of our ever-deepening friendship, we learnt the story of Günther and Ruth.

It was in the days when that sinister black cloud had not yet completely blotted out civilisation in Germany. It was during the year 1934, in Hamburg. Though Ruth was slightly younger than Günther, they were both pupils in the same class at the gymnasium. And one day the two of them arrived late at the door of their classroom – separately, but at the same moment; and both of them were out of breath through having had to hurry. They grinned ruefully at one another and each asked the other whether they should go late into class or slip out of school together and sit in a sunny park nearby to await the next class.

So Günther and Ruth sat in the park telling each other

their stories, as adolescents have done throughout the ages. And from then on they were in love with one another – he an orphan from an artistic Social Democratic family, and she a Jewish girl from one of those cultured German Jewish homes where the members seemed to breathe literature and music and art.

For almost a year they knew the joy of sharing the ecstasy and agony of growing up in that world poised between hope for a new ordering of society and despair at the rising barbarism around them.

And then Ruth's family emigrated to Palestine, settling in the beautiful coastal city of Haifa at the northern limit of the Carmel mountains. There Ruth was cut off from news of Günther, first by the Nazi restrictions and then by the second world war. And there she also drifted into a marriage with a man who proved to be both selfish and cruel. When this man eventually divorced Ruth she was left to care for her two sons, who grew up to be both handsome and clever. Sadly for her, however, the eldest of them was killed in Israel's war of 1967 against the Arab states. And, perhaps even more painful, her brilliant younger son not only quit the country on account of Israel's unbearable chauvinism, but was then seduced into following the false guru, Rajneesh, of Poona in India.

But many times, during the years between, Ruth's heart had turned towards the memory of the young man with whom she had been in love in her girlhood days. She often asked herself what had happened to him, and this question exercised her so insistently that she decided to try to find out: she inserted a notice in a German newspaper asking if anyone could give her news of her old schoolfriend, Günther Lys.

In view of the cataclysm that had overwhelmed Germany 30 years previously, Ruth had not been specially hopeful that her enquiries would bear fruit. But to her delight they did; she managed to contact Günther. And what, in the meantime, had the cataclysm done to him?

Since he was a Social Democrat by conviction, and a pacifist to boot, it was only to be expected that Günther's path in Nazi Germany had proved to be a thorny one. As he later told me, he had always refused to say, '*Heil Hitler!*', commenting humorously that '*Guten Tag* is good enough for anyone'. What precisely happened to him between the outbreak of war in 1939 and Germany's surrender in 1945 we never discussed, beyond the fact that he spent virtually the whole war in concentration camps. From Ruth I further gathered that Günther had been tortured and had been subjected to various medical experiments. Typically the book which he published anonymously concerning his years in the concentration camp is very modest, even undramatic, in the sense that he always seems to be pointing towards certain currents of humanity and wisdom flowing beneath the terrible outer happenings – currents which are deeper and more abiding than the inhumanity. Also he made a film entitled *One Day in a Concentration Camp*, to which he even gave certain humorous touches since, as he once explained to me, 'no matter how terrible a situation may be for human beings, there is always a chance of something happening which they will find humorous'.

Such was the man for whom Ruth sat waiting in the airport at Tel Aviv after 30 years of separation. Her decision to invite this now-unknown figure from her past to come and visit her had provoked scepticism among nearly all her friends. 'As soon as he sees you he will realise the folly of your meeting again', said one of them. 'He will catch the very next plane back to Germany.'

But the wiseacres were proved wrong. For, as Günther told me, 'The moment we saw each other, even after all those years and even though now we were both old, we knew that this was how it should have been always. And ever since, it was wonderful.' From Ruth I learnt that she had said to Günther as they left the airport lounge, 'Here is where we wait for the bus to Haifa'. 'A bus', said Günther. 'Why wait? Let us take a taxi.' 'Oh no!' replied Ruth. 'They are so expensive.' 'So what? We have already wasted too many years of our life. We will take a taxi so that the two of us can be alone.' And so they did; and they sat in the back of the taxi, just the two of them, holding hands, all the way to Ruth's flat in Haifa.

Whenever I have been with Ruth and Günther, I have felt so much at one with them in spite of their 'not being believers', to quote Ruth's own phrase. Once, indeed, she said to me with unquestioning confidence that I would not take it amiss, 'Religion can serve as a crutch for those who do not have Goethe and Beethoven and Mahler'. But, strangely enough, she did turn to me for help when her own heart became more and more broken over the behaviour of her younger son. And, in a sense, she has turned to me again from beyond death.

Last year, on Passover eve, she had yet another of her painful conversations with her son by telephone, after which she put down the phone, turned to Günther and murmured, 'I shall not survive this night'. Nor did she. Her heart was truly broken, and she was dead by morning.

Shortly afterwards Günther was explaining to us that Ruth had left her body to the Hadassah Hospital in Jerusalem for medical research purposes, and that her remains would become available for burial in a year's time. And that, he said, was a cause of concern to him because Ruth had insisted very strongly that she did not want any rabbi to say prayers over her remains when they were being interred – because she could not abide the narrow-mindedness of religious Jews. Moreover she asked him to see that she was laid to rest in a graveyard where Jews and Christians and Muslims and unbelievers could all be buried together. Granted the all-pervading fanaticism of the religious in Israel, how on earth was poor Günther to find such a spot? There was no such spot in Israel, he was sure; and so he asked me if I could find a place where we might bury Ruth's remains in accordance with her last wishes.

In between all my other tasks, I have searched high and low during the past 12 months for a solution to Günther's dilemma, but as this year's Passover drew near without any success, I began to feel rather desperate, envisaging an awful moment when we would collect Ruth's remains but have to stand with them helplessly, having nowhere to lay them to rest. What on earth would we do with them?

By the grace of God, however, almost at the last minute, we found the perfect place – a place that would furthermore symbolise Ruth's desire for all human beings of whatever persuasion to find peace together at the last. And from that discovery onwards, the whole action of burying Ruth's remains worked perfectly, moving through every difficulty with the smoothness of some ancient, well-practised ritual, from the moment yesterday when I asked the help of Yakoub and Abu Jihad until the end of the funeral meal in our apartment, where we all warmed our chilled bones with whiskey.

I needed Yakoub, my Christian friend, and Abu Jihad, my Muslim friend, to help me to prepare the grave because the weather had been stormy and bitterly cold, and the bottom of the grave was deep in water. They are strong fellows and know how to handle picks and shovels, how to deal with such eventualities. And I found it deeply moving to see how readily they responded to my request for help. Their immediate unspoken understanding of the occasion reminded me of the words spoken at the Introit for the Mass: 'I will go to the altar of God'. It was just as though my Arab friends were Mass servers, responding by declaring their readiness also to go to the altar of God.

Abu Jihad, in particular, without any fuss, conveyed by his every gesture a profound sense of the liturgical needs of the occasion. It may seem contrived for me so to describe his response, since Abu Jihad and I would on the surface appear to have little in common. Driven from his native village by Jews over 30 years ago into a refugee camp, he still lives in that same camp where he has brought up 14 children. Many of his children work abroad, some as doctors. The ones that I know are a credit both to him and to the straight path of Islam. But Abu Jihad and I have been greeting one another each morning for several years now in a liturgical fashion: '*Sabah el kher, ya sheekh*', '*Sabah e nur, doktur. Kif halak?*' '*Mabsut el hamdo' l' illah. Kif inte?*' '*Ana mabsut, nushkur Allah.*' ('Morning good, O sheikh', 'Morning of light, doctor. How are you?' 'I am well, glory to God. And you?' 'I also am well, thanks be to God.') We never say more; nor could we, because my knowledge of Arabic is as scant as his knowledge of English. But from those few economical words, repeated each morning, an understanding has arisen between us, a respect for each other's dignity grounded in our reverence for God.

Hence there was no ill ease or hesitation between us after we had eventually made our way over the soggy, clay ground to the grave and Abu Jihad for a moment assumed a hierarchical role superior to my own. With the confidence and assurance of an experienced priest of burials, he jumped down into the grave in order to place stones in position so as to raise the coffin above the water. And from down in the depths he controlled the labours of the rest of us like a priest shepherding altar boys. As he stood there in his rough clothes and gum boots, I thought of the Jewish saying, 'I learnt holiness from the very limbs of my teacher'.

Once his handiwork was done, and after I had spoken appropriate words, Abu Jihad gracefully withdrew, once more into a minor hierarchical role. Standing by my side and looking down in the heaped grave, he said in a low voice, almost whispering, 'That is the way of all human beings, doctor, the way of us all'.

But what were the 'appropriate words'? On the previous occasion – when I conducted funeral prayers for Mary Rudolf in Santa Cruz – at least Mary and her friends were in some sense believers, and so it had been possible for me to fulfil the priestly role: that is, to speak to God on behalf of the mourners and to the mourners on behalf of God. But now, out of loyalty to Ruth's wishes, I could not do the same. Instead, I addressed Ruth as one still living among us. At first, when I pronounced her name boldly and directly, I sensed a tremor run through those gathered around her coffin, as though they had not expected her to be present. But almost immediately it seemed perfectly natural, both to them and to me, that we should be thanking Ruth for her life of goodness and loving-kindness.

As we were slowly picking our way through the mud, out of the cemetery, Günther gently took my arm and, his eyes wider than ever, said in his hoarse voice, 'Every word you spoke, Donald, seemed to come out of my own heart'.

ৰু *16 March*

Once more, having spent a lifetime trying to explain matters by way of words, I discover that it is the events of life itself, rather than words, that lead to clarification. I am thinking of recent events surrounding our Shepherd's Hut. They have done more to illuminate for me an aspect of a certain Protestant mentality than all the books on Protestantism that I have studied or the lectures I have listened to.

What set off the train of events was the impending departure over a year ago of our librarian, Brother Bartomeu, as a result of which I had to search for someone to replace him. Since we needed someone with linguistic and theological skills similar to Bartomeu's, the search proved difficult and even began to seem hopeless until Father Peter mentioned the name of Brother Gabriel.

Brother Gabriel was a most learned Frenchman, a Jesuit of Jewish extraction, who had received permission from his superiors to pursue the hermit life out in the Judaean desert, in the remote wadi of Ein Fara. According to my friend, Father Peter, he was an excellent librarian and Peter suggested that he might be willing to come and direct our Institute library if only we could set up a hermitage for him within our grounds. At first that sounded to be a way-out idea, until I suddenly thought of our Shepherd's Hut. Although the Hut (actually a stone structure) was at that time almost buried in a blanket of nettles and looked as though it was scarcely more than a heap of rubble, I decided at least to examine it and give the old building a chance of renewed life.

When I did so one morning of bright wintery sunshine, it was as if the Shepherd's Hut itself responded and opened itself up to me to reveal its beauty. I noticed for the first time how snugly it rested in a quiet corner of our grounds, hidden so deeply, both by the folds of the land and by the olive trees, that some scholars have been known to spend a whole year in the Institute without ever discovering its existence. Its stonework blends comfortably into the rocky ground about it, and its proportions are so harmonious as to set one into an attitude of prayer the moment one enters. Standing outside, you look directly across the Judaean desert towards the mountains of Moab in the far distance, while once inside, the play of light and shade from the windows induces a feeling of being safe and at peace. Further, towards the rear of the hut, almost invisible, there are a few steps leading down to a cave, in themselves an invitation to penetrate even deeper through the heart of the cave into the cave of one's own heart. With its earthen floor so beautifully dry and its thick walls to protect one from the rain, the wind and the burning sun, our Shepherd's Hut was itself waiting to be adopted as a place of prayer.

And that is how I described it in the letter I sent to Brother Gabriel offering him the Shepherds's Hut as his hermitage if he would agree to come and serve as our librarian. But he never received my message. Two days after I had dispatched the letter, the dear man's body was discovered at the base of the cliffs in Ein Fara, directly below the cave on the cliff face which had served as his hermitage. Apparently he had slipped and fallen to his death.

Saddened as I was at the news of the good man's death, my thoughts scarcely ever turned again towards the Shepherd's Hut until one bright, sunny winter's morning when my path took me near it and my heart was suddenly moved, almost as though Brother Gabriel were touching me in order to tell me something. Straightaway I realised that, as an act of *pietas* towards him, I was being called to restore the Shepherd's Hut: it was meant to become a place set apart for silence and meditation and prayer. I straightaway shared my vision for the hut with my colleague Tony, our administrator, who in no time was working out the details of our project.

Confirmation of the vision's authenticity was given to us soon afterwards by the four young Muslim workmen to whom we entrusted the work of restoration. Without words, intuitively, they caught on to the vision we had of the Hut's purpose. All those four workmen live in the wretched Deheishe refugee camp nearby, and yet, in spite of the squalor in the camp, and the continual harassment they have to endure from Jewish soldiers, those young men remain unbowed. And they undertook the work with a sensitivity and respect for what they were about. During the months that followed they were always ready to listen intelligently to our proposals for the interior fashioning of the hut, and they would often put forward suggestions of their own, which almost always proved to be just what was needed. And all these exchanges they carried out with the quiet dignity of men who have been formed with a sense for the sacred.

So it did my heart good to see the bright gladness in their eyes when I thanked them and congratulated them on having worked so hard that the hut was all finished and beautifully appointed by 20 February, Ash Wednesday. That was the day we had chosen to celebrate the inauguration of the Hut.

And how powerful was that experience of Ash Wednesday! A little before 8 p.m., in the darkness of the night, we picked our way over the rocky ground south of our main building, stumbling along, holding on to one another, in the direction of the Shepherd's Hut. By the light of our torches, we managed to carry safely all the equipment needed for the Eucharist and the distribution of the ashes. For a good part of the way we also carried Jill, who suffers from multiple sclerosis. And perhaps it was the carrying of Jill which released the current of healing that palpably flowed through the whole community during the subsequent hours. Whatever may be the explanation, everyone present sensed the sacredness and solemnity of that moment when the Shepherd's Hut was being consecrated to a new life in the light of the still flames of the candles, as Lloyd celebrated the Eucharist according to the Anglican rite, and as the Roman Catholic priests then passed around reverently from one to another of the faithful who were standing with bowed heads, and signed them on their foreheads with the cross of ashes. It was enough to move you to tears to hear the quiet responses of everyone as they were asked to remember in their prayers those who had contributed to the blessedness of this special moment in this special place: among them the shepherds who for 200 years had sheltered here; Brother Gabriel, whose death was the inspiration for our restoration; and our Muslim brothers from Deheishe whose skilful workmanship was even then being highlighted by the radiance from the candles.

In all the years I have lived here, I have never known a moment of such healing as the one we experienced on the night of Ash Wednesday.

Yet now I hear that, after I leave Tantur, the Shepherd's Hut is to be made available for a commercial re-enactment of the Last Supper.

I was stunned when rumours of these plans came to my ears, but now I have come round to seeing them as a sign of a great gulf between an extreme Protestant view of the world and the Catholic or Orthodox view. For the former, the sacred is not that which in Hebrew is described as *kadosh*, set apart, the sign among Jews of holiness. There is little stress upon the fact that, in the order of the sacred, there are places set apart for the glory of God; that there are times set apart for special prayers; and that there are people set apart for special service – vessels set apart, vestments set apart, signs of the sacred.

Likewise there are special blessings for places, times and people, as we know from the woman who is blessed among women; for, as David Jones sang, 'She that loves place, time, demarcation, hearth, kin, enclosure, site, differentiated cult, though she is but one mother of us all: one earth brings us all forth, one womb receives us all, yet to each she is other, named of some other'. And in a further poem David gives voice to his fear that these special places might be reduced

> to a common level
> till everything presuming difference
> and all the sweet remembered demarcations
> wither
> to the touch of us
> and know the fact of empire.

↪ *17 March*

Often one recognises one's priorities not by sitting down and working them out but by reflecting on one's behaviour and, through reflection, coming to recognise one's priorities. An instance of that process was the way in which Dorothy and I tried to make sure that all the official farewell ceremonies of today were not going to prevent us from saying goodbye properly to Salman Arab. Immediately after an early breakfast, we went up the hill to the exposed spot where in his tent he has endured all the fierce rainstorms, gales, snow and cold of this winter.

As we approached his tent we were greeted by several rounds of loud, staccato barking on the part of the dog which he has recently acquired. But the dog quietened down; and having made our way through the rubble to the tent, we peered inside. We saw that he was not lying huddled on his camp bed as he has been doing throughout the whole of the winter. He was not there, and the tent seemed ominously empty. For a moment a sharp fear came over me that perhaps he had been taken ill and had gone to hospital, or even that he had died during the last few days. But then I glanced around the hill-top and saw him, about 20 yards distant. In his blindness and deafness unaware of our presence, he was crouching beside a rock, defecating. Hanging down, clearly outlined against the white rock, I could see the old man's genitals. In his nakedness and vulnerability he stood for me as a symbol of the frail creatures that we human beings are. I was reminded of the words spoken to Edgar by King Lear on the heath, the night of the storm: 'Unaccomodated man is no more but such a poor, bare, forked animal as thou art'.

And yet, after we had waited quietly for him to finish cleaning himself and I went over to him to take him by the arm and lead him back to his tent, and he realised who we were, I, in turn, realised that Shakespeare's troubled humanism shatters on the rock of Islam. The old man has never lost his dignity throughout all his trials. Not for a moment has there been even the slightest hint from him of a plea for pity. And when the moment came for us to say our final goodbye, he blessed us with complete composure, assuring us that the recording angel had quite literally written down every kindness that we had done towards him.

As we walked away from the dear old man, to whom I now felt so close, I could not help asking myself a question that went through me like a sword: how many of us on the hill opposite, in the Institute of Tantur, who talk day in and day out about God and spirituality, have enough faith to have endured what he has endured, without bitterness or animosity or any questioning of the will of God?

❧ *19 March*

On the flight from Tel Aviv to Manchester

Although we have now gone through it so many times, we still find ourselves bewildered and emotionally drained by the whole process of bidding farewell to a place where we have lived very intensely among others also living intensely, and where we have made deep friendships not only with individuals but also with the peoples who dwell in the land and, indeed, with the landscape itself.

Sitting here in the plane, recollecting the appreciation and love which has been shown towards us during these weeks of farewell, there are two occasions which keep presenting themselves before my mind's eye. The first was at the Rainbow Group two weeks ago. Before the evening's programme of this Jewish–Christian group began, the chairman, my friend Rabbi Jack Cohen, surprised me by asking me to stand up so that he could wish me well on behalf of the Rainbow. Having done so very warmly, he came over to me and presented me with two Israeli coins. One of them, he explained, was to help me on my journey outwards; and I was to be allowed, according to the traditional custom, to spend it. The other I was to keep to sustain me when I returned to Israel. It symbolises the heartfelt desire of the members of the Rainbow Group that I should one day come back to the land. Only a brief ritual, one may think – even trivial – but I found it moving and meaningful.

The second occasion was more emotional, as befits an Arab happening. It took place last Saturday morning.

Without any need to discuss the matter, Dorothy and I and our Arab staff decided independently that we and they wanted to bid each other farewell on our own, just the Arabs and ourselves, with no Americans or Europeans present.

The Arabs of this district, even after all the centuries of foreign incursions and the floods of tourists, still retain an instinct for how to conduct themselves according to the occasion. In other words, they have maintained a culture, in contrast to representatives of modern secularised cities who do not know how to behave. On Saturday morning this meant that all of them, cooks, handymen, receptionists and office workers, were sitting around our music room waiting to greet us in what I can only describe as a hierarchical fashion. The order in which they were sitting, and the manner in which they held themselves, were reminiscent of the somewhat solemn attitudes adopted in church. One knew, without having to be told, which of them would take the lead in making a speech, who would translate, and who would make the presentation of whatever lay within the large parcel resting on a side table.

Since I knew that I would be expected to say more than a few words on such an occasion, this solemn atmosphere constituted a slight problem for me: how could I speak in a dignified fashion while at the same time lightening the atmosphere which threatened to become oppressive? I thought I had solved the problem reasonably well with a few humorous reminiscences that I made towards the end of my ten-minute response to Issa's address – until the very last sentence, when I turned towards Dorothy to ask her to say a word of gratitude.

That did it! The cheerful smile on my face vanished when I looked into Dorothy's face; her eyes were filled with tears and her voice was choking as she began to express her affection for all of them. She had hardly got a sentence out before she was unmistakably weeping; and that set me off, and many of the Arabs present also began to weep.

In a way it was marvellous, a truly Arab occasion with plenty of speeches and many demonstrations of emotion leading to a welcome catharsis, finishing up with everyone sitting around, restored to cheerfulness, unashamedly tucking into the coffee and the mountains of cake.

ঙ্গ *6 April*

Letter to the **Tablet** (*written in early March*)

Dear Friend,

Here it is now night on the Mount of Olives, where I have come as the most propitious place from which to respond to your request that I should send you a final letter on the eve of my departure from the Holy City. I have chosen to come here because this Mount of Olives has never ceased to be a place of mystery for me. So I wanted to discover if I could somehow penetrate into its mystery by remaining here alone in the silence and the darkness, peering over the Kidron Valley towards the Old City of Jerusalem. Because I knew before – and know even more forcibly now – that the mystery of this place is the mystery of Jesus, the man with whom humankind can never come to terms.

For no matter how many times or in how many ways humankind may strive to capture Jesus, whether in words or painting or music or any other mode, he always escapes. The gospel says about Jesus's home-town crowd's attempt to fling him over the cliff: 'But passing through the midst of them he went away' – and still to this day he cannot be grasped, although now he will never go away. Of course, there are many people who wish he would. Some of them have written learned books to show that he never even existed; others have written equally learned books to prove that he was no more than a Galilean rabbi; yet others have tried to reduce him to the rank of a mere prophet. But it is no good. After all those words and all those arguments and definitive statements, this ever more mysterious Jesus remains, gazing steadily at each one of us.

And I know of no place where that steady gaze is more inescapable than at the altar within what the Roman Catholics call the Holy Sepulchre, and what the Orthodox more truthfully name 'the Life-giving Tomb'. Over that altar there is set an icon surrounded by a metal casing. And perhaps it is from the metal casing that the unflinching eyes of Jesus catch a certain glint of sternness, as if to remind us that this man is not to be trifled with. Having seen it all, yet he did not flinch. Those eyes are saying, 'Behold, man! Now you know what it takes to be a man.'

And here, on the Mount of Olives looking down upon Gethsemane, you can more readily envisage what it took in those

223

days to be a real man in the earthiest sense. I am sure you remember, dear friend, the day that we stood here and pondered together on the nitty-gritty details of those days after Palm Sunday, when Jesus lived on this very patch of the hill where we were then standing. His feet must have been bruised, for you cannot walk through the Judaean desert barefoot or in sandals without constantly striking your feet against rocks and stones and pebbles. Probably his skin was cracked; and likely enough he had fleas on him from riding the donkey. He and his disciples had sweated on the long pull up from Jericho; they must have all smelt of dried sweat, since there were no showers in those days and no daily changes of clothes. And we asked ourselves, how did they manage to clean themselves after emptying their bowels, since toilet paper and water closets were not yet invented? In the way still favoured by the Bedouin?

People who live at a distance from the Mount of Olives may hold such considerations to be irrelevant. But they are far from irrelevant if you wish to stand in the sandals and enter into the mind of the man Jesus, this northern provincial of Galilean accent, as he sat on the Mount of Olives and gazed across at that sky-scraping Temple, which was not only the centre of bloody sacrifice in the name of religion but was also the treasury, the centre of money-power, and of Israel's men of learning. And hard by, in uneasy alliance, stood that terrifying symbol of military power, the Antonia fortress of the occupying Romans.

As he looked across the Kidron Valley towards all that concentration of power – religious, financial, intellectual, political, military – the man from Galilee must have wondered sometimes whether he had gone clean out of his mind to confront such a concentration and take it upon himself, by Spirit alone, to destroy every part of its edifice even to the foundations, so that for all ages there would remain of it not one stone upon a stone. And most agonising of all, he would have to do it alone. Because he, who knew what was in men's hearts, knew that his own disciples would desert him and deny him, and that he would die transfixed between earth and heaven, seemingly rejected by both men and God. No wonder that he trembled, and shook so much that, despite the cold night air, his sweat fell upon the ground like great drops of blood.

These are some of the thoughts which for the hundredth time went through my mind yesterday as I sat on a wall reading the Gospel narratives of the Passion. The sun was warm, but underneath, as so often in these harsh Judaean hills, there blew a chill wind from the north, really biting. So not surprisingly there happened what constantly happens in this land as one reads the Scriptures: the meaning of the words seemed to stand up from the page and strike me between the eyes, like a blow from the fist of a heavy-handed labourer, leaving its meaning ringing in my skull.

For the Passion narratives are extremely primitive, all about money, bread and blood, about hunger and thirst. Just read them again, thinking of what I say and you will discover, even in your London flat, that what I say is true. Think, for example, of the widow's mite, the ejection of the money-changers, the price of the jar of alabaster, the purse kept by Judas, the 30 pieces of silver. 'Money and blood', I thought to myself yesterday, after I noticed a rivulet of blood running in the gutter at the side of the road as I was walking back from the Mount to Bethphage. Looking to discover where the blood came from, I saw a group of children gathered in a garage around a man who had just slaughtered a sheep which he held in his left hand, while with his right hand he brandished a large knife. The man was sacrificing a sheep because his new house was now finished, and the next day his son was to marry and bring in his new bride. Once the blood was outpoured, God would not begrudge him his wealth and his houses, so the man thought.

As for thirst, the Judaean desert impressed the deeper meaning of that upon me once more two days ago. Not long after sunrise, I set off to walk through the desert on my own and I spent the whole day alone until sunset. The only people I spoke to were two Bedouin shepherds whom I came upon at midday. They invited me to share their wonderfully refreshing sugary tea which they had boiled between some stones. Soon afterwards I ran out of water. And as I clambered up and down the wadis in the burning sun, I could feel my whole body becoming dried up and withered. For the last two or three hours of the day, my mouth was completely parched and I could think of nothing except water. Then I found a piece of orange peel which I gratefully chewed. What I experienced for an hour or two is everyday life for millions of our fellow creatures.

As for bread and hunger, they are symbolised for me in this land by the Musrara. The Musrara you may remember as that open space between the rather splendid hostel of Notre Dame and Nablus Road. It is there that crowds of workless Arab men gather each day at first light, in the hope that someone will hire them and enable them to put bread into their own mouths and into the mouths of their wives and children or of their aged mothers and fathers.

On no single occasion nowadays do I travel through the Musrara without thinking of Jesus' parable of those labourers who were standing idle in the market-place because no one had hired them. Often it is not at the eleventh hour but after midday that I go past them all; and by that time certain of them, both young and old, are sitting silently on their haunches by the roadside. From their eyes you can see that they have now abandoned hope of work and bread for the day. I remember with special vividness one day when we swept past them in the Institute car, on our way to a full-dress occasion in the Anglican cathedral – the consecration of a new bishop. And throughout the beautiful liturgy in the cathedral, my spirit was unceasingly troubled by the thought that before coming to seek his presence in the cathedral, Jesus had meant us to seek his presence among the poor men whom no one had hired.

Knowing that here I am simply echoing the feelings expressed by Mary, the mother of Jesus, in her prophetic Magnificat, I am led to tell you that what my sojourn in this land has changed as much as anything else is my image of Mary. In previous years, that could hardly have been any other than what I have received through Piero della Francesca's paintings or Gerard Manley Hopkins' poems or Gounod's music – the image of some dreamy, ethereal young lady, untouched by everyday toil.

But since that time I have met the peasant women of Galilee. So now the image that comes spontaneously to my mind is of a woman with strong hands, sinewy through much work; and of a face whose skin is rough from exposure to the sun and the wind; of feet that are broad-spread through climbing the hills around Nazareth barefoot; but above all, of eyes that are steady and a mouth that is firm through enduring the sorrows of the refugee, the poor and the oppressed.

On reading the above, my good friend, I can see you frowning and asking yourself whether my stress upon the earthiness of Mary and of Jesus may not be leading me – and not for the first time – to ignore the heavenliness of Jesus. But do not

226

fear. I realise more each day that the hidden and secret wisdom which we have received is about what no eye has seen nor ear heard nor the heart of man conceived, and that if we are to penetrate ever deeper into the deep things of God we have to be led by the Holy Spirit. It is simply that, through contact with this land, we learn that we can only search everything, even the deep things of God, once we allow everything in our own lives – and indeed the lives of all creatures – to be measured by the mystery of this man Jesus.

How truly he is the mystery at the heart of all mysteries burst upon me three weeks ago beside the Sea of Galilee. The weather at the time was stormier and colder in Tiberias than has been known for a generation. The waves on the sea itself were sweeping in violently and crashing over the promenade as we struggled against the fierce wind towards the little church of St Peter. Once inside, we found a haphazard congregation numbering no more than seven or eight persons. The priest, seemingly of Eastern origin, made his way painfully through the rite of Mass in a mixture of Latin, pidgin English and what seemed like broken Italian. Everything pointed to a most unpropitious occasion.

Then came a moment of truth, when the priest raised the host at the elevation. 'This is my body.' In an instant I realised with complete conviction that the body being raised was the same body who had indeed sailed the sea just outside nearly 2000 years ago; who had calmed that same sea one night when it had been stormy as now. He is the body whom we can only come to know through the sufferings of our own body, through attending to the sufferings of other bodies, and through sharing bread. That is why the man Jesus will for ever remain the mystery of mysteries whom nobody can fathom.

Peace and love, Donald.

The Testing of Hearts

An ancient Irish prayer

Mo theora ucse forsin Eig
intan noscairiub frim chri:
nimraib dorat i coibsi,
nimraib nama,
nimraib ni.

(Three wishes I ask of the King
when I shall part from my body:
may I have nothing to confess,
may I have no enemy,
may I have nothing.)

III.

Testing unto Death

1996–1997

·Ҽ 1996

[This final part consists of two sections. The first section was recorded by Donald on tape in August and September 1996. While this was done over a period, he listened to it as a whole and lent it to family and close friends. It ends with the passage on gratitude. This is followed by genuine 'jottings', written by him in far briefer form in a notebook from October to March 1997. A. H.]

·Ҽ August–September

When Dorothy and I spoke this morning to Mr Deakin, the consultant, we talked about the decisions that we wanted to make about my not having chemotherapy and being allowed to die at home. I was very pleased when he said: 'Well, if I were in your position I should do exactly as you are doing'. In the meantime Dorothy had suggested that I record one or two reflections that I had been sharing with her in the last few days. They are not, in one sense, intimate reflections – but they are reflections that perhaps might help someone else who is in the position that I am in now.

I have to go back a bit and say that when I was pretty sure that there was something very seriously wrong with me, I began to think about the first occasion in my life that I became much concerned with death. I was about 15, and I was reading the life of St Thomas More, a biography written by R. W. Chambers. I read that, when More was being tried and was under threat of execution, the man who was questioning him, Lord Rich, said to him: 'Well, look, you know that if you won't take an oath to the king, then you are going to have to leave behind your lovely home in Chelsea and your wife and your children, and it's only a question of taking an oath, otherwise, well, you will die'. And More replied: 'Well then, I die today, my Lord, and you will die tomorrow'.*

* More actually said these words to the Duke of Norfolk (R. W. Chambers, *Thomas More*, Fernhill (1973), p. 300).

That seemed to me to be a wonderful response, a controlled response and calm.

Of course, the other martyr in that year, along with More, was St John Fisher, who always has one strike in his favour since he's a Yorkshireman. On the morning of his execution, he was dressing and he asked the Lieutenant of the Tower to hand him his furred tippet – a little cloak – and the guard, who had obviously rather fallen in love with Fisher, said: 'Well, my Lord, you are not going to need that much longer', and Fisher said to him: 'So long as God gives me my health, I intend to preserve it'. Again, such a common-sense, and yet very saintly, answer.

A word of Muhammad occurs to me which has come into my mind quite a lot lately. Muhammad said: 'You must die before you die', meaning that, at least to some extent, we have to go through a kind of process of dying while in this life if we are going to live life properly, because then we are living it with the recognition that we are all going to die.

The next period when I became particularly exercised by this business of what we do with our lives was after the war, when I went to Germany. What struck me most about that time was the number of people in the German resistance movement who had been so calm in face of execution by Hitler. People like von Moltke, Alfred Delp SJ, Bonhoeffer – all those wonderful people. We have a volume, *Dying we Live* (Harvill Press, 1956), in which many of their last letters are collected, and they are witnesses to the triumph of the spirit.

This awareness of the spirit as triumphant in the face of death was enhanced for me when I translated the life of Edith Stein, the Jewish philosopher who became a Carmelite and who died in Auschwitz. The book records the way in which she encouraged the other people who were in the train that was taking them to Auschwitz, and has a lovely photograph of her. Looking out of the photograph is her face with these beautiful, beautiful eyes, as though they have seen further than almost any human being has seen. Often it's the eyes that count so much, a gaze: that's why I have around me now photographs of so many holy people who have accompanied me on my journey through life – like the Hindu sage, Ramana Maharshi, who has the most beautiful expression on his face.

When I start thinking about the relationship between spirit and matter, I realise that matter is secondary to spirit – that is to say, it is spirit which creates matter in the first place, matter is not self-creating. I am reminded of the observation of the Native Americans who once said to some Westerners: 'Of course, nature is an invention of you Westerners; where you see nature, we see spirit at work'. And as you look at the story of creation, as I've written about it in my article 'The ascent of love',* you can see that the created universe, the universe of matter, is a risk taken by the Spirit, the Spirit of God creating this universe, of which J. B. S. Haldane, the biologist, said: 'Not only is the universe more mysterious than we imagine, it is more mysterious than we could possibly ever imagine'. And in every act of creation there is a risk that things will go wrong, and obviously they have gone wrong in some respects in the universe.

The way I see it, the only way in which the risk involved in creation can be put right is through an initiative on the part of the Creator of the first spirit, and this is what our traditional religion teaches us – that somehow or other the one who took the risk has now to redeem the situation, and so the Holy Spirit breathes spirit into human beings. But of course for animals like ourselves, even though we are inspirited, so to speak, it is extraordinarily demanding to live at the level of the spirit. Very few human beings have so far managed it, and they are the witnesses. The Greek word *martos*, martyr, means witness to the spirit.

The difficulty was emphasised by Simone Weil when she said: 'Concentration is the essence of prayer'. And you have to live in a very concentrated way if you are to live at the level of the spirit. She went on to say: 'Distraction is the root of sin'. Which is a bit harsh, I think, but I know what she means: that the world as we have it today is a world given to distraction, because people do not want to face up to the demands of living at the level of the spirit. Many people try to do so, and try to help others to do so who are not quite up to it, but lately I have come across a prayer by a man who is Spirit-filled. He is another Jew, Martin Israel – a South African Jew who became a Christian. And here is a prayer which I have found very helpful in recent days:

> Let the healing grace of your love, O Lord, so transform me that I may play my part in the transfiguration of the world from a place of suffering, death and corruption to a realm of infinite light, joy and love. Make me so obedient to your

* In *The Beatitude of Truth*, Darton, Longman and Todd (1997), pp. 135–9.

Spirit that my life may become a living prayer and a witness
to your unfailing presence.

Martin Israel's use of the word 'presence' there reminds me of a
reflection which has been intriguing me for the last few days. And
that is about thought or thinking. About 50 years ago, I overheard
a Jungian psychologist who didn't know I was within hearing,
saying: 'I am sorry for that tall young man; he thinks too much'.
I was a bit put out when I heard this remark, thinking to myself,
well, you can't think too much. But I have now come to see that
you can, and that thinking is a sign of imperfection. I don't mean
to say that one doesn't have to think, but it is a sign of imperfection; for if you know, you don't have to think.

Similarly, for example, if you are in the presence of the
loved one, the presence of beauty, you don't have to construct
thoughts about beauty or about the loved one: you just have to
gaze. It's like when you are listening to music: you don't keep
thinking, you lose yourself in the music. In fact, it would be absurd,
wouldn't it, to meet the beloved whom you have been wanting to
meet for ages, and when you get there you read out to her or
to him the thoughts about him or her that you have been having?

That shows the absurdity of imagining that thought is the
last thing. Presence, total presence of one to another, is what is
ultimate, so there comes a time when, having come into the presence, you have to stop thinking, otherwise you lose the awareness
of the other. Isn't it true that sometimes one person doesn't even
notice another person because of being preoccupied with his or
her own thoughts?

I imagine that one reason why I've been *thinking* along
these lines is that, in my present situation, thinking is not all that
great a help. What is helpful is the presence of others, obviously
one's intimate loved ones, but also the pictures of Father Anthony
Ross, St Seraphim, Edith Stein, Ramani Maharshi. It is the icons,
the images, that are most helpful: the immediate awareness. You
don't have to be grubbing around in your thoughts for some kind
of consolation, help, support. Like that marvellous Father Jenko
who was a hostage in Beirut and seems to have behaved absolutely
wonderfully; and then last winter he had cancer, and his obituary
said how he showed everyone, not intending to, but by second
nature by this time, how to die at peace and with dignity.

I want to record something out of my native West Riding.

You would hear people say when they met: 'Hast ya baan?', which is the same as '*comment allez-vous*?', of course. And the answer would sometimes be: 'I'm nobbut just keeping band in't nick'. This image is derived from the weaving-shed, when you had to make sure that the band going round the pulleys remained in the nick, for if it came out, then the whole machine would stop and be wrecked.

And I find this is true of my days now; that what is crucial for me is that I must keep band in't nick. I mean, I must be centred at all times, in a state of what the New Testament calls a state of unceasing prayer. Not allowing emotions to throw me off balance, otherwise I'll finish up like one of the weaving machines when band has fallen out o'nick.

There is one further image I would like to record, and that is that when the consultant said to me on Monday that he wouldn't be needing to see me any more, I could just go home, and so on, there came into my mind the thought – well, now my sails are set for the journey home. And I remembered Jesus' words as a farewell to the disciples, when he said: 'I go to prepare a place for you'.

And that's what going home means: you go to the place that is prepared for you. And I am also hoping that, in some measure, if you are a follower of Jesus, you can also do something which he does, that is to say, prepare a place for your loved ones who are going to follow after. Going home means also preparing a place for others to come when their time arrives.

But there is no possibility of our finding a home, we are lost, lost in the universe, unless we have the faith that the universe is not a hostile place to us, is not in the last resort hostile to us. On the contrary, the centre of the universe is a loving heart, and we are responses to that creative, loving heart. Which means that the last word is not with corruption and death and nothingness, but with love, just as the first word of creation is love. If we have that faith, we can then trust ourselves, with our bodies and our spirits, to the universe, to the centre of the universe, to the heart of the universe.

That's not to deny, of course, that there are terrible things that happen in the universe. It's inevitable in any act of creation, especially the act of creating life, that there will be a risk. Life means vulnerability, whether through injury or death, anguish or tragedy, and all those kind of things. I remember some years ago – about 20 years ago, I think it was – when I was being tested to see whether I had cancer and, there was a discussion of whether they would find that it was benign or malignant. And I remember saying at the time, I would not describe any cancer which was to afflict me as malignant because this gives the impression that somehow there is a malign force in the universe which is attacking me.

On the contrary, any kind of thing that goes wrong is a sign that there is something deeply wrong with what has happened with our life on earth, and all life on earth, and in the human family. So I think of the cancer which is in me at the moment as part of that whole risk which is inseparable from life, and that part of my job is to accept all that that involves, and in some ways that it is part of a process of joining my suffering with the suffering of people throughout the earth; and if we accept it in that way, instead of its being malign there can be a redemptive quality about it.

There's a wonderful word from Paul Claudel who said that Jesus did not come in order to explain suffering but in order to fill it with his presence. And years ago, I remember, especially when I was in depression, I felt that I could somehow or other join in the business of redeeming the evil in the world by accepting whatever suffering was being sent to me at that time, as my contribution to the whole business of redemption.

And not until this very moment have I realised that when I came out of that depression, I began to do something which I think has helped me and the telling of which might help other people. I began to plan to write a book of gratitude for all the communities which had nurtured me throughout my life: our little family to begin with, and the village and the school and the Church and the university and the army, and so on. And I've dictated something like 16 hours on to cassettes about this, but unfortunately I am not able to complete it; and I have never actually arrived at the point of talking about the gratitude which I feel towards Dorothy and our beloved children who have taught me so much, and are absolutely the most wonderful children.

But one of the interesting consequences of doing that talk on to cassettes, talking all the time about my gratitude towards these different communities and people who have nurtured me in my life, is that I feel now such gratitude for the whole of my life; and although I can remember, if I try very hard, bad things that people have done to me and unfair things that people have said about me, and so on, I don't spontaneously remember them – and even when I try, the sting of the bitterness has gone out of it.

It's a bit like trying to see the shapes in a faded old photograph, because I am so filled with gratitude there isn't room for bitterness or recrimination or anything like that. In fact, I am reminded of the remark of Tyutchev, one of the two or three greatest Russian poets, who once said that gratitude is the purest form of love. It may not be the highest form of love, but it's the purest. Why? Because when you are full of gratitude, there isn't room for anything else: there isn't room for recrimination, and desire for revenge, and things like that.

So, in a sense, that depression which went on for four or five months or whatever – I wouldn't wish it on anyone, but in fact I think it contributed to my impulse to record my gratitude and that has in a way transformed my life, in the way I look back at my life. I am so full of gratitude.

☙ *October*

The thoughts of a serene man are themselves prayers.

'Jesus' is the word . . . Word through which . . . whom . . . we are called to enter into the very life of God.

I am bound to feel much isolation because, for everyone I meet or speak with, my death represents one event among many others – tomorrow's engagement or the holiday planned for Christmas, etc. – whereas for me my death is *the* event. And, of course, it is nearer for Dorothy to *the* event than it is for anyone else. *The* event is the sundering of one's body from the Spirit. No one living can teach me about death – no living person has experienced it. Some people are in a better position to guess about the experience than others – those who have watched many deaths with *eyes of compassion* – Mother Teresa's Sisters, certain hospital workers, etc. But they cannot *know* the experience.

The only people who might teach one about death are those who have died, and who in some way have witnessed to the experience. It is the martyrs (witnesses) who at least show us *how* to die. We call upon them and upon the ancestors to take us into their company. What they teach us, above all, is to go into death wholeheartedly, to embrace the experience with one's whole heart and in *joy*.

In his last letter to his wife and children, dated 13 July 1943, the day of his execution, Kurt Huber writes:

> Lord, my Lord, I am prepared.
> Guided by thy hand I go
> Joyously into eternity.

And the last recorded words of Dietrich Bonhoeffer are: 'This is the end – for me the beginning of life'.

The Hindu scriptures speak about 'The Further Shore'. One of my two 'big dreams', as the rabbis call them, was about the further shore: when I was walking on a journey, I came to the edge of a river, a very wide river, running fast and turbulent. To my right I saw a big steel bridge, all straight lines and massive bolts holding it tightly together. The road over the bridge was wide and smooth. To my own astonishment, I took off all my clothes and threw myself into the rushing waters of the river. Immediately I was thrown here and there, upside-down, breathless. I had no control over where I was being swept. The shaking by the waves went on and on, until suddenly I was flung on to the further shore and lay there calm, on my back, feet pointing towards the river. Looking towards the left, I saw that the bridge had collapsed completely leaving a great gap in the roadway.

Hindu wisdom says:

> Whoever clings to ignorance is lost
> And whoever clings to knowledge is even more lost.

It seems certain also that nothing whatsoever can be taken to the further shore except what can be contained in a pure heart – which means pure love. Not fame or the unstable judgements of human beings or one's 'achievements' – these count as *nothing* in the realm of grace, where there is no 'mine' and 'thine', and so no obligations or debts. All is grace and grace is all.

The love that is to be contained in pure hearts is the love referred to when it is said that 'God is love'. Which means loving your enemies, doing good to those who hate you, blessing those who curse you . . . Only by the grace of God can any creature love like that.

'There are times when good words are to be left unsaid, out of esteem for silence' (St Benedict). 'Silence is the sacrament of the world to come' (St Seraphim). When people are together in profound silence, they are bestowing sacrament on each other, a healing.

Although I had read James Alison's *Knowing Jesus* quite carefully some time ago, it is only in recent days that it has made its full impact upon me, revealing how often I have established my *identity* in a 'pharisaical' way by contrasting my 'just', 'good', 'innocent' self with others – e.g. the 'good' Northerner against the 'selfish' Southerner, or 'the victimised working-class boy' against the 'uncaring middle-class people', etc., etc. Jesus, the truly good, innocent victim has blown away that subterfuge as a way of being.

I have been most impressed by the *Testament* of Father Christian de Cherge, the Cistercian prior murdered in the Atlas mountains, who says of his impending martyrdom that he cannot claim innocence – he, like all of us human beings, is involved in the evil which infects the world.

And it is only too easy for believers to bolster up their identity by contrasting the good, i.e. believers, with 'the world', i.e. unbelievers.

Jesus teaches us that true love, the love which is God, is *unconditional*: no creature is outside the love and mercy of un-conditional love. If we establish conditions for our love, then we are not talking about the sort of love which the Gospel points to – the love which abides when everything else we can claim vanishes.

Waiting for the end of life ... waiting is almost the defining 'activity' of poor people – refugees, wives of prisoners, exiles. In that sense we are all exiles, but some are exiles in a far more biting sense.

Waiting makes one begin to feel useless, superfluous; so we have to remind ourselves that 'they also serve who only stand and wait' (as Milton wrote). And G. M. Hopkins also paid tribute to the lay brother St Alphonsus Rodriguez, the doorkeeper who for 40 years just 'watched the door'.

Last night I suddenly saw many things illuminated by Alison's *Knowing Jesus* ... some of them chastening. I saw, for instance, how *horrid* much of the life was in university senior common rooms – a lot of men who, since childhood, had been shaped to emulate clever men and had been placed as rivals for others who were being similarly shaped, and they were gathering each day to prove that they were superior in cleverness to the others who were there.

I was saved, in so far as I *was* saved, from the desert this process created by such people as David Jones, Edwin Muir, Scomo and Father Anthony Ross and Father Conrad Pepler – none of whom had been infected by a university education. (NB James Cameron gave up philosophy and became a poet, like my 'saviours'. When reviewing *Recent Thought in Focus* (1952), although he commended the book he ended his review by saying that he thought 'Nicholl is really a poet rather than a philosopher'.)

Jesus always addressed his whole being to the Father. And although the term 'Father' is completely inadequate as a description of the Creator, God, nevertheless it does contain a quality that enables us creatures to live in relationship with our Creator. Because the foundation of a relationship with one's father is *trust*. A child is defenceless, vulnerable, totally dependent on father, and so we have to become as little children, especially when we are ill and defenceless and vulnerable, and to trust *utterly* in God our Father.

Coming closer to Jesus

I sometimes think that the time I first began really to believe in Jesus was one day in a barrack room, and I saw the beams as shaping a cross. And I said to Jesus, 'I don't care if there is a heaven, still I shall follow you'.

I did not know then the Spanish poem,

> *No me mueve, mi Dios, para querer Te el cielo . . .*
> *Tu me mueves, Senor,*
> *Mueve me tus afrentos y tu muerte.*

(Do not move me, my God, to seek you in heaven . . .
But move me, Lord,
To seek you in your humiliation and death.)

One of the reasons why we may feel distant from Jesus is because we do not have a picture or description of him, and so he is in danger of becoming a third person in our lives and not 'thou' or a 'you! Jesus!' Jesus becomes our intimate personal friend when we *share* his suffering for the redemption of the world. Perhaps only then can we also share his joy.

240

'Father, out of the abyss of space and time you have spoken to us through Jesus.'

How strange, even eerie, it must have seemed to those present that Jesus, who had shown himself so skilled in debate, should have chosen not to defend himself. And, by contrast, how much of our energy most of us expend precisely in defending, protecting our *selves* – our *self* which we imagine is our true identity.

For a long time now I have been aware of the danger that faces me on account of the laudatory letters, etc., we have received, and on account of the repeated expectation expressed that I would, almost easily, make a good job of dying. The public awareness of my situation threatens to introduce an element of performance. Today's gospel about hypocrisy and acting, putting on an outward appearance, pinpoints the danger. I can only ask God to preserve me from that danger. So instead of entertaining the danger I shall just laugh in the face of it, and remember Jesus' command so frequently repeated, *Fear not*. And I shall keep before my heart's eye the *abhayah mudra* common to Buddhism and Hinduism – now taken over by some Christian Indian iconographers: *Fear not. Peace.*

Now that I am so defenceless I recognise the need to 'Fear not', and therefore to be able to live defenceless and in peace. My only 'defence' (not defence at all in the usual sense, i.e. wealth, health, intellect, connections, weapons, a sharp tongue, etc.) is the peace that passes all understanding which is a gift from God. Hence, 'Fear not'.

(NB The more defences you establish – e.g. the state of Israel – the greater your *fear*! Because you are saying to yourself, 'I must have enemies in large numbers if I need all these weapons'. In order to save one's life one has to lose it.)

One of the finest Hindu teachings is that one should not look for the fruits of one's actions or prayer (cf. the gospel words about not letting the right hand know what the left is doing – or vice versa?). I am being taught that lesson since much of my recent work will not appear until 'afterwards'.

'*Hat es ein echo gefunden*?', the words of Walter Lypgens in 1949(?) after I had published a translation of his article on Romano Guardini (*Dublin Review?*). There was something offputting about his concern for an 'echo', and something genuinely pathetic about his concern (like a little boy who wants to be liked).

All of us writers are a bit like Walter. And though it is easy to see why our concern is often the expression of egotism, there is also a positive side – like the concern of a singer to know whether he/she is striking the true note.

The positive aspect arises out of the true notes which Alison speaks of in *Knowing Jesus*: *gratis*, forgiveness, communication.

- *gratis*: we receive our creation and our salvation *gratis*;
- if we gladly accept our creation and salvation, we at the same time recognise that we have been *forgiven*. And this further shows itself in our turn, *forgiving* others *gratis*. We are now, by this time, in the realm of *grace*, freely receiving and freely giving;
- consequently we are *inspired* to communicate the gifts we have received to *everyone* whom we meet or know of. *Bonum est diffusivum sui*. (Goodness is self-diffusive.) So if we do not have any desire to communicate, that is a sign that *we have failed to accept the gift freely offered*.

While the temptation to be a showman or showwoman has to be overcome, so has the temptation to hide one's light under a bushel. Shyness is often the sign of a lack of courage disguised as a virtue. *To live out a human life is not quite the same as strolling across a meadow*!

I promised, at the beginning, to try to go on witnessing to the end. But to what am I to witness? *not* to my ability to 'die a good death', as they say, but to witness to the grace of God, his Presence.

❧ *27 October*

This last period of my life is its culmination (*culmen* means 'summit'). Now is the time for me to *validate* everything that I have claimed as true either by my speeches or my writings or my actions.

However, I am now virtually deprived of the capacity for speech, writing or action. I am powerless and defenceless. Therefore how can I validate what I have previously said, written or done?

Only, it seems, through fully accepting my weakness and powerlessness, my lack of ability to make any impression on the visible, tangible world. So from now onwards my life has to be 'hidden with Christ', hidden in Christ, so whatever may appear is not due to any initiative of mine. And, of course, nothing may appear. But whatever does, or does not *appear*, is no concern of mine because my life is hidden with Christ.

Perhaps I am feeling the same as Bernanos felt – though I wouldn't express it as he did – when he was heard to mutter, *'Maintenant! C'est à nous deux!'*

ॐ *28 October*

Last night, or – more exactly – the early hours of this morning, was not an easy time but proved wonderfully rewarding.

Looking at the photo of myself, aged seven among the 30 or 40 brickyard workers, I saw once more cousin Raymond (Mum's cousin), and began to think about him. How the consultant who fixed him with a voice box for his cancered throat had said, 'Mr Thornton is a perfect gentleman, always so courteous, always grateful and never complains'.

'A perfect gentleman.' Yet Raymond was brought up in a very poor family, in a one-up and one-down back-to-back house, next to St Thomas' Church, Claremount. Leaving school at 14, for the next 40 years he worked in the brickyard and brought up a lovely son and daughter with his buxom, cheerful wife, again in a one-up and one-down house. He was imbued with the formation of the Anglican Church. Sunday mornings, he was in the choir, later becoming the crucifix-bearer. Sunday school in the afternoon and then Evensong. Raymond gave the word 'meek' a good meaning, even though he could smilingly admire the bolder manner of my Dad.

I visited Raymond during his last days. And there he was, kind and gentle as ever, slightly excusing himself for the strange noises coming out from his throat.

He visited me in those early hours of today with an assurance of the communion of saints. And then, in the light of Raymond, I saw all these brickyard workers on the photograph as – not a *Lumpenproletariat* of the Marxists, but as redeemed by Christ, alive in the communion of saints.

Each time I pass a crucifix now, I touch the feet of Jesus and call to mind the words of Pascal: *'Jésus-Christ est en agonie jusqu'au fin du monde'*. And I think of the suffering people throughout the world, especially now in Zaïre. And I try to place myself amidst them.

✸ *30 October*

The word that came to me this morning was *ekenosen* – 'he emptied himself'. It is a word which helps me to make sense of the fact that my muscles are losing their power; they are being emptied of power. I must try not to object internally to this but take it as part of the emptying of my self, the fibres of my *being* being taken apart by God so that I may become a 'new creature'.

✸ *4 November*

In order for me to become a 'new creature', to be transfigured, my present corrupt body has to die. This body is *incapable* of eternal life. Only the eternal Father, the Creator of the whole universe, can endow me with the *capacity* for eternal life and sustain me in that life.

✸ *10 November*

Last night I once more had a dream about being dog-tired and trying to find some place to sleep. But when I went into the men's hostel, every time I thought I had found a corner I was told it was occupied. Then I came to rooms where there seemed to be places, but as soon as I prepared to lie down women came and said that here was the women's quarters.

I awoke and, heard in my head, 'The Son of Man has nowhere to lay his head' ... and I thought of the refugees in Zaïre ... of Pascal's saying, '*Jésus-Christ est en agonie jusqu'au fin du monde*'.

Laying awake I thought of St Stephen, the first martyr and, perhaps for the first time, the awful reality of what it must have been like to be stoned to death dawned on me.

ꝗ *13 November*

There is only *one* way of coming to know Jesus, and that is, to follow him. You can go on retreats and read books, etc., etc., perhaps as a *preparation* for following. But then you have to set off and *follow*.

Sometimes, after reading exaggerated remarks about myself, I say wrily to myself 'and at the end of the day I am just a Pennine village lad married to a Pennine village girl and we have five lovely children'.

ꝗ *14 November*

Often when I lie awake in the morning now, I wonder what is the point of getting up, and then I think, 'well, this is another day when I can express my love for Dorothy. Also, there is usually some occasion during the day when I can carry out my promise to God to be a witness to the end in some way.' But by the evening, the only connection I can make is with Pascal's remark and with the sufferings of the people in Zaïre, Iraq, etc.

ꝗ *18 November*

Every day now, and pretty well all day, is a struggle – with death on the horizon. As in every struggle, one hopes in the end for it to be over, with a victory. That is what enables one to keep going, to keep struggling – not so much for one's own sake (since there is so little in life except the struggle), but for the sake of those whom one loves who want one to stay alive.

That is motive enough. But the wonder, the miracle, is that Jesus gave up his life not only for his friends but also for his enemies – those who were intent on killing him.

ꝗ *22 November*

'Other refuge have I none.'
'Cover my defenceless head with the shadow of thy wing.'

245

I often hear these lines in my head. Because it is true that every creature is ultimately defenceless – without adequate defence against ultimate threat. Other sympathetic and loving creatures may offer *some* refuge of comfort, *some* defence, but in the end *no creature* has the *capacity* to provide total refuge, total defence. Only the Creator can do that.

The best that a creature can do is to point to this truth – that only in the Creator can we find ultimate refuge and protection. In that way, a creature may at least serve as a *witness*, one who gives a sign as to where ultimate refuge is to be found. The most convincing of such witnesses (martyrs) are those who themselves provide refuge, as much as they are able – according to their *total capacity* – to their fellow creatures, especially towards those most in need – widows, orphans, prisoners, the sick, the poor, etc. The refuge provided may be material, e.g. a house for the homeless, or emotional, for those in despair, or intellectual, for those tortured in their minds. But it is both foolish and unjust to expect another creature to provide ultimate refuge.

There is an intriguing Buddhist dictum: 'Despair is the last refuge/resort of the ego' (cf. 'Patriotism is the last refuge of the scoundrel'!), which means, presumably, that when one's ego has tried everything else in order to avoid acknowledgement, acceptance of one's 'Buddha-nature', then one's last resort is to take up, hide in, an attitude of despair – or in a defiant tragic stance.

That is to reject 'the peace which is beyond human comprehension', beyond the grasp of the human intellect. There has to be a surrender of the ego, and only then can there be that peace which passes all understanding. The surrender has to come before the peace can come.

Ego dormio sed vigilat cor meum – 'My ego has to sleep and my heart (which is infinitely deeper than consciousness) awakens', in the Heart which is the centre of the universe, the Creator.

Dante says: '*En la sua volontade è nostra pace.*' 'In his will is our peace.' How many times have I read and quoted that! But although I could find consolation/refuge in Dante only two or three months ago, that now seems aeons in the distant past – so far have I travelled since then.

◈ *27 November*

In *Testing of Hearts*, describing Dad's dying, I say that whatever can be saved from that situation cannot come from outside his bedroom. The same now applies to me.

No number of letters about me or for me, no telephone call – from the pope(!) or any other creature – can *really* help. Only the presence of God here in this room can save anything from the wreckage of my body and the *agonia* of my spirit. And the Spirit of God does dwell here in our hearts, especially in the love which Dorothy and I have for one another.

No message from outside can ultimately help, except in so far as they are themselves the work of the Holy Spirit. *Everything, everything* depends on God. *Tout est grâce.*

◈ *29 November*

Absurd as it may seem to say so, the main difficulty we have in believing in an *invisible* God is that we cannot *see* him!

The reason for our absurdity is that if we could *see* God in the normal sense of see, he would have to be reduced to the status of one object amidst other visible objects, instead of being the Creator of all objects including us who are doing the seeing.

Nevertheless we do speak of having 'glimpses' of God and of eternity, even though we are by nature time-bound. That is because our Creator has breathed into us the capacity for 'glimpsing' him in his creation – that capacity we call 'spirit'. And the more we strive to live by the spirit, the greater our capacity for 'glimpsing' God and eternity develops.

A few days ago I was granted such a glimpse. I was thinking about how Dorothy and I had been brought together as teenagers, and suddenly I was flooded with unutterable happiness at the realisation that we are married and that we have lived our marriage for many years. There is no way of saying how long the 'glimpse', the sensation – or whatever word you use for it – lasted because it was not time-bound, not measureable by time. Traditionally such moments have been described as 'timeless', and so they are. Since they are timeless they do not last, but the memory of them does. Which is why we continue to speak of them as 'glimpses' of God or 'touches' of God.

❧ *30 November*

I now realise why I find the media (radio, newspapers, TV) so constantly disturbing – *unpeaceful*. No matter what the words, the *tone* is almost always either combative or scornful or despairing or mocking. And I remember Dostoevsky's observation that a person can always tell what another person thinks of him by the *tone* in which he is being addressed (cf. the English class tones – servile, contemptuous, etc). The media expresses such contempt, etc. for its audiences.

What makes my present difficult mode of living worthwhile? Above all the chance to express my love for Dorothy, the family, callers, etc. At the end of today I can give thanks, for instance, that Harold Husemann has again come into our lives so affectionately, and that Richard has offered to go in search of Harry Uttley! *Deo gratias*.

❧ *5 December*

It was only today that I became aware of one of the 'deprivations', or diminutions which my particular form of dying, of cancer, has required of me. My awareness arose out of reading about the dying of Cardinal Bernardin and Henri Nouwen. They seem to have been able to function fairly normally until almost the very end. Almost all my life one of the activities most normal for me has been conversation, telling stories and listening to them. But very soon into my illness I was rendered incapable of continuing to do so. Occasionally it may have seemed to outsiders that I had voluntarily cut myself off from such intercourse. But the truth is that I am not able to maintain a conversation in my normal way – and in hardly any way whatsoever. It is a distinct ascesis of which I am only now becoming conscious.

∾ *6 December*

Today I realised a main source of confusion in my attitude. It is that often I am dealing with medics for whom death is the enemy and, therefore, all your energies have to be devoted to *fighting*, and so you can hardly be *at peace*. (cf. The way they refer to malignant growths, etc., a description which I have always objected to. NB Berger's study of hospitals which showed that doctors and nurses find every excuse possible not to go to the bedside of people who are actually in the process of dying. Their professional *raison d'être* is called into question by every death.)

Cardinal Bernardin said, 'Some people regard death as an enemy. I choose to greet death as a friend.' Hence he could be at peace.

The Macmillan nurse, from the hospice, is different. In the hospice, as opposed to the hospital, the atmosphere is one not of fighting against death but of living peacefully in acceptance of dying. Compare the panicky approach to serious illness on the part of the well-to-do in the nineteenth century, who could afford doctors and visits to Baden Baden, etc., and the way in which poor people often turned the approach of such illness as the beginning of the ritual of dying. Perhaps the insistence of poor people on having a little money stored away for a decent funeral was because the funeral was the last rite of their ritual act.

∾ *7 December*

Also, medics are concerned to *cure* you, i.e. to restore you to the condition you were in before your illness. But what we need is to be *healed*, i.e. rendered more whole than before for the rest of our life's journey. Twenty-five years ago I was not cured of colitis, I was healed through the experience (with the aid of the good doctors, of course).

∾ *16 December*

Speaking on the phone last night Anne Mathews said, 'You are my inner spiritual director'. In the course of my night walk I thought of the number of others who have said something similar, and that made me reflect how easily I could have come to think of myself as Somebody, someone special. And that perhaps only by dying could I overcome such a temptation.

When did the practice begin of awarding marks to people for their performance (in exams, etc.)? It has proved deeply corrupting because in the 'developed' world the inhabitants are for ever, as if by reflex, awarding marks both to others and to themselves. As a result they stop living! They become commentators.

I am reminded of an old student who was posted to live in a remote, all-African village. In a letter he said how refreshing he found it: 'Africans *live*. Westerners watch themselves living.'

Increasingly the human family has 'fallen into the hands of gangsters' (the phrase used by von Preysing at the time the Nazis took over Germany). These global gangsters are described as 'mafias' at a certain level, but they are scarcely distinguishable from the groups who govern many of the countries on earth – 'respectable' people who attend conferences and get themselves elected. There is an interlocking of arms dealing, drug dealing, media lying and monetary fraud of which the profits are 'laundered' into Swiss banks and other 'whited sepulchres'.

Such is the world order which Jesus came to replace by the Kingdom of God. Like all Christians I am called to be a *representative of the Spirit*, just as much as Bonhoeffer, von Moltke, the Scholls, Kurt Huber and others were called to be representatives of the Spirit in resisting Nazism.

❧ 17 December

In the *Observer* (15 December), 'Global Gangsters', concentrating on the Russian centre – with Israel, Britain, US mentioned. The 'optimists' in the West argue that the Russian gangsters will alter for the better in the next generation, 'sending their sons to British public schools and learning golf' (cf. the remark of a famous golfer: 'Golf is the social cement of capitalism'). This generation will become the next generation of Russian political figures, big businessmen, charitable benefactors and dynamic patriarchs!

In other words they will join the 'respectable' gangsters who already control the human family – US congressmen and businessmen, etc. They will be the new generation of those Herods with their 'easy speeches that comfort cruel men' – the same generation as crucified Jesus.

The Beatitudes – blessed are you when you are poor and weep and are gentle and hunger and thirst for righteousness, when you show mercy, your hearts are pure, you are peacemakers and are persecuted in the cause of right, because (at least *in so far as* those descriptions apply to you) you are *not* accomplices of the gangsters, and so are *already* sharing in the Kingdom, which will prove to be for your eternal joy. You are *already* blessed with a touch of that joy.

◈ *21 December*

As often happens at Christmas time it seems to me that what is unique to Christianity is a specific *note*, the note of joy.

In order for joy to be complete we have to be secure in joy; we have to be full of joy. It cannot be true joy if there is the knowledge that one day it is going to be taken away from us. Which is why, presumably, Jesus tells the disciples that their joy in him 'no man can take away' from them. One aspect of the bliss of joy is the knowledge, through faith, that this joy is never going to end. Joy is eternal, which is why human beings have always felt that they have been in eternity when they have received such a touch of joy.

◈ *Christmas Day*

Dossetti was buried recently in Bologna – a saintly man from the LaPira, Fanfani, Caretto group – how different Italy would now be if they had been listened to!

Father Aelred Stubbs lately read out to me over the phone the words of Sergei Averinstev about meeting me at the Oxford conference of St Theodosia's.

It seems ages ago now since I raised with Gerry [Hughes] the possibility that the *need* to think is a consequence of 'the Fall', and that we need, for our salvation, to *gaze* more as the remedy. Perhaps, therefore, as I draw so near to the end of life my need to think diminishes the nearer I come towards it. But, also, perhaps, gazing, if it is visualising, stimulates the need to think and so one does not so much gaze as *listen* to the Holy Spirit communicating in a mode beyond speech or words. We then *breathe* the Holy Spirit and there is no more to be said.

❧ *St Stephen's Day*

In the new Creation one's self-image has to dissolve, just as a lump of sugar dissolves when placed in pure water. So one's own *self*-image is dissolved in Love and one is a new Creation, wholly loving.

Since that is the case, it is easy to understand why flattery is a grave sin: it confirms a person in their self-image, but in the new Creation a person will live within the Trinity, any 'image' being the work of God, and not of self.

Once we realise this, we can relax all our efforts to build up or support our self-image, and can rest in the peace which is beyond the grasp of human beings.

❧ *29 December*

We tend to have a visual image of time spread out and eternity as enclosing time. Really, the eternal permeates time at every moment. Now is *eternity*.

'It's all a great mystery, nobody can fathom it' – Dad's last words. And though we can hardly avoid trying to 'fathom it' while we are alive, nevertheless the closer we come to death the more ready we have to *be* (to *be* eternal), to cease trying to fathom the unfathomable by way of speculation. And having accepted that truth, we are more ready to abandon ourselves in trust, faith, hope and love.

❧ 1997

❧ *1 January*

The one who is our companion and friend on the way <u>is</u> the all-mysterious one who draws us ever outwards into the unknown, the beyond, the infinite, the eternal.

Thus there opens out the possibility of the incursion by grace of that mystical prayer which is the gift of God alone.

Graham Smith (Spirituality Nov.–Dec. 1996, p. 382)

Even though I now look so haggard, I hope I may still bear witness to God's unfailing presence by smiling at life and the persons who come my way. Above all, to smile at Dorothy, my friend and companion, my beloved wife, whom I love ever more dearly each day.

❧ *6 January*

I am finding it more difficult to remember the foreign languages which I 'know'. Today, for instance, I could not remember the German word for 'silent'. Then I did remember. *'Wovon man nicht reden kann davon muss man schweigen.'* ('Whereof one cannot speak, thereof one must remain silent.') These failures I take to be a sign of preparation for the Kingdom where the 'language is silence' – not words, which obstruct communication.

❧ *9 January*

On this date in 1981 Mum died.

Independent Supplement: 'New Year, New Year, PLAY

TO WIN' – which recommends various strategies for taking advantage over other people, including, for example, flattery, etc.

At one time the members of the various groups of the human family all used to play games with one another, preceded by common worship of their God or gods. Afterwards they would all eat a meal together, followed by dancing and music in which all could join.

Then various individuals began to specialise in games, and became sportsmen who played while others were spectators. Sport was born. Eventually the sportsmen were paid to 'play' their sport while the majority of the people paid to watch them. Then the sportsmen began to be paid to move from one group to another: transfer fees.

So now the vast majority of the human family do not play games together but spend their leisure hours watching hired specialist sportsmen. They are organised into teams which have no loyalty to their own communities but are mercenaries in the pay of big businessmen, for whom the teams are their pawns in the 'game' of commercial warfare.

Hence so many human beings no longer worship or play together or dine together or make music and dance together. They are nihilists – nothing-ists.

In *Play* (appendix to *Recent Thought in Focus*), I was trying to show that God did not have a reason (need) for creating the universe but did so out of grace, freely. Having just now reread that short appendix, I am amazed at the insights given to me when I was young. I am having to try to learn them anew at greater depth in my last days.

ৡ *10 January*

The other evening Jean Vanier said that I should record some of my reflections from my present vantage-point.

The most prominent image in my mind is of my climbing a mountain on which the path gets steeper and steeper the nearer I get to the summit (culmination). Inevitably there are places where the path is so narrow that only one person at a time can tread that portion of the path. Equally inevitably, it means that one senses one's aloneness for a time, even knowing that others are around one.

But as the path gets steeper and higher so the vista –
what one can see, also becomes clearer and clearer.

In the light of what I now see I recognise, with sorrow,
how many of my actions in life were not wholeheartedly directed
towards the culmination because I had half an eye on other things
which were nothing to do with love, unconditional love – God.

ౙ *11 January*

I began thinking this afternoon about the billions of years
that the universe has been in existence, and that it is, apparently,
still expanding. Then, naturally, I began asking what is the significance of one human life of 70 years against this background?

There came to my mind the picture of what it would be
like if the universe were to run backwards again. It would reach
that point, infinitely small, from which, so it seems, the universe
began. Then it would vanish and there would be ...? No *thing*,
but only the One who *is*, the One who is not subject to time and
space but *is* eternal – not matter but eternal Spirit, who creates
matter, things.

Spirit created me and all the rest of the universe. Creatures could *never* comprehend, grasp, the nature of their Creator.
So, if we are ever able even to glimpse the nature of the
Creator, we can only do so if the Creator reveals himself in some
way. That has happened here on earth and the final revelation is
Jesus – the man who showed that love is stronger than sin and
cruelty and death.

So even if we are no more than minute creatures against
the background of time and space, nevertheless we have been
endowed with spirit, and are capable, through the Spirit, of sharing
in the nature of God. By grace we are called to share eternal life.

So when we are overwhelmed by the sense of our minute-
ness, we should remember that this whole creation emerged from
a point infinitely more minute; but like the minute hazelnut in
Julian's *Revelations*, 'It is all that is, because it has the *being* of
God'. So we, by grace, share the *being* of God, *utterly* dependent
on his creative power. Which is why we can only find peace and
rest in him, through Jesus who has sent into us the Holy Spirit.

❧ *17 January*

e. e. cummings speaks of 'thou unimaginable God', and how true that is!

J. B. S. Haldane says that 'the universe is not only more mysterious than we imagine but more than we could possibly ever imagine'. In fact, I can't imagine *the reality which I see before my eyes* (ears, touch, etc.) and whose workings we humans guess at and sometimes think we understand.

That is why knowledge can be fatal – when it blinds us to the truth of what cummings and Haldane say.

It is impossible for me to imagine the millions of human spirits who are entering into eternity at every moment – any more than I can *imagine* a million atoms or a million years – even though I know they are 'realities' or, at least, *concepta fundamenta in re*.

But in the middle of this mystery, I can know what I am meant to *do*, and I *know* that through *faith*, and *hope* and *love*.

❧ *18 January*

Strictly speaking one cannot 'prepare' for death because we cannot know or imagine what death does to us. But we can prepare to die by letting things happen to us without protesting, either outwardly or inwardly, against whatever happens in the course of every day.

That does not mean that we should not have in mind a pattern for the day, but that we should not protest when it is inevitably disturbed and the happenings are different from what one envisaged.

In *Testing* I spoke of how 'salvation' could not come from outside the room where Dad was dying. The implication is that salvation was to be found within the little circle gathered around him and particularly within himself – the *work* of the Holy Spirit.

So it is with me: I must not surreptitiously look for salvation in a phonecall from outside, or a letter, nor seek comfort in what people have said about my writings (e.g. wondering what Kallistos has said in his foreword to *Triumphs of the Spirit*).

I open the channel for the Holy Spirit, the comforter, to arise within me by repeating the name of Jesus: so I come closer to Jesus and, hence, to the Father. I relax into that 'rest' spoken of in Hebrews, surrendering myself to the happenings of every day.

ᏔᏂ *20 January*

My horizon – not death
but
Jesus resurrected, bearing the wounds of his crucifixion
now reigning in heaven
having endowed us with his Spirit.

ᏔᏂ *30 January*

The question occurred to me, 'Would you be glad if you were offered the chance to be restored to good health of body but with the mind and heart that you are in now?'

It goes without saying that I would be truly and profoundly glad to be with Dorothy more, and to see more of the children and watch our grandchildren growing up. But there are many activities I used to join in which I would not specially want to pursue again.

And if I retained the mind and heart as they are now, I feel that I would be bound to do many things which would make my heart and mind ache terribly.

Why? Because I have received intimations of what the 'new creation' might be, and what it might be to love unconditionally and I realise that such unconditional love is not altogether possible in this world for most of us. For me, certainly, I need to be bathed in the unconditional love of God which is heaven, plunged into the ocean of pure love so that my whole being is cleansed of my selfishness; and my ego is swept away entirely. I have a longing for that boundless love which would prove to be a constant ache if I were restored to bodily health.

❧ *9 February*

The date of Dad's death.

The agreement between Christ's teaching and Buddhism has been obscured by the way in which the experts on both sides have attached too much significance to concepts (both their own and the others') – in spite of the warnings in both their traditions against doing so.

At the end Buddhists are saying that the ego has to die so that the heart may be born – the heart that will be totally filled with compassion for all beings. The Bodhisattva does not choose to enter nirvana until the very last blade of grass has achieved enlightenment. How does this differ, essentially, from the Christian vision whereby the whole cosmos will be redeemed and '*all* shall be well and all shall be well...'?

At the practical level – level of practice – Buddhism teaches that one's meditation is not worth anything, one's pain is not worthily offered, unless it is on behalf of all beings. Compare St Paul's words about the vanity of giving our bodies to be burnt, etc., *unless* it is done out of love (for the whole creation) – with our sufferings making up for the sufferings that are wanting to the body of Christ (which surely cannot mean just the visible members of the body of Christ but the whole of God's creation?).

Is there one whit of difference between what Christians mean by love and the Buddhists mean by compassion?

❧ *11 February*

The small round piece of eucharistic bread is the point from which the whole creation emerges.

❧ *20 February*

I have long been uncomfortable with the phrase 'living in the present moment'.

Now I understand why – after coming across the remark that trying to live in 'the present' is like trying to sit on the edge of a razor!

How long is a moment?

Through memory we are able to draw upon the past ('the past has not passed away' but is present to us), and through faith and hope we live towards the future.

The present moment embraces the past and the future.

❧ *22 February*

Though he was a very calm man, Edwin Muir used to be irritated by the common usage of the word 'contemporary' – used to give a sense of superiority to the present generation or 'the spirit' of that generation.

I think I now understand better why he was irritated. It is because the usage implies that if you are not with 'the spirit' of the present generation, then there is something wrong with you – you are not really alive.

The further implication is that the past is dead, along with all those who 'belong to the past'.

But for human beings capable of memory and handing on memories, all those are 'contemporary', in the best sense, with whom we share the spirit – no matter at what time they may have been on this earth. In this sense, the holy ones of the past and by whose "spirit" we live are more part of our lives than those people who are now on the earth but are not alive in spirit.

This explains for me my instinctive dislike of the phrase 'the historical Jesus', which conveys a sense that Jesus belongs solely to the past when, in fact, he is the animating Spirit in many millions of people living on earth at this moment.

We are one in the Spirit with all our ancestors and especially with those who lived by the Spirit while on this earth – the martyrs in particular, the supreme witnesses to the Spirit (St Irenaeus, St Peter, Dietrich Bonhoeffer, Oscar Romero, Steve Biko, etc, etc.).

❧ *25 February*

Yesterday and today I have been reading the *Maryknoll* magazine and the book by Paul Glynn, *A Song for Nagasaki,* about Takashi Nagai, the professor/doctor who survived the A-bomb for three years.

When I read these incredibly moving stories about the heroism of such people who are inspired by the Holy Spirit, I ask myself why our generation gives itself to the phantasies of TV, tabloids and the Internet rather than attending to the wonderful, inspiring lives of these witnesses to the Spirit?

What a terrible impoverishment it is that our grand-children almost certainly know nothing about witnesses to the triumphs of the Holy Spirit. At one time, when faith was embedded in popular culture, everyone, no matter how ill-educated, would have been familiar with these witnesses from all generations. Nowadays what are they nourished with? The kind of stories that are the equivalent of Coca-Cola and potato crisps.

∽ 5 March

All this talk of cloning a human being, etc., being the opening of a new vista for humanity, etc., is so reminiscent of what we have heard so many times before – especially since the Idea of Progress so bedazzled the learned class and their middle-class patrons.

They all ignore the crucial point that *the* central issue for human beings is how we can have a change of heart and learn to love one another. They are in thrall to a mirage in a desert, and imagine that some trick or other (no matter how technologically sophisticated) will save humanity from unhappiness, suffering, warfare, etc. They ignore all the evidence that the struggle has to be won in the human heart not in the world of magic tricks. Applied science remains rooted in magic, whence it took its origins.

There is also a curious parochialism in the assumption that humankind can be in charge of their own destiny without regard for the whole vast cosmos of which our earth is only a tiny corner. Whereas all the world religions have recognised that our earth is part of an infinite universe, and that our struggle for redemption is just one aspect (though a crucial one) of the whole creation for the redemption of whatever it is that has gone wrong throughout the whole cosmos.

Our part in this struggle may be tiny, but it is none the

less crucial. That is why everything we do in our lives is of such importance.

If creation were to go into reverse, the expanding universe would contract, in a flash, until it vanished at the infinitesimally small point from which it emerged ... the point is like the hazelnut of Lady Julian's *Revelations* (Chapter 5): 'It is everything that is made ... I marvelled how this could be for it seemed to me that it might suddenly fall into nothingness, it was so small.'

As George Mackay Brown says of the Eucharist: 'The fires at the centre of the earth, the sun above, all divine essences and ecstacies came to this silence at the last – a circle of bread and a cup of wine on an altar.'

❧ *6 March*

Early this morning, soon after 3 a.m., I spent quite a long period in very deep peace. That peace was somehow connected with my thinking about Edwin Muir's indignation at the usage of the word 'contemporary'. And I realised, in the light of the true usage, that I am contemporary with all who try and have tried and will try, as I myself do, however weakly, to live by the Spirit. All such people, from our earliest ancestors till the very last human being on this earth, dwell in the same world, breathe the same Spirit. We are one in the Spirit – Abraham, Maximilian Kolbe, Edith Stein, St John of the Cross, Père Jacques de Jésus, Mary the mother of Jesus, my Dad and Mum, and so on, *ad infinitum*. I am one in the Spirit with all of these. They and I are contemporaries. We belong in the same world, whether we are alive now on earth or dead or yet to be born.

❧ *7 March*

How can we
Fettered by knowledge
Believe in
Such excessive Love?

Poem about Christ's coming among us.

๛ *14 March*

I sometimes smile wryly to myself when remembering the easy confidence with which so many in California (at the *Death and Dying* craze) spoke of 'Letting go', as though it is rather like relaxing into sleep at night. That is not the same as letting go of *everybody* and *everything*.

? 'Is enlightenment painful? Buddhist Rimpoche: 'No'.
'Is the process of enlightenment painful? Rimpoche: 'Yes'.

๛ *16 March*

The other day when I was finding the going rough, I heard in my head a voice with a firm Yorkshire accent saying, 'Keep gooin', lad'. I told Dorothy later, and she said, 'It was your Dad?' I bethought myself and then answered, 'No! It was Uncle Isaac'.

The words of D. H. Lawrence came back to me: 'The dead do not die. They look on and help.'

๛ *17 March*

St Aelred wrote that in heaven the joy of one person would be joy for all, and that *each* person would enjoy the *joy of all other persons*.

But no human being can enter fully into the sorrow of another human being – only God, who is nearer to us than we are to ourselves, can enter so deeply into our innermost being where sorrow takes us.

That is why it has been said that sorrow belongs to the fading countenance of this world and so has no place in heaven, which is joy – eternal joy.

Sorrow and joy are not equal in balance – do not ultimately go together.

✃ *20 March*

When people tell me that I need diversions of one kind or another they do not understand where I am. I am sailing between Scylla and Charybdis, two perilous features, and need my full attention to sail through without getting shipwrecked. I need to pay the sort of attention that Simone Weil speaks of in her *L'attente de Dieu* – as Jesus says, 'Keep awake – you know not the day nor the hour'.

It would be perilous, indeed, to allow anything to divert my attention, to distract me from keeping along the narrow channel between Scylla and Charybdis.

There are no outside sources (books, broadcasts, etc.) which can help me now, unless they evoke my own inner experience over the last 70 years. It is that experience, my guides over these years who have proved faithful, who can help me – the cloud of witnesses who have lived by the Spirit, my ancestors, friends and teachers. They have so much still to tell me, and so I listen to them. And I owe them so much that my thoughts of them become prayers for them and expressions of gratitude. ('The very thoughts of a serene man are themselves prayers.')

For them, as for me in these straits, Jesus is our lookout and the Holy Spirit is our helmswoman/man. It is to them that I have to listen, to pay attention. Otherwise I shall get diverted and go off course.

✃ *22 March*

Last night, or rather in the early hours of this morning, I experienced a great sense of peace for a time. It was connected somehow with the encouragement I received from Uncle Isaac's words to me (16 March). Along with Alois Pieris' statement that in the coming years he expects me, 'immersed in God', to serve as his guide for the rest of his life; and along with Lawrence's statement that the dead 'look on and help', it made me think that possibly one of the purposes of my keeping alive until now is to tell me that I shall have a vocation 'in heaven', acting as a guide for others during the last stages of their lives – I needed to learn my vocation 'there' while I am still here.

❧ 25 March

In my Minsteracres talks, I spoke of how you could imagine the expanding universe going into reverse and the whole of creation being sucked into an infinitesimal small point – then, nothing!

That connects with Lady Julian's hazelnut which seemed so small that it 'might fall into nothingness'. But it was revealed to be *everything that is made*'. But 'it lasts and ever shall last, because God loves it. And in this fashion all things have their being by the grace of God.'

'God made it – God loves it – God keeps it.'

cf. G. M. Brown's words concerning the Eucharist: 'The fires at the centre of the earth, the sun above, all the divine essences and ecstacies came to this silence at last – a circle of bread' ('and a cup of wine on an altar').

When we look at the bread of the Eucharist we are looking at the *point* of 'everything that is made' (Julian) – God embracing everything that he/she has made.

I have often felt uncomfortable at the use of the words 'detachment' and 'attachment'. It is as though all creation, all creatures, are an *obstacle* to our union with God. Of course, they often prove to be so, especially in the way we regard them. But it is also true that creatures make a way for us to have union with God – all creation by its *being* praises God. It is the way that we regard other creatures that determines whether they are obstacles on the way to our union with God.

❧ 26 March

Yesterday I awoke from my post-lunch sleep with a heavy burden upon me and the words, 'utterly . . . utterly . . .', repeating within me. It was because of a terrible dream in which I had felt utterly abandoned by everyone and everything.

The only response I can make is to abandon *myself* utterly to God, who subjected himself to Gethsemane and Golgotha for our sakes, willingly.

◦ℰ *27 March*

Bill Vanstone has a chapter on 'the grace of God' (Epistle to Titus) which is wonderfully illuminating – by grace God is revealed as attractive, not forbidding and threatening, etc. And I thought of what I say about Seraphim – his very presence was healing and attractive because grace had become his second nature.

The opposite of gracefully is grudgingly. The world of stern duty, as opposed to grace and freedom: Ivan Karamazov, who always kept an account of the money spent on him by his foster parents whereas Alyosha never enquired about the matter. Ivan was grudging. Alyosha was graceful. (cf. Ivan's lopsided way of walking!)

Vanstone reminded me again why we called our youngest 'Hilary' (*diligit Deus datorem hilarem: God loves a happy giver*).

'Doing good' for someone ('I'm doing this for your own good'!), giving them 'help', etc., has to be done gracefully – otherwise the person who is expected to receive your 'good' advice or your 'help' or your 'gift' *cannot* accept it because there is no flow of *grace* from you to them. Some people *radiate* goodness, and none but the very hard-hearted fail to respond.

How *un*attractive so much of what has been done in the name of Christ has actually been! cf. 'I learnt Torah from the very limbs of my teacher'.

◦ℰ *29 March*

What happens to me is not my business; it is God's. Mine is to respond to what happens with as much grace as I can muster. My response has to be inspired by the example of Jesus through the Holy Spirit.

◦ℰ *31 March*

Perhaps my final jotting. For centuries Christians (and others) have tried to teach others by every imaginable means the *compulsion* of law, government, excommunications, logic, bribery (food, money, status, etc.) – all of them *forms of violence*, violating the integrity of others.

A number of Christians have shown us the only way to end violence and injustice and ignorance, etc. (Francis, Seraphim): it is by *grace*, attracting others through freely giving oneself to all. The attraction of goodness is the only way to draw others out of the world of injustice, violence, conflict and unhappiness.

Not forcing others, but drawing them gracefully into communion with oneself and all creation.

X X X

Donald died in the evening of 3 May.
He had been holding Dorothy's hand
quite firmly and then, at the moment
of death, relinquished it.

❧ Breaking the Thread

Is this the last line I can write that you can read?
For still your days go drifting long and slow.
Your voice has weakened as you lie in bed.

Against the rasping sheets they turn your bones.
It's months since all we had to say was said
And still your days go drifting long and slow.

We long to ease the breaking of the thread.
The words I try to form you already know.
You read them smiling, see me in your head.

The loving that we have will never go.
Nothing now can change when life has fled.
And still your days go drifting long and slow.

I visualise you turning in your bed.
The words I try to form you already know.
It's months since all we had to say was said.

We long to ease the breaking of the thread.

Hilary Elfick, 22 March 1997

ঌ Dear Donald

Dear Donald
These are the words which you would not let me speak
When, in that room, back bowed, for once
Cut low from those aspiring heights where always I had seen
    you
You summoned me for our goodbyes
And, as I struggled with the love and thanks which rose
Together in one breath for one to whom I owe so much
Your gaze, clear and steady as it always was, and your quiet
    words
Stilled me, seemed to say
As in all things the natural time will come

And so it has
Now, from four corners of my life, the memories return
How once, years ago, I walked with you, skipping childlike at
    your heels
As the long strides outpaced me, down a leafy lane
And, dazzled by the moment, giddy with ideas and tumbled
    thoughts
I spilled my noisy mind to your patient ears, heedless, veering
    on and off
The straight path you trod, with my oft-repeated 'What I really
    think . . .'
And stepped before a car, and you, reaching out
Plucking me easily back, 'Be careful of the road', you said
'Or you'll not think at all', and in that moment seemed
To anchor for a lifetime my scholarship in sense

In those years
I wondered why you spurned what I most prized, as, ever
    distrustful
Of the picked argument, the need to conjure things from words

You headed off my clumsy overtures with 'Is it warm today?'
and
'Would you like some tea?' to bring me from philosophy to
something
Nearer home. There, your children, lifted high and laughing on
your shoulders
Saved you from such deceits, and farmers they would be, and
foresters, you said
Yet, as I left, casual-seeming and with a smile you gave a
compass-bearing
'Have you read such-and-such?', you said, and closed the door
And left me in unfamiliar silence, stopped the hard hammer of
my mind
And instead, and for a lifetime, set seeds growing

Years later
Your loyalty undimmed, the letters with their 'peace and love'
neatly inscribed
The conversations, slower now, and the writings with their subtle
patterns traced
Were landmarks in a far country. Then as the loss, bitter and
haunting, struck
At my life, we met again, as if you sensed when to replenish
where my life's spirit
Sweetened by your company, had drained. And there you sat,
fresh from preaching
Holding the table's fond attention, gently mimicking, your eyes
twinkling
With some mischief story as I came late to join you, and turned,
asking me directly
How it had come to be. Now there were no words, just my pain
and silence as
You watched, and then said simply 'It happened', and in that
steady gaze freed me
Showing, for a lifetime, how to keep safe a private grieving

In later times
I saw you less, but still we talked, and I could see always in my
mind
Your tall back, venerable as oak, arched down to the enquirer,
your eyes sharp

The Testing of Hearts

Heard still in your voice, quavering now, the hesitations longer,
   the words elusive
Your kindness and concern, the old fastidious taste for truth.
   Now again my life
Took fresh paths and uncertain I sought your help, expecting
   after so many years
A token offering. And yet you called, wrote letters, tested my
   resolve
Giving the spur I needed, yet obliquely, as if we worked together
   for the aim
So that I never felt the debt, until that day when, taking your
   leave, touching
With a smile the lofty plans and purposes, 'It will be exciting for
   you', you said
Setting me joyful, leaving a lifetime's inspiration

Dear Donald
These are the words which you would not let me speak
Which, in that room, you saw was not their time
These are the lessons which I learned easily in your company
But never knew till later I had learned them
These – the common sense that walks with intellect and is its
   guide
The gentle nurturing of thought which finds its own conclusion
The glad acceptance of love and loss alike finding no blame
And the courage to learn and move on – these were the gifts
   you gave me
Which I could not tell you as you died, and here today
These words, and thanks, and all I touch with them, are yours

Charles Evans